THE LIBERAL ARTS COLLEGE

THE
Liberal Arts College

~~~~~~

A Chapter in
American Cultural History

GEORGE P. SCHMIDT

R U T G E R S   U N I V E R S I T Y   P R E S S

New Brunswick   *New Jersey*

1957

Manufactured in the United States of America
by Quinn & Boden Company, Inc., Rahway, New Jersey
Designed by Leonard W. Blizard

For Irma

Preface

If present trends continue, the numbers of young people who will be attending the colleges and universities of the country will within the next few years rise to staggering proportions. Promising as this prospect is for the future of American civilization, the benefits will be fully realized only by those alert enough to take full advantage of the opportunities offered. To achieve this, they will among other things need to understand the purpose and know something of the origins and the present organization of the system of higher education from which they expect so much.

By far the greatest number of the millions seeking some kind of education beyond high school will spend the first few years in something called a college of liberal arts, or of arts and sciences, or just "the college." This college was the original institution of higher learning in America. In the three hundred years since it began in the struggling British settlements on the Atlantic seaboard the college has undergone many changes, but it is still a reservoir of culture and the all-important gateway to the professional and vocational studies through whose mastery the student hopes eventually to launch a career and earn a satisfactory living. Parents of prospective students, especially those who have not been to college themselves, may wish to find out why the liberal arts college is so highly recommended for their children and to satisfy themselves that it is worth the time and money invested. But those too who are college graduates to the third and fourth generation may find it worth their while to refresh their memories and compare their own college experience with that of their children.

This book then is the story of the liberal arts college. The first six chapters depict the age of the old-time college when that institution dominated the educational scene and dispensed the classical tradition from dignified halls of ivy on scores of campuses stretching from Maine to Missouri. This period lasted until the late nineteenth century, when the single-minded classical college gave way to the emerging complex university. Today in the twentieth century the liberal arts college is trying to maintain its identity and to keep from being smothered by the multitude of professional schools of the dynamic university which surrounds it. This recent development is the theme of the later chapters.

Limited as it is to the liberal arts college, this book cannot be considered a general history of higher education. Many aspects of the larger subject are treated lightly or not at all. The professional schools, medicine, theology, law, engineering, and the more recent ones of education, journalism, and business; the wide field of research; the important issue of finance; the rapidly expanding program of adult education—these and other aspects of higher education are dealt with only insofar as they affect the fortunes of the liberal arts college.

To examine in detail all of the eight hundred-odd liberal arts colleges of the country was impossible. Instead, I sampled, choosing among those I considered most important. These included not only the large and prominent universities but also a number of the smaller colleges. The latter were selected partly to indicate regional distribution, partly because I thought them typical of general conditions and trends. Of necessity, numerous excellent colleges are discussed briefly, or not at all. Among the smaller New England colleges, for example, I paid closer attention to Amherst, though Williams would have served as well. Western Reserve in its early days was subject to much the same influences as Oberlin, which I examined in greater detail. Of the state universities, Indiana might have been selected instead of Wisconsin, and Nebraska instead of Kansas.

In putting the story together I have tried to be clear and accurate, but no doubt errors of fact have crept in. It is likely also that some readers may take exception to my interpretations of the facts. Here too I may well be mistaken, and can only reply that I had to put things down as I understood them, after wide reading and considerable reflection.

GEORGE P. SCHMIDT

New Brunswick, New Jersey
Spring, 1957

Contents

THE LIBERAL ARTS COLLEGE

Chapter One

Colleges in the Wilderness

On the face of it, the American liberal arts college had a most casual beginning. When, on the 28th of October 1636, the General Court of Massachusetts Bay colony was droning through its fourth day and had disposed of such routine items as an increased stipend for the marshal, the choice of a cannoneer for Boston, the prohibition of the sale of lace for garments, and the summoning of Nicholas Simpkins "to give satisfaction for his misdemeanour," as one of its final acts "The Court agreed to give 400£ towards a schoale or colledge whereof 200£ to bee paid the next yeare, and 200£ when the worke is finished, and the next Court to appoint wheare and in what building." [1] This simple enactment marked the beginning of the institution which three years later was given the name Harvard College, and which was destined to be the forerunner, not only of the eight hundred-odd liberal arts colleges existing independently or as units of larger universities today, but also indirectly of the hundreds of technical and professional schools, which together are presently dispensing higher education to three million Americans.

The roots of this formidable establishment lie deep in the past. The European townsman of the thirteenth century was probably just as familiar with the words college and university as we are today, and perhaps a little less hazy as to their precise meaning. In the highly institutionalized Middle Ages the terms *collegium* and *universitas* were applied to the organizations or corporations of craftsmen and specialists of all kinds: the famous medieval guilds. The words themselves, as well as the practice they denoted, had come down from Roman times. As learning revived in Western Europe after the Dark Ages, its exponents, migrant scholars and lecturers, banded together for self-protection—a necessary measure in the feudal age—and for the reassertion of the privileges of the scholar, which from imperial Roman times had included exemption from certain civic obligations such as taxes and military service. To qualify for membership in a *universitas* of scholars, one had to be a master, or expert, in the liberal arts. Small groups within such a university might inhabit one building, endowed perhaps by a bishop or a nobleman, where they would have their meals in common, exchange ideas, say Masses in the chapel for their benefactor's soul, and eventually come up with a set of rules for all who wanted to share the common life. They were a *collegium,* a family group within the larger universal guild of intellectuals.

As the institution grew to maturity it began to vary in detail. The relative importance of *universitas* and *collegium,* for example, fluctuated from century to century and from country to country. On the Continent, generally speaking, the university came to dominate and the colleges tended to disappear,[2] but in England and Scotland the trend was otherwise. Here the separate colleges of Oxford and Cambridge, founded from time to time by churchmen, secular peers, or royalty itself, displayed greater vitality than the university organization of which they were a part. By the sixteenth century they had gone far beyond their original purpose of serving as living quarters for small groups of scholars, had in fact taken on the teaching and many of the other functions of the university itself. In Scotland and Ireland the watering-down of the university idea had gone even farther; Glasgow was essentially an arts college with only a rudimentary university organization, and the University of Dublin had no legal existence at all apart from Trinity, its one college.[3]

Of the colleges that constituted the University of Cambridge one of the best known was Emmanuel, dating from the late sixteenth century and dedicated primarily to the education of ministers of Puritan leanings. Graduates of Emmanuel predominated among the leaders of the great Puritan migration of 1630, and soon after their arrival in the Massachusetts Bay colony they established there a single college similar to the one they knew, as a connecting link between the higher education of the Old World and the New. This was Harvard.

A college it was, and a college it would remain for many years to come. Any lingering echoes of a larger university concept were gradually dissipated by three thousand miles of the Western ocean.

Colonial Americans, in Massachusetts and wherever else colleges sprang up, had neither the means, the leisure, nor that persistent scholarly interest which depends on continuous contact with the sources of culture, to establish and maintain any full-fledged universities. That development had to bide its time, until the centrifugal forces of the New World reversed direction. For sixty years Harvard was the only institution of its kind in British North America. When at the turn of the eighteenth century the scions of tidewater society in Virginia, and the inhabitants of the Connecticut towns, reached a point where they too were ready to provide for the education of their young people, the model before them was the little college in Cambridge. As second and third generation Americans, they knew little of European universities, but, especially in Connecticut, they did know Harvard, and that was what they copied. As for Virginia, even though a handful of planters had gone back to the homeland to study, and even though their own little institution at Williamsburg introduced a diluted Oxford curriculum, its form was that of a single college. Anything more elaborate would have been out of the question in the circumstances. And so William and Mary in 1693, and Yale in 1701, took their places beside Harvard as colleges, the three prototypes that set the pattern for the hundreds that were to follow. The provisional thus lengthened into the permanent, the makeshift became the standard, and the individual college, existing by and for itself, became the characteristic unit of American higher education, to remain dominant almost to the end of the nineteenth century.

Not all were content to call themselves colleges. The term university was in use quite early, for bumptious young America was not given to modesty in nomenclature. The results were confusing. Harvard assumed the broader title after 1780, when John Adams wrote into the new constitution of Massachusetts a chapter guaranteeing the rights and privileges of the "University at Cambridge."[4] Some slight justification for the grandiloquence might be found in the appearance, three years later, of a medical department; yet Franklin's College of Philadelphia had taught medicine for twenty years, and Columbia, which was not to be called university for another century, offered work in medicine as early as Harvard. In a reply, in 1816, to a circular letter from Governor Nicholas of Virginia asking the advice of distinguished educators on the best means of launching a system of higher education in his state, President Timothy Dwight of Yale commented on the confusion of terms, and gave examples of the indiscriminate and totally unstandardized use of the words university, college, and seminary. For good measure Dwight sent along to the governor a copy of what was still modestly called *The Laws of Yale College,* with the observation that they had had a "happy efficacy" in New Haven and would help get Virginia off on the right foot.[5]

The growth of colleges, in number and size, is part of the familiar story of American growth and expansion. There were nine colleges by the end of the colonial period,[6] but the great expansion came after the Revolution; it was then that the college really became a standard American institution. Many were the forces that shaped it. The church, the inherited cultural tradition, and the rapidly changing social and economic order all played a part, but first of all American colleges were local and provincial in character. Higher education in this country was not the outgrowth of any kind of central planning. It was a haphazard growth, a simultaneous and independent stirring in many corners of the country. This is clear from even a casual reading of the many college histories. Whatever else they may have been, colleges were local and community enterprises. Certain common factors were present, certain motives repeated themselves, but in ever-changing combinations and in endless variety. As colonists and later immigrants embarked on the long trek westward, as frontier after frontier emerged from its primitive phase, the moment arrived when leading citizens came to a consensus: This community needs an institution of higher learning; the prestige of our countryside, the maintenance of morals and true religion, the economic future of our children, all demand a seminary of learning. And so the campaign for a college was under way.

The story of the American college, with its insignificant beginnings but great expectations, its chronic financial crises, its headaches and heartaches, its blunders and triumphs, has been told many times over by loyal alumni, the authors of hundreds of college histories of varying merit but unwavering devotion. Here we can do no more than sample a few, for the flavor.

Harvard in its founding years experienced most of the vicissitudes that later befell its numerous progeny. Although it got off to a rather better financial start than some—a £400 appropriation plus an £800 gift made a tidy sum in the seventeenth century—the college had the rueful experience of many of its successors, for it never received the total amounts of these initial grants. The legislative appropriation came piecemeal, and less than half of John Harvard's bequest found its way into the college treasury. The first professor, Nathaniel Eaton, proved to be a misfit, who had to be dismissed after one year for cruelty and financial incompetence. He had held out on the students' allowance of bread, beef, and beer, had beat them twenty to thirty stripes at a time, had cudgeled the assistant master with a "walnut tree plant big enough to have killed a horse." Eaton left the college, and the colony, £1,000 in debt—having squandered some of John Harvard's bequest—and escaped to Virginia. When his estate was liquidated, all that was recovered was one cow. The college staggered under the blow, the students all left, and no instruction was given for a whole year. Then, in 1640 it reopened under President Henry Dunster, and has been receiving students ever since.[7]

In 1749 "twenty-four gentlemen of Philadelphia" voluntarily united themselves to found a college. Philadelphia, cultural center of British North America and third largest city in the empire, deserved a higher school. The twenty-four founders and trustees were of the "better sort," and included judges, merchants, physicians, plus one silversmith and "B. Franklin, printer." An earlier attempt at organization had produced a college building, at Fourth and Arch, which was thriftily designed to serve also as an auditorium for the traveling evangelist George Whitefield on his periodic visits to the city; it was also used by Baptists, Lutherans, and Presbyterians for church services, by the American Philosophical Society, and by a singing society, as well as for college classes; all on the theory that a public institution should be for the use of all. Contemporary critics who complain that our school and college buildings today are not being economically and efficiently used might look into this community service of the colonial College of Philadelphia. A college charter was secured in 1755, incorporating "The Trustees of the College, Academy, and Charity School of Philadelphia in the Province of Pennsylvania."

Money was of immediate concern, and it was hard to get. The managers of a provincial lottery loaned £800, the city council promised £50 a year, and a London banking firm donated £100. Later the first provost (the title president was not used), William Smith, went to England for two years to solicit funds. There he met agents of King's College, newly founded in New York, on the same errand. They joined forces and collected successfully from all classes of so-

ciety, beginning with the King, who gave £400 to his namesake and
£200 to Philadelphia. During the Revolution the college fell on
hard times, was suspected of Tory sympathies and briefly replaced
by an abortive, but intelligently conceived, state university. Even
after its return to favor with the triumph of the conservative faction,
the college was in straits. The state of Pennsylvania never assumed
responsibility for the institution, and contributed only rarely, and
then for special purposes. The student body, except for the medical
school, remained small, the maximum enrollment between 1800 and
1820 ranging from fourteen to thirty-one. It was not until the organized alumni, founded in 1835, began to take an active interest in its
fortunes after the middle of the century, that the college shook itself
out of the doldrums and started on its way to become a university.[8]

Although the War for Independence temporarily retarded the
progress of the colleges, its achievement, complete national independence, intensified the ardor and increased the numbers of the
enthusiasts for higher education in all regions of the land. A characteristic product of such regional zeal was Union College, whose
very name suggests cooperation and joint enterprise. A petition
signed by nine hundred and seventy-five inhabitants of northern
New York, representing "the first really popular demand for higher
education in America," led to the establishing of an academy which
in 1795 obtained a college charter from the state legislature. Support
came from all social levels, racial stocks, and religious denominations
in the Hudson and Mohawk valleys. Dutch Reformed, Scottish Presbyterians, and New England Congregationalists participated, the
terms of the charter preventing control by any one. The analogy of
the new federal union in the political field was in everyone's mind.[9]

More narrowly denominational than Union, and yet in a very real
sense a people's college, was Amherst. Some three decades after the
launching of the Schenectady institution, seventy-one lay and clerical
delegates from thirty-seven towns in western Massachusetts met under
the chairmanship of Noah Webster to see about a college for the
Connecticut Valley. A fund of $50,000 was projected—and actually
collected—with individual contributions ranging from $3,000 to $8.
It did not all come in the form of cash: Watermelons and turnips
found their way into the college coffers along with banknotes! Later
subscription campaigns brought in many pledges of a dollar each,
with one enthusiast, according to tradition, pledging six cents a week
for life. Three trustees ultimately assumed payment of these smallest

pledges. The request for a charter met with opposition, fomented in part by a sister institution across the Berkshires, and sturdy lobbying was required before it was finally granted, by a legislative vote of 114 to 96, in 1825, with a proviso that the grant was never to be construed as a pledge of pecuniary aid from the state. A building was erected, and classes began with fifty-nine students. But the money was used up fast, and the initial enthusiasm began to sag after a few years, as did the enrollments, so after an auspicious start, Amherst entered its time of troubles. Then there came a turn for the better with new gifts and a stop-gap legislative appropriation. Energetic administrators took hold, the debt was paid, and soon after the middle of the century Amherst was solvent.[10]

Meanwhile, down in the North Carolina piedmont, the Scotch-Irish community was bestirring itself. Having built an academy as a feeder for Princeton as far back as 1760, it now wanted a full-fledged college of its own. Under the leadership of the Concord presbytery, but with wide popular support from the "friends of education," $30,392 was collected from six counties in five months, four hundred and sixty-nine acres of land were bought, and a building was put up with volunteer labor and homemade brick. And so Davidson College got under way, in 1837, with sixty-five students and a faculty of three. A few years later a windfall, a gift of $200,000 from Maxwell Chambers, a Salisbury merchant, provided Davidson with one of the stateliest college buildings in the South, if not in the entire nation. In the Greek revival style with forty-five-foot columns, it was considerably larger than Nassau Hall at Princeton, which at the time of its erection in 1756 was reputed the largest structure in North America.[11] The building was used hard for three quarters of a century, then burned down. But by this time Davidson could take the loss in its stride.[12]

And now an example or two from the Old Northwest. Education-minded settlers from Wisconsin, Illinois, and even Iowa, gathered in Beloit in 1844 for a series of meetings which led to the chartering of Beloit College the following year. In this frontier village five hundred miles from a railroad, fifty miles from a bank, and three days' drive from the nearest city, the citizens subscribed $7,000 for a building. The town gave ten acres, an eastern friend donated an additional one hundred and sixty, and a Connecticut man contributed $10,000 for a professorship. There was more grubbing later; campaigns for funds, large and small, had to be repeated over and over before the college was firmly on its feet. To secure and maintain broad popular support, the trustees of Beloit were evenly divided between clergy and laity, Presbyterians and Congregationalists, Illinois and Wisconsin (Iowa had proved to be too remote). By way of emphasizing the democratic and independent character of the institution, its first president, Aaron L. Chapin, exulted in his inaugural address that American colleges were "free born." Untrammeled by wills of founders or acts of parliament, "our colleges are free to become and to do whatever the true interests of learning require." [13]

For a final instance of local concern for higher learning we turn to Michigan. Here, only a few years after General Harrison had made the Northwest Territory safe for democracy at Tippecanoe, the following remarkable piece of legislation appeared in the territorial statutes: "Be it enacted by the Governor and the Judges of the Territory of Michigan that there shall be in the said Territory a *catholepistemiad,* or university . . . of Michigan [which] shall be composed of thirteen *didaxiim* or professorships. . . . [These included] chairs of anthropoglossica, physiognostica, iatrica." [14] The backwoods sage who palmed off this bit of pedantry on a helpless legislature was Territorial Judge Augustus B. Woodward. For all of Woodward's classical zeal, there was still a long and rocky road ahead before this bizarre and theoretical *catholepistemiad* was transformed into the University of Michigan.

These random examples of origins portray the typical. What happened at Harvard, or Beloit, or Davidson, especially in the initial stages, was, with local variations, the experience of all colleges. And they soon numbered in the hundreds.[15] The unbridled enthusiasm of the "friends of education," especially in the first half of the nineteenth century, led to a mushrooming of schools of all descriptions in virtually every state of the union. It was that age of optimism and bombast referred to variously by historians as Jacksonian democracy, the age of the common man, the rise of Tom, Dick, and Harry. Everything seemed possible to the young and confident nation, in every field of endeavor. The spirit was most pronounced, and the record is most familiar, in the field of business enterprise. There private initiative and individual risk-taking reaped the greatest rewards; there brilliance and foolhardiness were both on display, producing shining successes and dismal failures, and magnifying the normal business cycles into lurid and spectacular sequences of boom and bust.

Education was like business. The same strange mixture of courageous idealism and competitive recklessness that animated many business leaders, with an almost total absence of any estimates of long-term trends, was to be found in the promoters of colleges. A college was desirable for more than narrowly scholastic reasons. It raised the general tone of the community, added luster and prestige, and was good for business. And so colleges were founded, especially in the West, with the same naïve confidence and absence of sound financial support as wilderness townsites and wildcat banks. Since the founders were always long on faith and usually short of cash, the mortality rate in the ensuing struggle for existence was appalling. Of forty-three institutions of higher learning established in Ohio between 1790 and 1860, twenty-six had closed their doors and were defunct by the latter date; corresponding figures for Georgia were forty-six and thirty-nine, for Missouri eighty-five and seventy-seven.[16] Such a record should not cause too much astonishment. "College" was still a slippery word before the Civil War, of no precise significance; and these figures represent every attempt, successful and abortive, to set up in a given state something that could by any stretch of the imagination be called a school of higher learning.

Once a college had been determined upon, there was likely to be keen competition among the towns of the region to have it located in their midst. The story of the western county seat which had to be satisfied with the university when it had really been after the state penitentiary may be apocryphal, but it suggests the sort of thing that went on. All kinds of arguments were advanced to secure the prize: climate, accessibility or remoteness, as the case might be, virtue and morality. One is impressed, in reading the inviting prospectuses, with the vast number of American towns and villages that had the most salubrious climate in the world. Numerous New Jersey towns competed for the school the Presbyterians were planning for that province in the 1740's. New Brunswick at one time seemed to have the inside track, but it failed to meet the requirements of £1,000 cash, ten acres for a campus, and two hundred acres of woodland for fuel. Princeton did, and got the college. When a few years later the Dutch settlers of New Jersey promoted a college of their own, New Brunswick, not to be caught napping again, made an adequate offer and this time secured the prize: Queens College, later Rutgers, with its royal charter of 1766. For years after the Rutgers catalogues boasted of the "mild and proverbially healthy climate of New Brunswick," and its "frequent and rapid communication" with New York. They were right about the latter.[17]

Albany and Poughkeepsie competed and intrigued for the possession of Union, but Schenectady came through with the necessary $35,000 clincher. When Bowdoin was looking for a suitable location, Portland, Freeport, and other Maine localities put in their bid. The ensuing debate disclosed a difference of viewpoint which one encounters again and again. Portland urged the advantages of a city (it had a population of two thousand) for polish and refinement, while the representative from North Yarmouth pointed up the importance of securing the boys against the extravagance and dissipation of a seaport. His village, by contrast, had little trade, was no county seat; hence "all of his constituents were virtuous and . . . most of them were pious." [18] Preponderance of sentiment was on the side of piety, and most college sponsors held out for the small town off the beaten path. Kenyon was recommended for its location six miles from a stage line and only twenty-five from the National Road. Besides, it was of course the healthiest spot in Ohio.[19] So was Yellow Springs, when Antioch College was to be located there. Also, its citizens pledged twenty acres and $30,000. The place chosen for what was to become Indiana University was Bloomington, where the mail came in regularly once every week, unless it rained or the roads were bad. And as late as 1899 a Methodist conference in Arkansas located its brand-new college in the remote village of Siloam Springs, because of its climate and its fruit farms, and because "the moral environment is not surpassed anywhere else." [20] Occasional dissenters held out for the city. Columbia in New York City, committed to an urban existence, perhaps made a virtue of necessity when in 1854 a committee of its trustees reported unfavorably a suggestion that the institution be moved to the outskirts. A country location, they argued, though presenting some advantages, would lead to frivolity and vices, gaming and extravagance. In the city the number of students affected by such vices would be comparatively small, for home and church influences would act as restraints. As the Columbia trustees saw it, the "commuting" student lived a more normal, and therefore a more moral life.[21]

State and local politics sometimes played a part in the choice of a location, especially if the institution was to be publicly supported. The University of Missouri found a home only after a lively contest among six river counties. Boone was the victor, having subscribed

$82,381 in cash and $35,540 in land. These contributions came from over nine hundred individuals, nearly a hundred of whom gave $5 or less. The largest single amount, $3,000, came from a man who had to sign his pledge with an X. The College of South Carolina was located at Columbia, in the center of the state, as a result of a political compromise between the wealthy tidewater and the impecunious but rapidly growing piedmont. When at times a new institution encroached on what an older college considered its legitimate territory, the competition became acrimonious. Princeton was not at all pleased to see Dickinson College move into Carlisle in the heart of the Presbyterian belt; and supporters of Williams lobbied actively in the Massachusetts legislature to prevent the chartering of Amherst. The news of the founding of Bates was not received with joyous acclaim by Bowdoin and Colby, its neighbors in Maine. Four denominations in Illinois, each with a college in the planning, were cutting each other's throats until the leader of one, wiser than the rest, suggested that they combine forces and put an omnibus incorporation bill through the legislature, chartering all four.[22]

Once a college had outgrown its infancy and could look back on a few decades of continuous existence, it could begin to count on a new source of support: its graduates of the earlier years, the alumni. Few contemporary American colleges or universities would have come as far as they have, and many would have disappeared long ago, had it not been for the help of loyal alumni. The alumni association as an organized force to support and strengthen the alma mater is an American phenomenon, virtually unknown in this role in European university circles. By the middle of the nineteenth century this new force was beginning to make itself felt. The alumni association of Princeton dates from 1826, that of Pennsylvania from 1835, that of Harvard from 1842.[23] The intelligent concern, the financial sacrifices, and the plain hard work of college and university alumni over the past hundred years offer one of the most gratifying examples of altruism and social conscience in all of American history. No one can know, nor is there any way of measuring, what loyal sons and daughters have done to keep *their* college, if not in the van, at least in a respectable place in the academic procession. On the surface this support sometimes took a sticky sentimental form, thick with misty-eyed eloquence of loquacious old grads, who were moved by hallowed memories or the festive nature of the occasion. "A venerable institution of culture . . . becomes . . . a hallowed influ-

ence, partaking of a religious sacredness which causes men to trans-
figure and to translate into a plane of unapproachable holiness, the
shrines whence emanated those influences of culture." [24] This came
from below the Mason and Dixon line, but the sentiment might just
as well have been expressed in New England or Illinois or California.
Rhetoric opened the floodgates of contributions for scholarships,
endowed chairs, new buildings, and all the manifold blessings that
alumni have showered on their chosen colleges. The contributions
have not always been unmixed blessings. As alumni associations grew
in numbers and influence, their ideas of what makes colleges great
began to differ at times from the aims of the educational and administrative leaders; and alumni have a way of making their demands
felt. Today, as all university administrators know, the alumni have
become a familiar and equivocal asset: Their support, so welcome
and necessary most of the time, can on occasion be embarrassing.

It may be alumni pride and loyalty, too, that induces some colleges,
unlike individuals, to give themselves out as older than they really
are. Those of colonial vintage are especially sensitive to dates. Yet
the early years of some of them are nebulous and shadowy, with no
more substance than the Cheshire cat. Harvard was founded in 1636,
but continuous instruction dates from 1640. The University of Pennsylvania celebrated its bicentennial in 1940, though its first effective
board of trustees was organized in 1749 and its college charter was
not granted until 1755. Yale and Princeton led a will-o'-the-wisp existence before they settled down in their present locations. The University of Georgia got a charter in 1785, but for the next fifteen years
nothing happened. Then, early in the nineteenth century, a president was chosen who, while waiting for the college building to be
finished, gathered in his home such virtuous and intelligent youths
as he could round up from a constituency which was "illiterate, irre-
ligious and happy." Queens, with a 1766 charter, suspended operations twice, the second time from 1816 to 1825, when it was revived
by Henry Rutgers, a New York merchant, with a gift of $5,000 and
his name.[25]

To keep the colleges running, whether in the eighteenth century
or the twentieth, the greatest single need has of course always been
money. The history of virtually every American college and university, from its beginning to the present day, has been one long, repeated, often desperate, search for funds. Large or small, renowned
or obscure, none has been immune. Looking back over the past of

a small but reputable mid-western college, the author of a centennial history summed it up: "The history of Illinois College has been one long succession of financial crises." [26] The sources of income were gifts and pledges from individuals and churches, more rarely appropriations of public funds; and the tuition fees of students. Most of the larger gifts, naturally enough, came from the Atlantic seaboard, where capital had accumulated, and took the place of the pre-Revolution European source of largess. Like the canals, railroads, and banks of the West, education too depended upon the creditor East. The occasional institution that was carefully nursing a productive endowment found it a slender reed, likely to be blown away by the next financial panic.

Nor were the so-called state institutions any better off. In the late eighteenth and early nineteenth centuries the distinction between state universities and privately endowed institutions was not as sharp as today. There were state universities then: Georgia, founded 1785; Vermont, 1791; North Carolina, 1795; South Carolina, 1805; Indiana, 1820; Virginia, 1825; Alabama, 1831; Michigan, 1837; Missouri, 1839. But the states rarely assumed responsibility for the institutions they had called to life. Georgia gave forty thousand acres and a loan at a high rate of interest, then set its university adrift. As a result it was possible for "private" colleges in Georgia to educate students for less money than the state university could. Emory, for example, boasted in 1839 that the over-all annual cost to a student for tuition, board, lodging, and incidentals was only $135 as against $150 and up at Athens. The state university at Chapel Hill faced similar largely unsubsidized competition with the church colleges of North Carolina. Missouri, founded in 1839, got its first state appropriation in 1867. The reasoning of the politicians there was that the university should live off its income from federal land grants plus tuition, for the state needed such money as it could afford to dedicate to education for its proposed system of public elementary schools. In their twenty-third annual report the regents of the University of Michigan complained that while the legislature was showering ample and regular appropriations upon its reform schools and lunatic asylums, the university at Ann Arbor, older than any of these other institutions, had not, in the twenty-three years of its existence, received a red cent. The College of South Carolina was the first in the United States to get regular appropriations for plant expansion and current expenses from the state treasury. This was done, to be sure, in that aristocratic state, at the expense of a public school system.

On the other hand, private colleges, that is, institutions maintained by churches or groups of private citizens and governed by trustees independent of state control, did not hesitate to ask for public support. Harvard and Yale were really public institutions in the colonial period, for at that time the distinction between public and private, especially in New England, had little meaning. In the early nineteenth century the regents of the University of the State of New York repeatedly distributed public funds among the colleges of the state: Columbia, Hamilton, Hobart, and Union. Various colleges in Pennsylvania received sporadic grants from the legislature of that state. Federal land grants for education were occasionally diverted to privately controlled colleges, as, for example, Miami in Ohio and Cumberland in Tennessee, giving these institutions a semipublic character. A group of church colleges in Georgia, and another in Virginia, combined to ask for legislative aid, but were unsuccessful.[27]

One other source of income was widely resorted to until it fell into bad repute, and that was the lottery. All the pre-Revolutionary colleges, and a good many others, kept themselves financially afloat at one time or another by conducting a lottery. For one of these, conducted by Princeton, Benjamin Franklin printed eight thousand tickets. Lotteries for the benefit of higher education were similar in purpose and principle to bingo for charity. But the technique is unfamiliar today, and a closer examination of one such lottery may be in order. By a close vote, and in the face of much opposition, the legislature of New Jersey in 1812 authorized the trustees of Queens, in New Brunswick, to conduct a lottery designed to net $25,000, one fifth of which was to be paid into the state treasury, the remainder to go "towards the finishing of the new college edifice, and the purchase of a library and philosophical apparatus." Newspaper advertisements launched the campaign, in which 15,000 tickets were to be sold at $7 each. There were over 5,000 prizes, one of $25,000, one of $10,000, and so on down to 4,900 of $10 each. Each prize was subject to a 15 per cent deduction, which would, it was hoped, provide for expenses and help fill the quota intended for the trustees. The big prizes were staggered so that not all of them would turn up in the early drawings. The public appeal was frankly to greed and the gambling instinct, as in many give-away programs of radio and television today.

In the end, neither the public nor the college got all it was looking for. Precisely how much, the fragmentary records and the amateur bookkeeping of that day make it difficult to determine. Estimates range from nothing to about $11,000 of the promised $20,000. At any rate the building was completed; it is still in use today. Ten years later the trustees petitioned, and the legislature grudgingly consented, that the lottery be revived. This time a professional firm took over the management for profit, and the whole procedure was more businesslike; the college eventually got about $20,000. Even so there were charges of abuse which caused the attorney general to intervene and the governor to secure an injunction, which stopped the whole proceeding. As the result of experiences such as these, the civic conscience turned against lotteries, and colleges dropped them, for they were no longer respectable.[28]

Fortunate was the institution that had a financially literate president and board of trustees, for much of the money so laboriously collected from devoted friends of education was wasted by incompetence, occasionally lost through dishonesty. Great expectations were often followed by hard times, when the college had to reduce its commitments, the trustees gave personal mortgages, presidents threw their personal savings into the hopper, and professors agreed to share the annual net income—if any—in lieu of their salaries. Sometimes the troubles were simply a matter of slovenly bookkeeping and could be corrected by energetic and efficient financial measures. Rarely was it necessary to resort to such heroic cures as one institution felt obliged to adopt. This school, once among the leaders, had lost prestige and drifted into financial difficulties. It was rescued by a determined treasurer who discovered that students were not paying their bills and no effort was being made to force payment. He accordingly had himself sworn in as deputy sheriff, and on registration day, as the students filed into his office, he laid a revolver on the counter and kept it conspicuously in view. Miraculously, collections improved; in three years they rose from $4,000 to $16,000, and from a student body that had not meantime increased in numbers.[29]

The real momentum behind the seemingly reckless competition among the colleges was the grass-roots conviction that the average citizen was entitled to a chance at higher education and that this could be best achieved by regional and decentralized institutions of learning. Under such a system bright boys would not be put to the expense, which only the rich could afford, of the long trip east and the costly education at Harvard or Virginia. With educational opportunity widely distributed, any deserving young man could go to the college on the hill in his own community and graduate, a better American and democrat. In these "people's colleges," as President Tyler of Amherst called them, "the rich and the poor not only meet together, but they commence their intellectual struggle under the full knowledge of the fact that no hereditary dignity or inherited wealth . . . can entitle to special privileges and honors, nor . . . repress the aspirations of genius." [30] These same arguments were to be used in the last quarter of the nineteenth century in support of the new midwestern state universities, as opposed to some of these same "people's colleges" of an earlier day, which had meanwhile evolved into prestige institutions for the privileged few.

Higher education in pre-industrial America, then, was fragmented and particularistic. Colleges were local growths, and each was a law to itself. There was no general plan, nor were there any national standards. This is not surprising, since the educational system merely reflected American life as a whole. Until after the Civil War the United States was a loosely organized federal union of presumably sovereign states. Its population sprawled thinly over a vast territory, with widely separated areas of concentration. Effective social action was local and regional, the national interest weak and remote. There were many who deplored this near-anarchy in cultural as in political life. In the first flush of national enthusiasm following the winning of independence and the adoption of the Constitution, influential voices were raised in appeal for a national outlook. Benjamin Rush, versatile and public-spirited Philadelphia physician, urged, in his *Thoughts upon the Mode of Education Proper in a Republic,* a uniform system of education to promote national homogeneity and enlightened patriotism. Similarly Noah Webster, in articles in his *American Magazine* and elsewhere, outlined his educational theories for a New World republic, going as far as to suggest a new American language, consciously different in spelling and pronunciation from English. Webster's famous speller and, later, his dictionary were promoted as means to this end.

The American Philosophical Society, ambitious American counterpart of the various European societies and academies for the promotion of the arts and sciences, also had a plan. Founded on the eve of the Revolution, this organization included in its membership not only intellectuals but also nearly every prominent man in the country. David Rittenhouse was a member, and Joseph Priestley, but so were Washington, Madison, and Hamilton. Franklin was its first president; Jefferson held the office later. By no means narrowly nationalistic, the society prided itself on its liberal cosmopolitan outlook. In the third volume of its *Transactions* it listed ninety-six American and sixty-eight European members. Yet the main spur to its energies was the new country with its infinite possibilities. By way of helping to make the United States culturally respectable, the society promoted a contest, offering a $100 prize for the best plan of a system of education "adapted to the genius of the government of the United States." The judges eventually divided the prize between two contestants: Samuel Knox, teacher and minister and occasional practitioner of medicine, and Samuel H. Smith, scholar and editor. The two plans, though differing in detail, had certain common features. Both philosophical gentlemen, as true sons of the Enlightenment, were contemptuous of tradition, and insisted on an open, liberal approach offering opportunities for growth and progress for every type of citizen. Then, paradoxically, but equally in keeping with eighteenth century thought, they proceeded to confine this philosophical freedom in a most rigidly symmetrical frame of organization. There was to be an elementary school in every settled community (Knox spells this out more completely than Smith), an academy in every county, a publicly maintained college in every state, and, at the apex, a national university. The best obtainable scholars were to be appointed to the university faculty by a national board of education, and given permanent tenure. Requirements for admission to any level and for promotion to higher grades were to be uniform throughout the system; uniformity extended to the qualifications of teachers and the choice of textbooks, even to the format and binding.[31]

Not only visionary intellectuals, but hardheaded politicians and practical statesmen, were thinking nationally about higher education in those early years. President Washington, in his first message to Congress, suggested the creation of a national university as a suitable topic of deliberation for the national legislature; eight years later, in his last message, he bracketed the university with a military academy: "The desirableness of both these institutions has so constantly increased . . . that I cannot omit the opportunity of once for all recalling your attention to them." [32] Jefferson, too, as President favored a national establishment for education, but had constitutional scruples and suggested that an amendment might be necessary to achieve it. Madison echoed Jefferson's sentiments. A national seminary of learning would, so he told Congress, promote enlightened opinions, expand patriotism, diminish sectional jealousies, and strengthen the foundations of free government. John Quincy Adams, most nationalistic of all our early Presidents, revived Washington's original plea with double emphasis.[33]

But nothing happened. President Jackson, who followed Adams in office, was not interested in a national university or system of education in general, and no President after him saw fit to revive the issue in that form. National sentiment was still too weak, and the struggling federal government in Washington had other more pressing concerns. Its prestige was low, its income insignificant. By the time both these lacks had been remedied, late in the nineteenth century, the country's higher educational needs had been filled in another way, by the creation, as opportunities arose, of great numbers of independent as well as state-controlled colleges and universities. Perhaps it was just as well.

In the absence of any central direction it was all the more necessary for the many budding colleges to be closely identified with, and understood by, the communities from which they sprang. To achieve and maintain this desirable liaison, American higher education evolved an ingenious administrative device: the governing board of trustees. As the corporation charged with the execution of the charter which gave an institution legal existence, this nonsalaried, usually self-perpetuating, uniquely American body of public-spirited citizens proved an effective instrument for keeping the college in touch with its constituents. Historically, it was an outgrowth of medieval practice. In the universities of the Middle Ages the members of a *collegium,* that is the resident masters who taught and lectured, customarily also administered its external affairs. The practice was democratic. The masters, or faculty as we would say today, governed the college, choosing one of their number as titular head. As for the students, they were mostly planning to become masters themselves, so their interests were more closely identified with those of the masters than are the interests of an undergraduate student body of today with those of their professors. The founders of Harvard, familiar with this form of organization, set up the usual corporation of the president and fellows. By way of insuring due subordination to the Puritan commonwealth, however, they added a second governing body, the overseers, and thus established a bicameral system.

When Yale was founded some sixty years later, only one governing body was provided in its charter, consisting of the president and a number of trustees.

Yale's single board was to become the pattern for American colleges generally, the bicameral plan of Harvard being copied by only a few.[34] Moreover, this single body was made up, not of professors and tutors, but of clergy, government officials, and prominent men of the colony, men *external* to the faculty. Here, too, Yale set the pattern for the others. More and more colleges were organized with external boards of trustees; the last tutors and professors disappeared from the Harvard Corporation by 1806; [35] William and Mary, which had tried to function under the English form of government by resident masters, succumbed to the same external pressure. Although the college retained the outward traditional form of a governing body under a charter, the substitution of outsiders for the teaching faculty completely changed its character. Under the new auspices, American higher education became something quite different from its English prototype.

No conscious plan to create anything new was involved here; certainly no deep-dyed conspiracy to enslave the faculty, as more than one professor, outraged by some particularly objectionable action on the part of his board of trustees, has been inclined to suspect. It was necessary to strengthen the weak structure of higher education in the New World with popular support, and a board of trustees made up of representative members of the community answered the need. Without such support, most colleges would have gone under. This was a young country, with little in the way of accumulated financial endowments for the peaceful pursuit of scholarship and less reverence for its traditions. No national government strong or concerned enough could be appealed to. The only appeal was to the leaders of opinion themselves, in the community, the region, the state. To arouse these interests, often in cutthroat competition with others, and to translate visions and blueprints into bricks and mortar, classrooms and libraries, was a rough-and-tumble task for which the average academician had little stomach. Had the government and maintenance of American colleges been left to their teaching faculties alone, it is doubtful if one in ten would have survived, and most of our great universities would not be what they are today.

There have been other consequences, not all of them happy. When presidents and trustees were actuated by a high sense of personal integrity and social responsibility, the system worked fairly well, but in the hands of power-hungry autocrats a college could easily degenerate into a tyranny. The degradation of the independent teaching master and scholar to the status, in extreme cases, of a hired hand whose job depended on the whim of his employers, did not make for higher standards of achievement or raise an institution's prestige. Then, too, the trustees, with an ear to the ground and closer to public opinion than the cloistered pedagogues, might demand educational changes and innovations which the latter viewed with alarm. Actually, over the years, trustees have done very little of this, being happy, usually, to delegate such matters to the president and the faculty. Yet they could, and the mere threat produced situations of tension on many a campus. That on the whole the system has worked so well is perhaps a tribute to the reasonableness of the participants in the whole enterprise of higher education.

Besides the trustees, who held the individual institution together, there were other unifying forces which counteracted the absence of all central direction. Common traditions and internal similarities existed which more than made up for the disorderly individualism of the external growth of the American college system. The unifying forces were primarily two: the influence of organized religion, as evidenced in the character of the control and in the expression of aims and objectives; and the inherited intellectual tradition as it was reflected in the curriculum.

Chapter Two

Higher Education,
the Child of Religion

~~~~~~

"Education in colonial America was the child of religion." [1]
Education had always, from the beginning of the Christian era, been
a concern of organized religion and controlled by the church. The
masters of the medieval universities were clerics, and their students
were destined for the same profession. The Reformation intensified
this interest of the churches in education. The new Protestant denominations as well as the reorganized Roman church all felt under
pressure to justify their chosen positions. Whether achieved through
the dialectic of a dynamic leader or maintained by the logic of history, the philosophical and theological foundations had to be upheld
against all attacks of rival systems. It thus became increasingly necessary for each church to secure the future by establishing its young
people in its own tenets, whether of Wittenberg, or Geneva, or
Trent. If such confirmation in the faith was desirable for the rank-
and-file lay membership, it was doubly important that the clergy of
the future be well armed for the years of conflict ahead.

It is not surprising therefore that that portion of the militant
Calvinistic church which established itself on the shores of Massachusetts Bay in 1630, at the first opportunity attended to these pressing problems of higher education. In the words of the chronicler of
New England's First Fruits: "After God had carried us safe to *New
England,* and wee had builded our houses, provided necessaries for
our liveli-hood, rear'd convenient places for Gods worship, and setled
the Civill Government: One of the next things we longed for, and
looked after was to advance *Learning* and perpetuate it to Posterity;

dreading to leave an illiterate Ministery to the Churches, when our present Ministers shall lie in the Dust." [2] The same religious motive actuated the Bishop of London's Commissary, James Blair, and his associates in Virginia, when they began to agitate for an institution of learning for the tidewater colony. Results were a little slower here: It took eighty-five years as opposed to six in Massachusetts; for Virginia was built under Anglican auspices, and although in its early years Puritan discipline was not unknown, the aggressive drive of a dissenting church was missing. Then, too, some of the patrons back home were not at all convinced that a college for the training of ministers and the saving of souls was necessarily a function of the colony. "Damn their souls, let them make tobacco," was a sentiment that delayed the charter of William and Mary to 1693.[3]

A powerful factor in the founding of Yale was a suspicion that the Massachusetts brethren were departing, if ever so slightly, from the path of true orthodoxy, and that the pious youth of Connecticut had better be entrusted to the more reliable theologians of the New Haven persuasion.[4] And so it went. The two New Jersey colleges of the mid-eighteenth century, at Princeton and at New Brunswick, were by-products of the Great Awakening, tangible fruit of the preaching of George Whitefield, Gilbert Tennent, and Theodore Frelinghuysen.[5]

Yet for all their preoccupation with religion, the colonial colleges were not theological seminaries, or given to the education of ministers exclusively. At no time did all or nearly all of the graduates enter the ministry. Such compilations as are available make this perfectly clear. At Harvard, 52 per cent of the graduates and 40 per cent of all students in the seventeenth century became ministers, probably a smaller proportion than at Oxford and Cambridge in the same years. Of four hundred and seventy-eight students who graduated from Princeton during the incumbency of President Witherspoon, 1769 to 1794, the percentage was less than 25. A later compilation, made in 1850, showed that about 25 per cent of the graduates of Harvard, Yale, and Dartmouth up to that time had become ministers.[6] Secular interests, in other words, had never been entirely absent, and they were beginning to encroach on the theological. The eighteenth century was crowding the seventeenth. Whatever else Harvard may have been intended for, it was from its beginning, as one of its founders put it, "a nursery of knowledge in these deserts." The phraseology of the various college charters indicates a breadth of interest that was anything but narrowly theological. William and Mary, in addition to propagating the Christian faith among the Indians, was to educate youth in good manners. The Yale charter, though safeguarding the Protestant Christian religion, goes on to emphasize instruction in the arts and sciences so that the students "may be fitted for publick employment both in Church and Civil State." Oddly enough the two New Jersey institutions that were the direct product of a religious surge, Princeton and Queens (Rutgers), displayed no theological emphasis. On the contrary their charters are couched in broadly tolerant phrases stressing the liberal arts and sciences and guaranteeing equal rights to students regardless of denominational affiliations. A similar catholicity of spirit characterized the founding of Kings (Columbia). In a general "advertisement" its first president, Samuel Johnson, linked the knowledge of God in Jesus Christ with virtuous habits and useful knowledge which "may render them creditable to their Families and Friends, Ornaments to their Country and useful to the public Weal in their Generations." Among the most sweeping provisions were those of the College of Rhode Island (Brown): "Into this Liberal and Catholic Institution shall never be admitted any Religious Tests," but "Youths of all Religious Denominations shall and may be freely admitted to the Equal Advantages, Emoluments and Honors of the College or University." And in Franklin's College of Philadelphia the religious motive was entirely absent. Its sponsors were interested in what was "most useful" and "most ornamental." [7]

The relaxation of theological rigor was a reflection of the times. New York and Philedphia were bustling seaports with a mixed religious population and a growing breadth of intellectual interests that was approaching cosmopolitan proportions. Titles in libraries and bookshops, where theological volumes had predominated, were becoming increasingly secular. No one denomination controlled either town. As for Princeton, Rutgers, and Brown, the conciliatory language of their charters is in part to be accounted for by the fact that all three were sponsored by dissenting minority groups: Scotch Presbyterians, Dutch Reformed, and Baptists, who felt it advisable to speak softly in order to gain their ends. These were still pre-Revolutionary times. The various minorities had not yet made common cause with other colonial Americans in a united resistance to British measures of imperial reorganization; they had not yet become the Founding Fathers and the ancestors of the Sons and Daughters of the American Revolution.

Still, they were rapidly moving in that direction, with the result that political interest began to crowd out the earlier religious motivations. This change in emphasis did not leave the educational institutions unaffected. With few exceptions college leaders ranged themselves on the side of independence, and the students were usually more radical than their professors. At Harvard, early in the controversy, students in the debating club declaimed on "the pernicious practice of drinking tea." While Princeton's president, John Witherspoon, was helping to organize the Continental Congress, his students were making life miserable for classmates suspected of Tory tendencies; and at the end of the war the class of 1783 had the thrill of delivering their commencement addresses to an audience that included General Washington and most of the members of the Congress. Jacob Hardenbergh, first president of Queens, was a hunted man throughout the Revolution because of his strong stand for independence. The College of Rhode Island showed its colors by giving an honorary master of arts degree to General Greene. Nathan Hale, patriot spy and martyr, symbolized the spirit of his alma mater, Yale, and similar sentiments prevailed at William and Mary, where the wartime president, Bishop Madison, even referred to heaven, not as a kingdom, but a great republic. On the other hand, the colleges in Philadelphia and New York were not so uncompromisingly identified with independence; the former temporarily lost its charter because of the supposed pro-British leanings of its leadership; and loyalist president Myles Cooper of Kings was saved from a radical mob by the eloquence of his former student Alexander Hamilton.[8]

Patriotic motives and political considerations were thus joined with the earlier religious drive to give to higher education, as to American culture in general, a new dimension. It was thoroughly in keeping with the new orientation that the charter of Hampden-Sydney, the first college incorporated after the Declaration of Independence, and whose very name breathes defiance to arbitrary power, should contain the following provision: "And that, in order to preserve in the minds of the students that sacred love and attachment they should ever bear to the principles of the present glorious Revolution, the greatest care and caution shall be used in electing such professors and masters, to the end that no person shall be so elected unless the uniform tenor of his conduct manifests to the world his sincere affection for the liberty and independence of the United States of America." [9] Having just subverted the royal government, the Virginians had no intention of letting subversion go any further. Patriotic and generally secular motives, which were uppermost in the founding of state universities in the South, were strong enough to move Thomas Jefferson from the high ground of disinterested scholarship. When selecting the faculty for his University of Virginia, he insisted on getting competent scholars, even if they were Europeans, but departed from this principle in one instance. The professor of moral and political philosophy had to be an American, for neither he nor the board of visitors wanted any "European gospel" in this course, which "gives tone and direction to the public mind." [10]

To claim that the colleges were leaders in the movement for independence would be taking in too much ground, even though much of republican theory was formulated on the campuses, or at any rate by campus leaders. More often it was the other way around: Whatever the current orientation of the cultural elite, whether religious, political, or, as in later years, economic, it sooner or later affected the purposes and practices of the colleges.

Politics had temporarily overshadowed theology, but the religious drive, though henceforth modified by patriotic and other secular motives, had by no means exhausted itself. For a while it was pushed into the background, biding its time in the lax post-Revolutionary decades, when deism, rationalism, and "French infidelity" seeped into the colleges. It was in these years that Yale students playfully took the names of French atheists, and a president of Harvard found it necessary to deny publicly the vicious charge in a Boston newspaper that his professors were poisoning the minds of the students with Gibbon's *Decline and Fall of the Roman Empire*. Saintliness at Princeton reached such a low ebb after the war that students put on plays, took fencing lessons, and danced to the violin. They did the same at the University of Pennsylvania, but then Franklin's college had never claimed to be pious.[11]

The temporary eclipse of religion soon came to an end. The fires of religious zeal kindled in the Great Awakening of the mid-eighteenth century had never completely burned out, but had continued to smolder through the years of triumphant deism. Now, at the turn of the nineteenth century, they flamed up again in a new series of revivals and camp meetings which swept the country from the Atlantic to the Mississippi. This form of religious emotionalism, a natural concomitant of frontier living and cultural dispersion, became a chronic feature of American Protestant Christianity, to last almost to the end of the nineteenth century. Not all denominational leaders approved, but few could resist it. Seasons of revival were an immediate, if temporary, stimulus to flagging religious zeal, and set the evangelical churches off on a crusade of reform and expansion, which, its optimistic leaders firmly believed, would win the nation and the world over to Christianity and Progress.

The intellectual effects of the crusade were something else again. Unquestionably it strengthened religious orthodoxy and stopped the spread of deism and rationalism, for the time being. It was on the whole a simple gospel that the revivalists preached, one that appealed to the emotions and minimized intellectual difficulties. Not all of its symptoms were as crude as the jerking and barking and general hysteria which followed in the wake of some of the early Kentucky camp meetings. The movement was more complex than that and had its sophisticated levels. Yet its general effect was to fan the fires of faith and discourage cool rational speculation. One of its critics— to adopt a drastic change of metaphor—has compared the evangelical surge to a massive intellectual glacier, pushing west and south from its sources on the eastern seaboard, and crushing every warm expression of religious and philosophical liberalism in its icy path.[12]

Whatever the influence of the evangelical movement on intellectual life, its effect on higher education was profound. In their collective and sometimes competitive bid for the souls of the west, the various denominations, working out of eastern centers of population and wealth, used schools and colleges as effective instruments. Nowhere was the militant fervor of the Christian churches of the nation, especially those of Calvinistic origin, more effectively displayed than in this fight to retain and advance their religious and cultural heritage amid the primitive and inhospitable environment of a newly settled country, where nature well-nigh forced man to live on bread alone and where success in life consisted in little more than achieving the bare minimum of existence. Local and community efforts to launch a college were likely to succeed to the extent to which they could enlist the interest and tap the resources of eastern sponsors. Just as the colonial colleges had sent agents to England and Scotland and Holland for contributions, so the institutions of the Mississippi Valley looked over the mountains to the East, whence came their help, both financial and intellectual. When finally established, an institution, so sponsored, was likely to be a compromise between the desires of its local supporters and the plans of its eastern patrons.

In the educational activities of the churches, local demands for democratic equality and patriotic sentiments accumulated since 1776 were by no means overlooked. With considerable skill and complete integrity, religious leaders appropriated these sentiments and wove them into one seamless garment of responsible Christian democracy. Lyman Beecher's widely read and influential *A Plea for Colleges* is a prime example. In a republic, Beecher argued, the intellectual and moral culture of the nation must become universal and elevated, demanding an increase of professional men and of institutions to train them. As the great equalizers of society, where the rich and the poor meet together, the colleges of the republic are worthy of general support. But, he declared, if republican enthusiasm is not to degenerate into a leveling radicalism that breeds innovation, insubordination, and hate, the literary institutions which train the leaders must be conducted under religious auspices and directed by a religious philosophy.[13]

As we follow the churches in their educational mission we can discern two main streams of development. The first emanated from Congregational New England, the second from the Presbyterian strongholds of New Jersey and Pennsylvania. Both moved west. New England was well prepared for this sort of thing, having the oldest homogeneous culture in the United States and possessing a superb political and economic instrument for cooperative planning in the town meeting. Since Yankees usually migrated in groups to previously surveyed locations, as they had been doing ever since Thomas Hooker led his flock out of Boston to the Connecticut Valley, they outgrew the primitive phase of frontier life faster than did the haphazard settlements made by other Americans, and were ready all the sooner for the things of the mind and spirit. The roster of Yankee colleges is most impressive. Beginning with their own frontiers, Yankees had by 1800 founded Williams, Bowdoin, and Middlebury. And they never flagged in their zeal for education as they moved west. New York, Ohio, Michigan, Wisconsin, and Minnesota were soon dotted with New England colleges, milestones in the path of empire. Union was a cooperative enterprise of Presbyterian and Reformed churches. Farther up the Mohawk Valley, Samuel Kirkland's missionary school for Indians expanded to become Hamilton College in 1812. Beyond New York, in the old Connecticut Reserve on the shore of Lake Erie, transplanted Yankees established Hudson (now Western Reserve University) in 1826. Eight years later came Oberlin, destined to be one of the most individualistic and influential institutions in the land. The movement reached the Mississippi Valley with Beloit, in Wisconsin, and Illinois College, founded by a band of theological students from Yale and a group of interested citizens of Jacksonville. The movement crossed the Mississippi to found Carleton in Minnesota, and reached its farthest western outpost in Whitman College in the Oregon country. There were many others.

Paralleling the New England advance, but a few degrees farther south, were the Presbyterians. When the Scotch-Irish wave rolled down the Appalachian valleys into Virginia and the Carolinas and broke through the passes into Ohio, Kentucky, and Tennessee, it flooded the countryside with academies and colleges. Many of these owed their existence to the vision and vigor of a single pioneer minister, for the Presbyterians, like their Congregational brethren, were firmly committed to an educated clergy. Most of these trail-blazers were from Princeton, which along with Yale deserves the title of mother of colleges. To mention but one of the many who deserve recognition, there was Hezekiah Balch, Princeton 1762, who founded Greeneville College in Tennessee with $1,352 in cash and some books and mathematical equipment which he had begged together in the East and carried back over the mountains, and who was such an earnest searcher after truth that he was cited sixteen times for heresy and schism before the local presbytery, four times before the regional synod, and once before the general assembly of the church.[14]

First of the Presbyterian foundations were Hampden-Sydney and Dickinson. Farther west in Pennsylvania two small institutions in neighboring villages, Washington and Jefferson, were combined under the joint name. Some of the brethren there had conscientious scruples about naming their institution after the notorious deist Thomas Jefferson, but were mollified when it was pointed out that Jefferson had, after all, more than made up for his skepticism by his staunch opposition to the notorious federal whiskey tax.[15] In the founding of Allegheny in northwest Pennsylvania joint influences were at work; here the first president was a Yankee from Harvard, but the constituency was Scotch-Irish. In the southern piedmont, Davidson in North Carolina and Oglethorpe in Georgia marked the

Presbyterian educational effort. In the Northwest Territory, Ohio University at Athens and Miami at Oxford were among the first. Hanover and Wabash in Indiana followed. Organized support for both Presbyterian and New England institutions came from the Society for the Promotion of Collegiate and Theological Education at the West, whose general secretary, Theron Baldwin, kept the interest alive by issuing annual reports for twenty-six years on the general educational situation from his headquarters in New York.

The Episcopal church suffered under a handicap. Though interested in higher education, it had lost prestige during the Revolution as the Tory church. Its colonial college, William and Mary, had suffered correspondingly, in spite of its intelligent curricular innovations, and both college and church were slow to recover lost ground. But in time the Episcopalians sponsored Geneva College in New York, soon to be renamed for Bishop Hobart, and Kenyon in Ohio, product of the untiring efforts of its missionary bishop, Philander Chase. Trinity in Connecticut, originally named Washington, preceded both Hobart and Kenyon.

Growing awareness of educational needs in the Lutheran church was reflected in the two Pennsylvania colleges, Gettysburg and Muhlenberg, the latter named after the great leader and organizer of the colonial Lutheran church. An early nineteenth century migration of Lutherans into the Mississippi Valley produced a string of collegiate institutions modeled originally after the German *Gymnasium*.

Methodists and Baptists, largest and fastest growing of the American sects, were slow in taking up the educational challenge. At the outset neither body thought highly of an educated ministry. With the fox-hunting parsons of colonial days fresh in their memory, the Methodists demanded tangible evidence of conversion and dedication in their circuit-riders, rather than proficiency in Latin and Greek. When Cokesbury College, first Methodist attempt at higher education, burned in 1795, all efforts ceased for a time, and Bishop Asbury doubtless breathed a sigh of relief as he recorded in his *Journal:* "Cokesbury College is consumed to ashes. . . . Would any man give me ten thousand pounds a year to do and suffer again what I have done for that house I would not do it." But as other education-conscious churches forged ahead to wealth and prestige the Methodists changed their tune. By 1831 John P. Durbin, one of their leading clergymen, was urging the brethren to build or acquire colleges of their own so that they, like the Presbyterians, might exert a cultural influence commensurate with their numbers. The latter, Durbin maintained, because they controlled a "large majority" of American colleges, were producing editors, authors, and teachers in great numbers, who were to be found everywhere in positions of trust and authority. This was only natural, he felt, for it was the purpose of these institutions to train for leadership. "The President of a superior college has it in his power to do more harm or good than the President of the United States."[16]

Even under such provocation the Methodists proceeded cautiously. In 1840 their General Conference resolved that common instruction for the many must precede a university for the few. Methodist colleges, when they did come, should be within reach of all the people. They came, eventually, and Randolph-Macon, one of the first, was recommended by a church paper as a "cheap literary institution" whose trustees were determined to keep expenses down. Similar circumstances attended the founding of Wesleyan, in Connecticut, and its later namesakes, and of Indiana Asbury (now DePauw). The Methodists also acquired a few moribund institutions of other denominations and gave them new life. Dickinson and Allegheny are examples, both taken over from the Presbyterians. Theological seminaries, however, and all specialized training for ministers were still frowned upon. In Methodist pulpits exegetics and dogmatics would not be allowed to deflate the joyous testimony of the sanctified.[17]

Cultural awakening among the Baptists, where educational interests had lain dormant since the founding of the College of Rhode Island in 1764, followed a similar course. The Baptist custom of the lay preacher who farmed on weekdays and exhorted on Sunday put a premium on inspiration at the expense of scholarship; and the complete autonomy of the local congregation made educational planning more difficult than it was for the Methodists with their episcopal centralization. Nevertheless, Baptists, too, read the signs of the times and entered upon a college program. Among their earliest institutions were Madison University (now Colgate), protégé of the Baptist Education Society of New York; Columbian (now George Washington) in the national capital, supported by a literary society under Baptist auspices; Mercer, creation of the Georgia Baptist Convention; and Granville (now Denison), by the Ohio Baptist Education Society. Coming late into the competition, Baptist schools needed all the support the denomination could muster, which may account for editorial appeals like the following: "Where are your sons, Baptists of Ohio? Are they in Granville? . . . Baptists must . . . patronize their own institutions. It is rare that a Presbyterian will patronize a Baptist institution, though he be located in the same town. . . . What will Baptists do?" [18]

An educational campaign similar to that of the Methodists and Baptists early in the nineteenth century was undertaken near its end by the Roman Catholic church. By that time the rapidly growing Catholic population was able to give moral and financial support to an expansion program launched by the bishops, with the aim not only of propagating the faith, but also of realizing the Catholic intellectual heritage in the New World and securing place and prestige in American life. Earlier in our history Catholic colleges, like Catholics themselves, were few and far between. Georgetown, founded in 1789, and under Jesuit control from 1805, represented the first efforts of the cultured tidewater planters, under the direction of Bishop Carroll, to provide "a pious and Catholic education to the young to insure their growing up in the faith." Its college charter, a Congressional grant, dates from 1844. Notre Dame, pioneer college in Indiana, recalled the days when the French were empire-building in the Mississippi Valley. Some of the early Catholic schools exerted an influence beyond the borders of the church. Soon after its opening in 1822, Bishop England's classical seminary in Charleston numbered sixty-three students, of whom fifty-one were non-Catholics. A few years later the enrollment had risen to one hundred and thirty, and Protestant journals were beginning to warn their people against the "errors and deformities of Popery." [19]

The term church college, rather loosely used thus far, requires fuller explanation. For the first three colonial colleges it had no meaning at all; they were hybrids. Harvard, William and Mary, and Yale received governmental, ecclesiastical, and "private" support. But as the colleges multiplied after independence the emphasis began to change. The line between state and church, still somewhat blurred, was growing more distinct. The ultimate outcome of this trend was to be the state university in the modern sense of the word. Meanwhile, there was no uniform type of control for the emerging church college. Patterns varied considerably. The charter might provide that the board of trustees, though self-perpetuating, must contain a definite proportion of members of certain religious groups. The sixteen original trustees of Beloit were as delicately balanced as are racial and geographic factors in a state or municipal political machine: eight clergymen and eight laymen, eight Congregationalists and eight Presbyterians, eight residents of Wisconsin and eight of Illinois. An example of more direct control was Davidson, whose charter empowered three neighboring presbyteries to appoint the board of trustees, one fourth going out every year. Similarly the Indiana Methodist Conference was authorized to fill all vacancies in the original board of twenty-five of Indiana Asbury, and to create a board of visitors besides. The Texas Baptist Convention appointed one third of the trustees of Baylor annually, and the charter of Denison provided that the self-perpetuating board should choose no one who was not a member in good standing of a regular Baptist church. Roman Catholic colleges were—and are—customarily operated by religious orders, but in the general framework of the authority of the church.[20]

Church control, by the way, however exercised, did not imply financial support. Denominations were loath to accept financial responsibility for their cultural offspring, and usually limited their support to occasional collections for special purposes such as a building or a professorship. Regular subsidies were rare, and many a disillusioned president had to content himself with formal resolutions of good will and rejoicing at the Christian courage with which he was struggling to keep his institution out of the red. Let anything go wrong on the campus, however, and the churches were prompt to criticize.

Indirect influence was often more effective for the churches than charter provisions. A community college in New England, unless otherwise specified, was *ipso facto* a Congregational college whether the charter said so or not; and wherever Presbyterians formed the articulate majority of a region, any college located there gravitated naturally into their control. Such control might extend to public, tax-supported institutions as well. The Presbyterians made no attempt before the Civil War to establish a college of their own in South Carolina, for they had captured the state college. Taking the lead in the surge of public indignation over the belligerent religious liberalism of South Carolina's president, Thomas Cooper, they saw to it that from the time of Cooper's forced resignation they had one of their own people in the presidential chair. Presbyterians had the inside track at the University of Missouri—which did not sit well at all with Methodists, Baptists, and Campbellites of that state. To meet the terms of a bequest the trustees of the municipal University of

Cincinnati maintained a required course in the Protestant Bible. In its first decades the University of Michigan was controlled by the clergy of the evangelical churches, and meetings of the board of regents were regularly opened with prayer.[21]

Even more effective in maintaining religious controls was the make-up of administration and faculty. The most important person on the campus was the president. More than anyone else, it was he who set standards and directed policy. Nine out of ten college and university presidents before the Civil War were theologians. There was little change in this ratio for one hundred years; the proportions in 1850 were about the same as in 1750. The great majority of the teaching faculty too were clergymen, rather than trained scholars or teachers. Some of them became both; but most of them would probably have agreed with Noah Webster when, at the cornerstone-laying of the first building at Amherst, he proclaimed that one of the chief purposes of American colleges was "to reclaim and evangelize the miserable children of Adam." [22]

Now the reclaiming of the children of Adam can be done in various ways. In course of time different denominational groups read new meanings into the concept, and a serious cleavage developed between two of the leading churches which had hitherto been harmoniously carrying on a joint educational program. Ever since 1801 New England Congregationalists and Scotch-Irish Presbyterians had been co-operating in church expansion and educational work on the basis of a plan of union formulated in that year. Colleges like Western Reserve, Miami, Illinois, and Knox were the result of such joint efforts. But the merger, though adopted in good faith, proved to be a union without unity. The original Scottish element, which took its Presbyterianism neat, stressed doctrinal orthodoxy and correctness of form, but in questions of social and civic morality tended to take on the color of its surroundings. The New England contingent, on the other hand, was inclined to be indifferent in theological questions, but took social reforms most seriously. With one faction waxing hot about total depravity and closed communion while the other was denouncing liquor and slavery, it was obvious that they were no longer speaking the same language. The church divided into a conservative and a liberal wing, but the New Englanders, finding even a left-wing membership too confining, denounced the plan of union entirely and eventually revived their own Congregational association of churches.

All this had a bearing on higher education. The New England-oriented social reformers tried to gain control of the jointly supported colleges and also founded new ones, with the purpose of using them as vehicles of propaganda and bases for their reforms. Chief exponent of this new direction was Oberlin, where traditional intellectual concerns were sternly subordinated to a way of life that linked a personal moral perfectionism with a comprehensive program of social and political improvement. A Yankee outpost in Ohio, its leaders and much of its financial backing came from New York and New England. The Reverend John H. Shipherd, principal founder and patron of Oberlin, had come out to the Western Reserve to save the people from "rum, brandy, gin and whiskey," and the church from "Romanists, Atheists, Deists, Universalists, and all classes of God's enemies."

From the outset Oberlin was thus committed to a philosophy of reform and progress. Asa Mahan, its first president and a scholar of note, proclaimed the new direction. Universal reform, he maintained, was not fanatic or dogmatic, but based on reason and open-minded inquiry. Oberlin would examine all sides of a question and then demand a practical correction of abuses that met the standards of the Gospel. Grounded in this philosophy, Oberlin went on to pioneer in many directions. Everybody knows that it was first to admit women to the same classes as men. It was also among the first to admit Negro students. Of great significance to its program was an early resolution of the trustees: "That the question in respect to the admission of students into this Seminary be in all cases left to the decision of the Faculty and to them be committed also the internal management of its concerns." This most unusual resolution led to faculty control and responsibility, which the faculty wisely shared with the students, who by the way were older than most college students of the time. Free discussion of all issues thus became a basic principle of which the college has always been justly proud.

When Charles G. Finney, the evangelist, succeeded Mahan as president in 1851, Oberlin really became "God's college." Finney had never been to college himself, but had studied law and entered that profession. He was a fine athlete, musically talented, a good dancer. But in his young manhood he had had a powerful conversion experience which he recalled in later years as "a wave of electricity going through and through me . . . waves and waves of liquid love . . . the breath of God . . . seemed to fan me, like

immense wings . . . literally moved my hair like a passing breeze."
The momentum supplied by that jolt carried him through a long
and distinguished career as revival preacher, crusader for perfection,
and successful college professor and president. Under Finney, militant reform at Oberlin reached its peak. A professor and several students went to jail for resisting the fugitive slave law; students and
faculty were active in both the radical and conservative branches of
the American Peace Society; wayward girls from New York City
were enrolled as students to be rehabilitated by the Female Moral
Reform Society, whose membership included both coeds and professors' wives; the Sylvester Graham diet of cold water, fresh vege-
tables, and brown bread was given a whirl; and the entire community set its face firmly against dancing, liquor, tobacco, coffee and
tea, cards, checkers, and chess. The ban against novel-reading and
the theater was relaxed a bit upon the appearance of *Uncle Tom's
Cabin.*[23]

This breadth and comprehensiveness of the reform interest was
not confined to Oberlin or, for that matter, to educational institutions. The second quarter of the nineteenth century was the flower-
ing period of perfectionism and optimistic social reform in the
United States. Societies to abolish slavery, to promote temperance,
to improve prisons, to achieve world peace, and to secure rights for
women, competed for public notice and support. The various drives
were interrelated: If you were opposed to slavery, you were probably also opposed to liquor, and you could be won over to a vege-
tarian diet and rights for women, and you were likely to have leanings toward pacifism. The same names appeared again and again in
all these crusades; the leaders moved in and out among them like
so many interchangeable parts.

On the campuses perfectionism and reform agitation became most
acute in those strategic institutions where the Scottish and the New
England strains met and mingled. Antioch College, south and west
of Oberlin, was such a spot. Named after the Syrian city where the
followers of Jesus had first been called Christians, it too was given
to the advancement of Christian reforms. Among other things, it
admitted Negro students. Its famous president, Horace Mann, insisted on this, and he had the support of his faculty, though the
trustees had their reservations. At Antioch the contending factions
were the "Christian" church, a Protestant splinter group, which controlled the trustees, and the Unitarians, whose leading spirit was

Mann himself. After some years of dissension it was decided to award the college to the group that would raise the most money. The Unitarians won.[24]

Other front-line institutions were Illinois College, Knox, also in Illinois, and Berea, in Kentucky. Edward Beecher, of the famous Beecher family and first president of Illinois, tried to convert it into an antislavery outpost. Though not as extreme as some of his colleagues, he was among those who stood guard over the abolitionist press at Alton the night before Lovejoy was murdered. Knox, in the northern part of the state, was for a while used for similar purposes. Contrary to the wishes of most of its constituents, President Jonathan Blanchard, a Vermonter who had begun his career as a reformer by smashing a jug of rum in his father's cellar, tried to train up a body of students to be vehement witnesses against liquor and slavery. "We want a martyr age of Colleges and Seminaries to send forth a host of young men at the sound of whose coming the whole land shall tremble." As for the faculty, it "ought to lead the students, both by precept and example, to take the simple ground of opposition to prevailing sins. . . ." Among such sins, as Blanchard pilloried them in many a public address, were of course slavery and whiskey, but also freemasonry, and the wrongs of Ireland. At Berea a group of former slaveholders, together with a few zealots from Oberlin, tried the impossible: the admission of Negroes to a college in a slave state. As a result, Berea's early history was one long chronicle of whippings, shootings, and mob scenes.[25]

The excesses of some of the crusading reformers led to corresponding emotional outbursts in defense of the *status quo,* in the schools as in the nation. The student debating societies in South Carolina College had been in the habit of discussing freely, and taking opposite sides, on such fundamental questions as slavery and secession; but toward the middle of the century it became more and more dangerous to take the unpopular, "subversive" side. Under the sting of mounting abolitionist criticism even its able president, the Reverend James Thornwell, was goaded into bitter denunciation of all who opposed the "peculiar institution" of South Carolina, and came to see American and world society in oversimplified terms of black and white, the righteous and the unrighteous. "The parties in this dispute," asserted Thornwell, "are not merely abolitionists and slaveholders—they are atheists, socialists, communists, red republicans, jacobins on the one side, and the friends of order and regulated freedom on the other." Nor was there unanimity on northern campuses. In conservative institutions like Princeton, or Dartmouth under President Lord, the extremism of uninformed zealots was deplored. At Amherst, after an undergraduate from Tennessee had slugged a classmate from New Hampshire, the faculty, "in the present agitated state of the public mind," ordered a student antislavery society to disband.[26]

Before long the reformers had to meet a challenge from another quarter. Oberlin, the rumor had it, was debasing intellectual standards and sacrificing solid scholarship to emotional orgies, and in eastern cultural centers classical eyebrows were being raised. Now it was true that the classics were subordinated to the Bible at Oberlin and the study of Hebrew took precedence over Greek. Finney, by his own admission not enough of a classical scholar to criticize the English translation of the Bible, resisted the effort of some of the professors to make it a literary institution at the expense of its religious character. Furthermore, the classic texts that were read had been expurgated (as in other places) and purified of all passages that "pollute and debase the mind." But things got serious when the American Education Society sent out a committee of inquiry in 1838 which reported that the Oberlin curriculum was deficient in the classics, whereupon the society resolved to render it no further financial aid. That hurt. The young college was now faced by a dilemma: What did it need more, consecration or cash? The impasse continued for a time; then, characteristically, a faculty committee was appointed to investigate "the present apparent lack of vital piety in the Institution as well as the very depressed state of the Treasury." Eventually Oberlin conformed to eastern standards and recognized the claims of scholarship.[27] The American Education Society, incidentally, was perhaps the nearest approach to anything resembling an external standard or an accrediting agency in the competitive anarchy of higher education in nineteenth century America. The society was dominated by Yale, and the voice of Yale carried far.

For other reasons, too, the fires of reform died down. With the end of the Civil War and the adoption of the Thirteenth Amendment, one of the main issues was removed from public discussion. The postwar period ushered in a new set of conditions and a changed social and economic climate, in which the old enthusiasms appeared dated. Scientific discoveries engendering new intellectual and philosophical problems turned the energies of the colleges into other and perhaps more legitimate directions, though to the regret of the old reform group. In his Phi Beta Kappa address at Harvard in 1881, Wendell Phillips, battle-scarred crusader, bemoaned the failure of the colleges to keep the lead in the agitation of the great social questions of the day.

With the decline of reforming zeal came a gradual relaxation of church control as well. By degrees the Protestant colleges came out from under the tutelage of the denominations that had launched them, to achieve either complete independence or else that casual, if sometimes uneasy, relationship which most of them enjoy today. In some of the older institutions the process of separation had begun quite early. At Harvard the turning point was perhaps the appointment by the Overseers of Henry Ware, a Unitarian, as Hollis professor of divinity in 1805, on the grounds that Harvard had been dedicated to Christ, not to Calvin. In successive amendments to the charter the ties between the Corporation and the Overseers, on the one hand, and church and state, on the other, were loosened until the connection was entirely severed and Harvard emerged an autonomous institution. Yale went through a similar process of emancipation.

At varying speeds and to varying degrees the so-called church colleges of the country followed this general pattern. Tests of orthodoxy for faculty and students were relaxed in the same way. Some had never had them. Student orthodoxy at any rate, that is, membership in a particular church, had seldom been required anywhere. This of course was simply good business in such a competitive field. Tests for professors, which had been more rigorous, were also gradually eased. At Bucknell, a Baptist school, the faculty from the beginning, in 1850, were expected to "exert a pure and saving influence," but without "sectarian peculiarities." The trustees of Northwestern University, under Methodist control, decided to elect their first faculty in 1855 without reference to church connection. A similar softening of the theological climate appears in the pledges exacted from the professors at Davidson. At its opening in 1838 every professor and tutor had to swear allegiance to the constitution of the Presbyterian church as faithfully exhibiting the doctrines taught in the Holy Scriptures; by 1887 this was watered down to a "solemn promise to be faithful in the discharge of my duty as a Professor in this Institution." [28]

Also symptomatic of secular trends were the names of colleges.

Few, except for Roman Catholic institutions, were named for saints or with any other ecclesiastical connotations. They usually took the name of the town in which they were located, often changing later to that of a prominent benefactor. The trustees, well aware of the importance of continued support by the local constituency, adopted names in gratitude for favors received or in lively anticipation of others to come.

By the last quarter of the nineteenth century denominational zeal was clearly flagging. The new science, the higher criticism, and increasing wealth and physical comfort all contributed. More and more professors were becoming specialists in their subjects, while fewer and fewer were ministers. Wealthy alumni in ever-increasing numbers and with larger and larger contributions to dangle before the trustees demanded more voice in the control of their alma mater, often at the expense of the church. Whatever the causes, it no longer seemed quite so important that a college be Presbyterian, or Methodist, or Baptist. Perhaps, too, administrators and teachers were coming to agree with Julian Sturtevant of Illinois College as to the role of state and church in higher education. Co-founder and for many years president of an institution where the fires of faith had once burned so hot that students petitioned the faculty to advance morning prayers from five to four-thirty to gain time for the Lord's work, Sturtevant expressed his reasoned conclusion, in 1860, that the state and the churches are alike constituted for other ends than the management of literary institutions, and the primary ends for which they exist will always be paramount in their proceedings and reduce all other interests which they may attempt to embrace and take care of, to a subordinate position.[29] Daniel C. Gilman, in his inaugural address at the opening of Johns Hopkins University, sixteen years later, was to voice almost the identical sentiments.

As piety receded, scholarship filled the vacuum. For a time the two were in uneasy equilibrium. They had to agree, for education was the child of religion and must remain in harmony with it. Or had the church brought forth a monster that would devour its parent? Once again the age-old dilemma of the medieval Schoolmen had to be faced: Which comes first, faith or reason? But college constituencies had to be kept reassured that there was no conflict and that all was well. This was the task of the presidents, in their public statements, their inaugural orations, and commencement addresses. And they performed the task with vigor and ingenuity. We want faith *and* reason *and* science, they said, for we are educating the whole man. And so they rang the changes, endlessly, on the old theme, varying only the phraseology as new issues arose and as the language slowly evolved. Here conservative and liberal Protestants were in substantial agreement with Roman Catholics. They could all subscribe to the Jesuit ideal of education as the full and harmonious development of the intellectual, moral, and physical powers of man, for they had all inherited Aristotle and Aquinas.[30] The body, the mind, and the spirit; knowledge, reason, and virtue; information, appreciation, aspiration—there is only one commencement address, for there is only one thing to be said. And that is so simple that it scarcely needs saying, but could be assumed as self-evident. Yet it must be said, for the peace of mind of students, professors, parents, and posterity.

Chapter Three

The Classical Tradition

More potent than the church in impressing American colleges with a common stamp was the course of study brought over from Europe and known as the liberal arts and sciences, or also as the classical tradition. As old as Western civilization itself, the liberal arts have undergone many changes in content through the centuries. Various fields of knowledge have at one time or another been included, only to grow obsolete and to be replaced by new ones. Underneath all such changes, however, a persistent idea remained intact. In all ages the pursuit of the liberal arts has meant the attempt of men to discover, by the free use of their faculties, something of the nature and meaning of the universe, man's place in it, and the highest values to which human life can attain. Put in another way, the liberal arts and sciences were those subjects of general interest and importance that were considered the indispensable intellectual equipment of an educated person. In form and organization they go back to the remarkable galaxy of talented and speculative individuals who flourished in Athens in the fifth and fourth centuries B.C. Most particularly it was Aristotle, that intellectual giant of the ancient world, to whom we owe both content and method of our thought to such a degree that even the categories under which we organize our knowledge, the "ologies" of today's college catalogues, are largely his formulation.

The path from the Athens of Aristotle to the New World Cambridge of Dunster and the Williamsburg of Blair is devious but recognizable. The Aristotelian body of knowledge and method of thinking was modified by Roman and Moslem additions, then almost lost to the Western world in the centuries of barbarism that followed the

disintegration of Roman civilization. It reappeared, diluted and fragmented, in the lectures of the masters of arts who were combining
in the thirteenth century to establish the University of Paris. Known
now as the seven liberal arts and the three philosophies, this heritage
was reconciled with the theological premises of the Roman church
and became the standard curriculum of the medieval universities.
They called it the *studium generale* and made it a prerequisite for
the study of theology and law and medicine. It passed from Paris
to Oxford, from Oxford to Cambridge. By the sixteenth century it
had lost some of its liberal qualities and degenerated into a logic-
chopping, preprofessional course for theologians. At that point it was
given new life and flexibility through the ferment stirred up by the
Italian Renaissance and the resulting introduction of polite letters.
This meant classical Latin and especially Greek poetic and philosophical writings, which were held to be a suitable cultural experience for that emerging new type, the English gentleman and public
servant. With these additions the standard university program of
studies was legalized for Cambridge in the Elizabethan Statutes for
1570 and for Oxford in the Laudian Code of 1636. Thence it was
transplanted to Harvard by the Reverend Henry Dunster and to
William and Mary by Commissary James Blair.[1]

In sparse language Dunster announced the first Harvard course
of study: *Primus annus Rhetoricam docebit; secundus et tertius Dia-
lecticam; quartus adjungat Philosophiam.* Rhetoric of course meant
Latin and Greek; dialectic or logic was conducted at first with Latin
texts, and so was philosophy or metaphysics. The purpose of it all,
in the language of the Harvard charter of 1650, was "the advancement of all good literature, artes and Sciences"; and all in the framework of eternity: "The maine end of [the student's] life and studies
is, to know God and Jesus Christ which is eternall life." In proclaiming these goals the charter was speaking not only for Harvard but, as
it turned out, for the old-time American college in general. A president of Columbia was to rephrase it over two hundred years later:
"Here in college is to be fashioned, in the highest attainable perfection, the scholar, the citizen, the good man, the Christian gentleman."[2]

The transplanted curricula of Dunster and Blair spread from the
first two colleges on American soil to all their successors. For a time
the colonial institutions managed to maintain tolerably successful
contact with Old World scientific and intellectual developments.

But in the little fresh-water colleges that marked the westward movement after independence, Europe as a source of intellectual stimulus faded into the background, and their courses of study came more and more to be replicas of those eastern colleges from which their presidents and professors had graduated: copies of copies. This accounts for the astonishing sameness of American colleges, which extended not only to the curriculum but to all aspects of college life and which lasted, with minor variations, until late in the nineteenth century. By the time Dartmouth came along, last of the nine colonial colleges, this uniformity had been thoroughly ingrained and the pattern was set. An even century separates the founding of Dartmouth in 1769 from the accession of President Eliot of Harvard, who broke the mold. This century with a few years' leeway at either end was the era in which the classical college, that unique American institution, dominated the field of higher education without serious challenge.

Rhetoric, dialectic, and logic, then, were to be the standard intellectual fare. In the heyday of the college this was expanded to mean something like the following. Freshmen and sophomores spent by far the largest amount of their time in class translating Latin and Greek classics and acquiring, it was fondly hoped, a disciplined mind and a free spirit in the process. The remainder of the program of the two lower years was made up of mathematics, rhetoric, and natural philosophy—lectures on the rudiments of physics and chemistry. In the junior and senior years the classics tapered off to give way to increasing amounts of logic, metaphysics, ethics, and polemical lectures on the evidences of Christianity, all usually taught by the president. Smatterings of modern foreign languages, history, political economy, zoology (then known as natural history), and geology rounded out the program. That was the nineteenth century version of a liberal education; inflexible and irreducible, it was required of all for the degree of bachelor of arts.[3]

It has been contended that Dunster's classical curriculum was already obsolete when it was introduced.[4] Such a suggestion, though undoubtedly true for the nineteenth century, would hardly seem fair when applied to the eighteenth. In one sense, to be sure, every college curriculum is always dated and obsolescent, for the logical organization of any body of knowledge for teaching purposes is bound to stop short of the latest developments in that field. In the nature of things it could not be otherwise. How far it stops short depends on the intellectual climate and on the alertness of the teacher. Today, a course in modern history that ended with the battle of Waterloo would admittedly be sadly out of touch with reality. But the colonial college was not so somnolent and antiquated as all that. The amazing advances in the science and mathematics of that age, for example, were known and appreciated on American campuses. Though hampered by a narrow curricular framework, Harvard showed a lively interest in science. In 1715 Yale received a library of some eight hundred volumes donated by English cultural leaders, including such men as Bishop Berkeley, and among its titles were many of the leading scientific and philosophical works of the day. At Princeton also science received considerable attention. Halley's comet and the Lisbon earthquake were intelligently discussed; telescopes and orreries were known, used, and even constructed in America. The English contacts of the Puritans, who, after all, had never been unfriendly to scientific thought, were not with Oxford, where science was in the doldrums, but with the dissenting academies, which were more alert to developments in this field, and with Cambridge, where, among others, Isaac Newton lent luster to the work in science. Newton, as professor of natural philosophy, never repeated the same course but always continued where he had left off the year before.[5] All in all, the many-sided gentleman of the eighteenth century was not so far removed from his college education as was the American businessman of a hundred years later from the classical college of his day. Thomas Jefferson and James Madison, Benjamin Rush, Ezra Stiles, and Joel Barlow were all products of American colleges.

There was another course in those days which, when given by a skillful instructor, remained in touch with contemporary thinking and the issues of the day. This was the course in moral philosophy, sometimes also known as moral science or simply as metaphysics and ethics. Aristotelian in form and origin, it supplemented and sometimes replaced the classics and mathematics in the senior year. The term moral philosophy does not suggest anything exciting, and when presided over by a droning pedant, the course was probably dull enough. But in the hands of an imaginative teacher it had possibilities. It not only included ethics in the narrower sense but contained the germs of political science, economics, psychology, in fact the whole range of what we today call the social sciences. Since it was taken by seniors as the climax of the four-year program, the president of the college usually made the course his special responsibility and took on the duties of the "moral professor" along with his administrative functions.

In its long passage from medieval Paris to the British North American colleges the course was exposed to various philosophical schools and acquired much additional intellectual baggage. Its heaviest debt was to a group of scholars in Scottish universities whose philosophical views were known collectively as Scottish realism or as the Scottish philosophy of common sense. Foremost among them were Francis Hutcheson of Glasgow, Thomas Reid and James Beattie of Aberdeen, and Adam Ferguson and Dugald Stewart of Edinburgh. All were professors of moral philosophy. Two Englishmen, not members of this school, ranked with them in popularity in the colonial colleges: William Paley, noted Christian apologist in the fight against deism, and Bishop Joseph Butler, famous author of the *Analogy of Religion* (1736). These were the authorities after whom the American professors patterned their courses. The lectures of the latter were mostly comments on the texts of the Scottish and English masters. These comments sometimes went far afield, but their point of departure was always the European authority. No original system emanated from American chairs of philosophy until Peirce, James, and Dewey fashioned pragmatism at the beginning of the twentieth century.

The Scottish philosophy was designed to liberalize Calvinism, but not too much. At the same time it protested from the conservative side against the futile materialism of Locke, the overly subtle idealism of Berkeley, and the corrosive nihilism of Hume. Locke's thesis, it will be recalled, was that man cannot know the material world as it really is but only as it appears to him through his senses, which are externally stimulated to create images or ideas of things in his mind. Bishop Berkeley carried the argument a step further by contending that inasmuch as one cannot know objective reality at all, one has no right to assume its existence. Matter as a rational concept does not exist; only ideas and the mind that perceives them are real. It was left for Hume to demonstrate, logically enough, that the human mind has no more reality than the world of things around it. Neither can be known objectively. Consequently the existence of neither mind nor matter can be postulated, but only that of ideas. At this point Reid of the Scottish school took up the argument and suggested that there are after all no such things as abstract ideas serving as intermediaries between mind and matter, except in the imaginations of hair-splitting philosophers. The reduction to absurdity is now complete: Locke has denied man's knowledge of the material world; Berkeley has demolished this world entirely; Hume has annihilated the mind; Reid has exploded the idea. Nothing is left, and the field is cleared for a new philosophy. What shall be its guiding principle? Common sense, said the Scottish school. That will lead philosophy out of the dilemma in which oversharp dialectic has entangled it. When logic and metaphysical abstractions result in palpable absurdities, all one can do is to fall back on reality as seen by practical common sense and start afresh.[6]

Common sense tells one that there are both mind and matter, good and evil, in the world, that man has freedom of choice as well as an innate moral sense, and that happiness is the goal of morality. A practical, not too profound philosophy that cut through many Gordian knots of metaphysics and ethics, the Scottish doctrine appealed to a young America preoccupied with action not contemplation, and came to dominate American academic thought. A few critics were unkind enough to suggest that it was a system with appeal only to those who, like King George III, were not particularly intelligent. In time, American texts proclaiming the same thesis came to compete with those of the Scottish masters, as professors from Columbia, Princeton, Brown, Mercer, Oberlin, and elsewhere, published their class lectures. Only a small remnant tried to keep Berkeleyan idealism alive, and later a few scholars introduced Kantian ideas. But even the idealists could not entirely escape the Scottish influence. Thus William Ellery Channing, Unitarian leader and link to Emerson, recalled as his most vital experience in college the idea of the dignity of man and the possibility of social progress, which he had derived from the Scottish texts.[7]

The American professors were by no means slavish imitators. While accepting the basic premises of the Scottish school, they enlarged or contracted, modified, deviated, and disagreed with complete freedom to suit the times and the needs of their students. The divergences are most apparent in their discussions of political, economic, and scientific matters, all of which could be drawn out of this protean course like rabbits out of a conjurer's hat. Thus President Samuel S. Smith of Princeton, who wrote one of the most complete treatises, showed unusual interest in man's physical origin. In the course of this discussion he went out of his way to explain man's physical characteristics entirely in terms of environment, even citing on what seemed to him unimpeachable evidence the example of a coal-black Negro in Maryland whose complexion changed in the course of a few years to that of a normal white man. Smith's purpose in stressing environmental factors, which he had also done in a formal paper before the American Philosophical Society, was to buttress the Biblical account of the creation and original unity of man in opposition to current European theories favoring diverse and multiple origins. All the American writers departed from their European mentors in denouncing religious establishments and class distinctions as unworthy of a free society. The impact of the new evangelical orthodoxy is discernible in some of the later texts, which began to hedge on the complete adequacy of human reason and brought revelation and divine grace back into the picture.

On slavery the American texts divided, those written in the North generally opposing it with varying degrees of vehemence, while texts like that of President Dagg of Mercer College in Georgia, widely used in the South, vigorously defended the peculiar institution as in keeping with the Bible as well as the common sense philosophy. Such thinking was in line with Professor Thomas Dew's lectures at William and Mary, as well as with the familiar *Pro-Slavery Argument,* of which Dew was the chief author. Southern colleges that used northern texts in moral philosophy would substitute the lectures of more reliable southern colleagues with the "right" point of view, when they came to this part of the course. At Randolph-Macon, for example, Francis Wayland's text was used, but when the topic of slavery was reached, the New Englander had to give way to *The Philosophy and Practice of Slavery,* a treatise written by Randolph-Macon's president, the Reverend William A. Smith, who taught the course.[8] Not only slavery but also the tariff, the currency, and other household words of nineteenth century history were likely to get an airing in this many-sided course. To cite just one of its unpredictable consequences, William Jennings Bryan maintained that his devotion to freer trade and his ideas on bimetallism had come to him in the omnibus course in mental, moral, and political philosophy which he took in his senior year at Illinois College under President Julian Sturtevant.[9] Had Timothy Dwight of Yale been able to foresee the emergence of such conflicting views, which proclaimed the inability even of moral philosophers to detach themselves entirely from their surroundings, he might have been more hesitant about insisting, as he did in his own lectures, that principles never bend to circumstances.

The vogue of Scottish realism, with its American modifications, reached its climax near the end of the nineteenth century, when President James McCosh of Princeton, himself a Scotsman born, proposed to raise it to the dignity of *the* American philosophy. Said McCosh in an address at the Chicago World's Fair of 1893: "Hitherto America has had no special philosophy as the ancient Greeks had, as the Scotch have had, and the Germans have had. But there is a philosophy lying before it, and it should appropriate it and call it its own—an advance beyond Locke, beyond the Scottish school—the American philosophy. This would be in thorough accordance with the American character which claims to be so practical. The change from the speculative to this thoroughly realistic philosophy would not be unlike that from the European Monarchies to the American Republics. Where could this be inaugurated so appropriately and auspiciously as at the World's Great Exposition?" [10]

McCosh's patriotic appeal recalls a similar gesture a hundred years earlier, when Joel Barlow of the Connecticut Wits announced that since America was destined to be a great country, it needed a great epic like the *Iliad* or the *Divine Comedy*, and out of a patriotic sense of duty proceeded to write one. But McCosh's appeal came too late. Scottish realism was already crumbling before the assaults of world-shaking new scientific theories and new precisions in philosophy. It had had its day, and it ceased to be.

Even at the height of its popularity the impact of the philosophy was probably confined to those college students fortunate enough to hear it presented by a competent and stimulating teacher; and not all enjoyed this good fortune. But there were occasional professors—so one gathers from fragmentary lecture notes and autobiographical reminiscences of their former students—who made an indelible impression by using this flexible course as a springboard to launch into whatever topic they wanted to discuss with the seniors before letting them loose on the world.[11] While students' notes are not necessarily the most reliable source for what the professor actually said, they do sometimes convey a flavor by recording the spontaneous comments and ad-libs and by suggesting overtones—all of which are carefully expurgated when class lectures are embalmed for publication. Through a student's class notes we slip into the lecture room of President Nott of Union College, one of the sprightliest of the "moral professors," and hear him hold forth, among other things, on the best way to handle mobs in town and gown riots, the evidence for the existence of ghosts, the relation between singing societies and early marriages, and the reason why Methodist ministers die young (they don't laugh enough). We also hear his warnings against the evils of drunkenness, buttressed by startling accounts of chronic alcoholics who burned to cinders, the victims of spontaneous combustion. Such a course and such a lecturer made up for years of dull recitation and routine translation of the dead languages.[12]

Whatever appeal the moral philosophy course may have had for the average undergraduate, a deeper though perhaps more unpleasant impression was left by another subject of instruction. By far the largest amount of his time and effort was devoted to the ancient languages, Greek and Latin. After practically monopolizing the student's time in the freshman and sophomore years, these "classics" continued as an important part of his program almost up to graduation. Along with mathematics they were the "core curriculum," the subjects that mattered. Other things were taught, but with the exception of the senior philosophy course they were fringe subjects.

The sciences received lip service and little more. Laboratory instruction was unheard of, but the demonstrating equipment of the better institutions was probably as good as could be had at the time; at any rate college catalogues consistently boasted of the variety and costliness of their mineral collections and "philosophical cabinets." There were some able men teaching science. Benjamin Silliman of Yale, Thomas Cooper of South Carolina, Edward Hitchcock of Amherst, and Joseph Henry of Princeton would have won respect in any scientific circle of their time. But except for such an occasional distinguished scholar, the scientists remained second-rate citizens in the academic world and their influence was negligible. For one thing there was no way of training them. Benjamin Silliman had the usual classical education and was studying law when President Dwight picked him to teach natural philosophy at Yale. His first move was to visit the University of Pennsylvania, which presented more advantages in science than any other school in the land.[13] Here he attended lectures in the medical school. Later he managed a few months of study in London and Edinburgh, being sent over on what might be called today a traveling fellowship. Few colleges were as generous as Yale to their incipient scientists. With this preparation, Silliman began his long career of teaching chemistry, mineralogy, and geology. Later, as distinguished editor of the *American Journal of Science and Arts,* which he had founded, Silliman presided over a bewildering range of scientific interests, as indicated by the titles of articles which appeared in the fifteenth volume, in 1829: "Salt Springs in the United States." "Volcanic Rocks." "Bleaching." "Fossil Organisms." "Account of an Orang Outang." "Falling Stars." "Iron in the Blood." "Christian Morals at Marseilles." "Drinking Ice-Water." "Yale Report on the Classics." "Earthquakes on the Mississippi." "Intensity of Light." "Population and Religion of Russia and France." This was no professional journal but a magazine, a storehouse, in the true sense of the word. Silliman's *Journal* was still addressing itself to the eighteenth century ideal of the universally cultured gentleman-scholar.

Not all students were so fortunate as to have a Silliman for a professor. Most of them seem to have remembered their classes in science, if at all, as a dreary routine of untested assertions or half-baked demonstrations with ridiculously inadequate equipment. Lyman Beecher, perhaps with some exaggeration, recalled the sad plight of the pre-Silliman philosophical equipment at Yale in his student days: "As to apparatus, we had a great orrery. . . . It was made to revolve, but was all rusty; nobody ever started it. There was a four-foot telescope, all rusty; nobody ever looked through it. . . . There was an air pump, so out of order that a mouse under the receiver would live as long as Methuselah. There was a prism, and an elastic hoop to illustrate centrifugal force. We were taken to see those dingy, dirty things, and that was all the apparatus the college had."

A similar complaint at Brown, many years later, was voiced by the student newspaper in 1870 when it alleged, perhaps for propaganda purposes: "A cabinet of comparative anatomy is essential to any college. . . . Every plant and animal is an expressed thought of God, and cannot be presented through the medium of a professor. Brown has one ghastly skeleton and two or three small charts, and a few promiscuous bones! Natural philosophy is also destitute of means for making the subject interesting, if it is possible to make it so. Juniors are edified with a clothes-line and a broken fiddle." Two years later a scientific school was launched at Brown.[14]

The sciences were new and insecure; the classics, on the other hand, of ancient and lordly lineage. In the Middle Ages, when the Schoolmen of Paris were blending Aristotle and Christian theology into the first university curriculum, the universal language of scholarship was of course Latin. It continued as such through the seventeenth century and then slowly gave way to the vernacular tongues as these acquired a scholarly vocabulary. The practice of printing the roster of college officers and students in Latin, with every name tortured into a Latin form, was discontinued early in the nineteenth, and our own day has seen the disappearance of that last vestige of the classical proprieties: the Latin on the bachelor's diploma and the Latin formula for the granting of degrees on commencement day.

Greek had never had as wide popular use as Latin but had nevertheless, since the time of the Renaissance, formed an essential part of the stock and substance of higher education. The two languages together were the medium for transmitting the inherited cultural tradition to posterity. Knowledge of Latin and Greek was the key to the understanding and appreciation of that grand body of history, science, and philosophy, as well as literary forms, which, together with Christianity, made up the substance of Western civilization. To know the classical age with its poets, philosophers, and statesmen was to know wisdom and the good life. That was the Renaissance ideal. Stiffened by Puritan concepts of duty and discipline, it was the ideal of the leaders of American higher education. So firmly imbedded was this belief that Provost John M. Mason of Columbia College could say with little fear of contradiction: "Experience has shown that with the study or neglect of the Greek and Latin languages, sound learning flourishes or declines. It is now too late for ignorance, indolence, eccentricity or infidelity to dispute what has been ratified by the seal of ages." And the faculty committee of which Mason was chairman was ready to dismiss as "naturally stupid or incurably idle" any student who could not take the classical medicine in full strength.

That was in 1810, and though in a sense consistent with tradition, it marks a lowering of sights for Columbia. Its first president, Samuel Johnson, a half-century earlier, had had a broader vision. He saw among the purposes of the new college not only ". . . to instruct and perfect the Youth in the Learned Languages" but also "in the Arts of reasoning exactly, of writing correctly, and speaking eloquently; and in the Arts of numbering and measuring; of Surveying and Navigation, of Geography and History, of Husbandry, Commerce and Government, and in the Knowledge of all Nature in the Heavens above us, and in the Air, Water and Earth around us, and of various kinds of Meteors, Stones, Mines, and Minerals, Plants and Animals, and of everything useful for the Comfort, the Convenience and Elegance of Life, in the chief Manufactures relating to any of these Things: And, finally, to lead them from the Study of Nature to the Knowledge of themselves, and of the God of Nature, and their Duty to him, themselves, and one another, and everything that can contribute to their true Happiness, both here and hereafter." Needless to say Johnson's program remained a soaring ideal which neither Columbia nor any other university has realized to this day.[15]

From its strongholds in the East the standard classical curriculum spread west and south, keeping pace with the building of new colleges and marking the advance of the cultural frontier. This frontier, by the way, showed little independence of judgment when it came to choosing a form of higher education adapted to its needs. Whatever originality it may have displayed in fashioning economic and political institutions—a point which the successors of Frederick J. Turner are still debating—in matters of higher education, the frontier was docile and receptive to eastern ideas.[16] At the first commencement exercises of Allegheny College in Meadville, Pennsylvania, then a frontier town of seven hundred, a local citizen gave an address in Latin, the president responded in Latin, and the graduating class contributed a Latin oration, a Hebrew oration, and a Latin dialogue. In Lexington, Kentucky, the "Athens of the West," youthful Transylvania University was warned by a writer in the *Western Review* that "should the time ever come when Latin and Greek should be banished from our University, and the study of Cicero and Demosthenes, of Homer and Virgil should be considered as unnecessary for the formation of a scholar, we should regard mankind as fast sinking into absolute barbarism." Blount College in Tennessee, chartered in 1795, began classes as soon as its president, the Reverend Samuel Carrick, had a respite from the more urgent business of shooting Indians. Yet in this environment the first backwoods graduate was examined in "Virgil, Rhetoric, Horace, Logic, Geography, Greek Testament, Lucian, Mathematics, Ethics, and Natural Philosophy." And the first catalogue of Beloit College, on the Wisconsin frontier, proudly announced in 1849 that its standard classical course of study was "drawn up exactly on the Yale plan." [17]

Exactly on the Yale plan. Bastion of the conservative forces was Yale, the largest and most influential college in the country. Princeton, intellectual headquarters of American Presbyterianism and second in influence only to Yale, was equally conservative. Both the classical tradition and the theological neo-orthodoxy of the early nineteenth century had their staunchest supporters in these two institutions; they stood for the *status quo*. But the *status quo* was not to be maintained without a struggle. America was after all a rapidly growing and changing civilization. Increasingly, not only in the West but on the Atlantic seaboard as well, the all-sufficiency of an inherited and unalterable educational formula was being questioned. New winds of doctrine, gentle and intermittent as yet, were stirring the dead air of tradition. There had always been some dissenters. The University of Pennsylvania had never conformed; in Virginia a state university with startling innovations was about to be launched, carrying the immense prestige of Jefferson's name; even Harvard was suspected of unorthodox leanings, as in fact it had been through most of its life. In the circumstances a vigorous reassertion of the merits of the old order seemed called for, and the task fell to Yale. Any educational pronouncement from Yale was certain of wide and respectful attention. And so President Day and his faculty, at the request of the Corporation, drew up a sweeping polemic designed to end the confusion once and for all. Written in 1827 and published as the "Yale Report on the Classics," the statement laid down the guide lines for the defenders of the classical tradition. It succeeded in insuring their continued control for the next half-century.[18]

The Yale report was an able document. It had a salty flavor and made short shrift of visionaries. Forceful in expression and rigorous in logic, it was a powerful plea for humanism and the liberal arts, or the genteel tradition, as then conceived. This meant primarily the classics, mathematics, and philosophy. The cultural values of science, it is only fair to say, were also vigorously defended. Yet many subjects accepted today without question as valid constituents of the liberal arts—English literature for example—were then without the pale. The central theme was the theory of mental discipline. After defining the chief end of a college education as "the discipline and furniture of the mind," the report went on to demonstrate that of the two, discipline was by far the more important. A trained intellect rather than a mere accumulation of facts was to be the goal. This is not so far removed from the goal proposed by a contemporary critic of the modern university: intelligence, capable of being applied in any field whatsoever.[19] The Yale faculty, Day went on, were by no means walking blindly on a treadmill but were constantly improving and enriching their offerings. They had no intention, however, of submitting to the popular cry. "From different quarters we have heard the suggestion that our colleges must be new-modelled; that they are not adapted to the spirit and wants of the age; that they will soon be deserted, unless they are better accommodated to the business character of the nation." To this the reply was that the object of college was not vocational and professional training, or superficial adjustment to passing popular whims. Therefore "we have on our premises no experimental farm or retail shop, no cotton or iron manufactory." Only those subjects have a place in a college curriculum that train the mental faculties, "that fix the attention, train thought, arrange the treasures of memory, and guide the powers of genius." And these subjects were the ones already mentioned, the ones that Yale was teaching at the time. None could be dispensed with, no new ones could be added. With this simple and compact program—the entire curriculum of the four undergraduate years required only one page of the catalogue for 1829-30—Yale was ready to face the world.

Certain corollaries followed from these general propositions. The entire course of study must be taken, and no choice of electives could be permitted. Modern languages, for example, though they were accomplishments and adornments, should not be required. If studied at all, it should be through their classical roots. To read Voltaire before Livy or Tacitus was "to reverse the order of nature." Class recitations, furthermore, should be from a single text to promote accuracy; wide reading in many books could only lead to confusion. In this last contention, once again, the report was strictly logical, for an educational system based on authority can brook no disagreement among its authorities. The general conclusion then: Let Yale persist in its present course. The balanced program which its faculty has so carefully constructed is for all conditions and all times, because it is founded on the eternal values.

The far-reaching influence of the Yale report can hardly be overestimated. Conservatives everywhere were encouraged to resume the fight against innovators and philistines. Yale had spoken. The issue was settled. In an eloquent address at Miami University in 1836 Lyman Beecher, leading exponent of the New England way of life in the Midwest, held the line "for God, for country and for Yale." The future of the nation, insisted Beecher, depended on the training of its college men in philosophy, logic, Greek, Latin, and the

Bible. Similar expressions by Methodist educational leaders Stephen Olin, president of Randolph-Macon, and Bishop Matthew Simpson, president of DePauw, indicated that the largest American church was swinging into line behind the Yale philosophy. President Benjamin Hale committed Hobart, an Episcopalian institution, to the same course.[20]

In the South the Yale proposals had to meet the competition of the indigenous and revered University of Virginia, but even here the Yankee notions made headway. A quarter-century after the publication of Day's report, Frederick A. P. Barnard, Yale graduate and professor at the University of Alabama, headed a faculty committee which succeeded in staving off the Virginia plan of free choice and retaining the required classical curriculum at that school. The committee convinced its colleagues that it would be a grave mistake to discard the latter "and to erect upon its ruins, a fabric of so loose a construction and so doubtful a character, as that of the University of Virginia." Barnard was still of the same mind when he moved on, a few years later, to become president of the University of Mississippi. Another graduate of Yale, President Alonzo Church, was meanwhile maintaining a similar classical regime at the University of Georgia. When Joseph Caldwell came down from Princeton, the other northern classical stronghold, to become first professor and later president of the University of North Carolina, he found a broad and flexible program of studies in force there. For this he gradually substituted the classical curriculum of his alma mater until, by the time he retired in 1835, North Carolina was thoroughly committed to the traditional order of things. A few years later James H. Thornwell, Presbyterian leader and president of the College of South Carolina, was proclaiming his policy: "While others are veering to the popular pressure and introducing changes and innovations which are destructive of the very nature of liberal education—let it be our glory to abide by the old landmarks." Shortly before this Thornwell had visited Yale, where he had been royally welcomed and had made a speech at an alumni dinner. One is tempted to speculate on what might have happened if the issue of southern secession had been left to the college graduates of the country. Perhaps the common classical heritage would have held the union together.[21]

The victory of the classicists, though sweeping, was temporary. The *status quo* is always a fragile thing, and the Yale report was really a delaying action. A most successful one, it must be admitted, for it was not until nearly the end of the nineteenth century that the system which it upheld finally collapsed. By that time the gap between theory and actuality had become too wide; or perhaps it would be more correct to say that by that time American opinion was no longer ready and American money no longer available to support that one brand of higher education and give it monopolistic control.

At no time had the critics been entirely silenced. Protests against the classical treadmill long antedated the Yale report, were in fact as old as the nation itself. Some of them led to interesting experiments which, while not always successful, were important in their day. First among the educational nonconformists was the University of Pennsylvania, brain child of Benjamin Franklin, who had never been to college. Even before it opened as the College of Philadelphia its first head, the Reverend William Smith, had written a utopian prospectus of a system of education for the New World. He called it *A General Idea of the College of Mirania,* and in it he struck a new note. The Miranians (presumably the Americans) "did not scruple to reject some things commonly taught at colleges, to add others . . . as best suited their circumstances." A daring concept in a classical age. And again: "We must not then, they say, bewilder ourselves in the search of truth, in the vast tomes of ancient schoolmen." In other words the Miranians would not be content to force their bright young men into the customary educational mold but would demand that that mold be recast to fit their actual needs. Smith could not divest himself entirely of his class bias. He was an English gentleman after all, and in translating his theories into practice he called for two types of education, one for the masses destined for the "mechanic professions," the other for the small elite of the governing classes: "the better sort." This aristocratic notion, which was to become the basis of most European systems of education, never gained wide appeal in America, for reasons that were beyond even such an enlightened eighteenth century gentleman as the Reverend William Smith. The Miranian college course was to run for five years. It subordinated but did not eliminate Greek and Latin; it added belles-lettres, history, and practical subjects such as scientific agriculture. Even though, for lack of funds and changing circumstances, Smith's ideas were never fully realized at his college, the birth of the University of Pennsylvania nevertheless marked a new departure in American higher education.[22]

What Franklin was to Pennsylvania, Thomas Jefferson was to the University of Virginia, which was to deviate even more from the norm. As early as 1779, in the midst of the Revolutionary War, Jefferson had proposed a complete system of state-controlled education to the legislature of Virginia with a university as the capstone. He first thought of the College of William and Mary in this role, but when the latter's sectarian character made it an unsuitable choice, he urged the founding of a new public university. This materialized in 1825 and was the last of Jefferson's great services to his country. Here his original educational theories found full expression. Here a student had a choice of any one of eight schools or departments, graduating whenever he had satisfactorily completed the work of the school in which he was enrolled. This might or might not take four years. With its considerable freedom of choice and its emphasis on content rather than form, Jefferson's university came to be a perennial challenge to the exponents of the classical and disciplinary school of thought. Until temporarily incapacitated by the Civil War, Virginia was the second largest college in the country, surpassed only by Yale, with whom it contended not only for the mind of the South but for the allegiance of educational theorists the country over.[23]

Similar attempts to break the classical lock step, but on a smaller scale, were made in various northern colleges. Union College, product of a real community movement, had never quite accepted New England Puritan leadership. Its very motto, *Sous les lois de Minerve nous devenons tous frères,* betrayed its erstwhile allegiance to the French Enlightenment. This was far removed from Harvard's *Christo et Ecclesiae,* to say nothing of Yale's *Urim* and *Thummim.* Under the vigorous administration of President Eliphalet Nott, the college broke with precedent, in the very year of the Yale report, by establishing a parallel course in which modern languages might be substituted for Greek. This little device of Nott's was widely copied and enlarged, so that by the third quarter of the century scores of classical colleges had set up parallel schools of languages and also of science. At the time of its introduction at Union it was so glaring a departure from tradition that Nott did not dare to grant the A.B. degree to his Greek-less mavericks, but only a diploma certifying the completion of a definite amount of work. Even so he was roundly denounced for his defiance of convention, and Union was attacked as the dumping ground of substandard students and scholastic derelicts from other colleges. Dumping ground or not, enrollments jumped in the upper classes of Union, so that they were larger than the lower classes, in complete reversal of the experience of all other colleges.[24]

While Union was kicking over the traces, a group of professors at Amherst, headed by Jacob Abbott, famous later as author of the *Rollo* books, persuaded their colleagues and the trustees to try out a more flexible curriculum of modern languages, English literature, history and political economy, and practical science, on the premise that it was absurd in a young, free, and constantly improving country "to cling so tenaciously to the prescriptive forms of former centuries." More revolutionary, if less influential, was the reorganization of the University of Vermont under James Marsh in 1826. One of the first American educators to be influenced by German thought and scholarship, Marsh proceeded on the assumption that the way to revive the run-down, bankrupt college of which he had been made the head was to give every student something interesting and significant to do. Accordingly he had them work in one or at most two of four departments: English literature, foreign languages (ancient and modern), mathematics and science, political, moral and intellectual philosophy. Thus the rigid class system fell away, and the degree was awarded, as in the University of Virginia, when the student had completed a stipulated amount of work, regardless of elapsed time.[25]

The West and South, too, had their innovators. Cumberland College in Nashville, Tennessee, chose as its president in 1825 Philip Lindsley, a Princeton graduate and professor, but an unusual one. Lindsley did not regard himself as a dedicated apostle of the Princeton scheme of values but was willing to give the people of Tennessee a rational system of education commensurate with their needs and wants. His concrete plan was for six colleges, some humanistic, some vocational, together constituting a university. In this plan classical studies would by no means be eliminated but would cease to hold the center of the stage.[26]

Foremost among the critics of the established order before the days of Eliot was Francis Wayland of Brown. Two insistent problems confronted Wayland during his presidency there from 1827 to 1855, one intellectual, the other financial. They were interrelated. The first was a constantly growing volume of complaint by college graduates and others that the classical curriculum was not getting the results its defenders claimed for it. The wisdom of the ages might well be contained in the writings of ancient Greek and Roman authors, but it was successfully concealed from the student by coming to him through the medium of a foreign language and a dead one at that. The kernels of classical wisdom and truth were imbedded in a hard shell of grammar and syntax, and most students never learned to crack the shell. College classes rarely got to the point of actually discussing the ideas of the writers they were supposed to be studying but remained bogged down in the preliminaries of form and construction.

Andrew Dickson White, later president of Cornell, summed up the charges neatly in recalling his student days at Yale. Though the work there, he admitted, was superior to that of a smaller college which he had first attended, much of it was still a waste of time. Class exercises consisted largely of recitation by rote, with most of the time given to structure and form. The system "made everything of gerund-grinding and nothing of literature." [27] That was the crux. The good student was one who spotted the ablative absolute, and excellence consisted in snappy recognition of that subtlest of all distinctions: the one between the gerund and the gerundive, the tweedledee and tweedledum of Latin syntax. A trained mind was supposed to result from all these mental acrobatics, but did it? Or were the pedagogues confusing ends and means, were they putting the cart before the horse? So the complaints ran. They may have been unfair to the more scholarly teachers and better students, but they had wide vogue and needed to be answered.

Wayland proposed to answer them. He was prompted by another and most practical concern. Brown, along with most other New England colleges, was losing students. In the face of a rapidly rising population, college enrollments were almost stationary.[28] This meant dwindling funds and loss of prestige. To the solution of his twofold problem Wayland brought freshness and originality.[29] Independent in judgment, he refused to accept institutions whose sole merit was their antiquity. When he found textbooks not to his liking, he wrote his own. When he reached the conclusion that the entire collegiate system of the United States was wrong, he persuaded the trustees of Brown to let him substitute a new one. Such a drastic change was necessary, he felt, because the colleges had lost their momentum, having allowed precedent and authority to obscure contemporary needs. "God intended us for progress"—the all-American slogan of the nineteenth century—"and we counteract his design when we deify antiquity, and bow down and worship an opinion, not because it is either wise or true, but simply because it is ancient." It was not surprising, therefore, that the public was withholding students and funds. "What could Virgil and Horace and Homer and Demosthenes . . . do toward developing the untold resources of this continent?" The time-worn argument for the classics as mental discipline, Wayland curtly dismissed as the lazy excuse of a poor teacher. What this growing country needed instead was suitable studies for all. "When our systems of education shall look with as kindly an eye on the mechanic as the lawyer, on the manufacturer and merchant as the minister; when every artisan shall be transformed from an unthinking laborer into a practical philosopher; and when the benign principles of Christianity shall imbue the whole mass of our people with the spirit of universal love,—then, and not till then, shall we illustrate to the nations the blessings of republican and Christian institutions."

To achieve all this, the college curriculum must first be enlivened with new subjects. But if that is done without removing old ones, the result will be an indigestible mass of subject matter and, inevitably, superficial and slovenly work. The student will acquire the habit of "going rapidly over the textbook with less and less thought," and cultivate "the passive power of reception instead of the active power of originality." This was already happening. As the best way out of the dilemma, Wayland urged the substitution of free electives for the old system of compulsion. Every student—and this was his final recommendation to the trustees—should henceforth choose his courses freely under faculty guidance. When he had completed a requisite number in any combination and passed a comprehensive examination covering all his studies, he was to receive the A.B. degree. This need not take four years; if the student worked hard and took enough courses, he might finish sooner. To give students sufficient variety of choice the course of study at Brown was to be enriched by the addition of modern languages, science, history and political economy, agriculture, law, and the science of teaching. The ancient languages, competing on an equal basis with all other subjects, would stand or fall on their merits. The trustees adopted Wayland's recommendations, introduced the new subjects, and established the degree of bachelor of philosophy for non-classics students. They also made it possible to earn a master of arts degree in four years. This had been a purely honorary degree heretofore. When these changes became effective, Brown differed more widely from the norm than any other northern college.

Quite different from Wayland's ideal but also a departure from convention was the program that Henry Philip Tappan tried to introduce at the University of Michigan. Tappan, who had studied in Germany, published his views in a treatise, *University Education,* which appeared the year after Wayland's report, and offers an interesting contrast to the latter. The aim of Tappan's projected model university was not vocational or civic training for the mechanic and the merchant but intellectual excellence of a kind that America did not yet appreciate. "In our country," Tappan maintained, "we have no universities." The way to get them was not by popularizing the colleges, as Wayland had suggested, but by raising the standards and intensifying the work for the qualified few. Tappan, in other words, would not broaden the base but raise a superstructure. Like Jeremiah Day in the Yale report, he hoped to train the intellect, but he did not propose to limit himself to the classics and mathematics as a means to that end, and he was not satisfied with the passive receptivity of the student implied in Day's scheme. Genuine university students should be above the close supervision and spoon-feeding of the average college. They should already have acquired the necessary general knowledge and formed habits of study and investigation which would "enable them to hear the lectures of professors to advantage, to consult libraries with facility and profit, and to carry on for themselves researches in the different departments of literature and science." Tappan believed it was a mistake to dangle college before the commercial and agricultural classes, for in America men did not need college to achieve material success. The many easy roads to wealth created "a distaste for study deeply inimical to education." Cheapening college therefore with a window dressing of practical subjects would not help. There might be a temporary influx of students, but only until the novelty wore off. The only proper incentive was "the satisfaction and distinction of a thorough and lofty education." With this aristocratic ideal Tappan set out for Michigan, in the heart of the democratic West.[30]

The range of these various educational programs was considerable, and the solutions were diverse. Some of the problems touched upon are not too different from those that agitate the educational world today. At the time, not much came of them. The net results of three decades of critical discussion of the historic curriculum were aston-

ishingly meager. Most of the programs vegetated or collapsed entirely. A modern student has called the period a false dawn.[31] Reasons for the failure were manifold. In the case of Tappan, whose
program never got off the ground, it was clearly a lack of perspective
which prompted the abortive attempt to graft a foreign system onto
a native growth that could not support it. The turbulent frontier
society of Michigan, torn by local jealousies and sectarian strife, did
not look with favor upon a state university modeled upon European
originals, nor did it appreciate the dignified and imperious president who liked to call himself chancellor and who flaunted an
eastern accent. His motives were misunderstood, his ideals ridiculed,
and his efforts to raise scholastic standards suspected as vaguely un-
American. He induced a reaction in his constituents not unlike that
of a recent Secretary of State in the junior Senator from Wisconsin.
"He has been hobnobbing with aristocrats," cried the editor of the
Detroit *Free Press* in alarm; "he is prussianizing free Americans.
Ann Arbor is not Berlin." And the Lansing *Journal* jeered: "Of all
the imitations of English aristocracy, German mysticism, Prussian
imperiousness, and Parisian nonsensities, he is altogether the most
un-Americanized—the most·completely foreignized specimen of an
abnormal Yankee, we have ever seen." [32] Coming in 1854 at the
height of the Know-Nothing movement, these editorial outbursts
poured oil on the flames of intolerant natonalism and materially
weakened Tappan's position. In the face of growing opposition he
held his views before the Michigan electorate for eleven years and
then was forced out. It was some years before Michigan caught up
with the ideals of its first great president.

Implied in the opposition to Tappan was a certain anti-intellectualism, which was nation-wide and not limited to Michigan. "Eggheads" were derided in the nineteenth century at least as much as
currently in the twentieth. When a bill to incorporate four denominational colleges in Illinois was up for passage in 1835, one of its
more vehement opponents in the legislature proudly proclaimed
that he was "born in brier thicket, rocked in a hog trough, and had
never had his genius cramped by the pestilential air of a college."
A few years earlier, in 1829, in an attack on Indiana College, the
precursor of the state university, it was locally charged that the president and faculty were Yankee intellectuals opposed to Andrew Jackson, and presumably not real folks and dyed-in-the-wool Hoosiers.[33]

Such resentment of the intellectual and, by inference, of the expert was not confined to the field of higher education. The body of popular beliefs that we loosely identify as Jacksonian democracy had almost elevated this prejudice into an ideal. In politics the belief that any decent citizen was competent to hold any public office soon degenerated into the spoils system. Suspicion of lawyers as the smooth-tongued parasites of the ruling classes is as old as our history. In some western states equalitarian distrust of experts in medicine was carried to such lengths that charlatans with no medical education could hang out their shingle without a license, pose as one of the people and accuse trained physicians of the community as being "arrayed against the people." [34] In his picaresque novel, *Modern Chivalry,* Hugh Brackenridge, writer of the Pennsylvania frontier, satirized the popular mood by having his leading character lose an election as a result of the charge by the opposition that he was seen reading a book.

A strange ambivalence in the American character is apparent here. Paradoxically enough, from the same communities that expressed their suspicion of higher learning came the enthusiastic support, the financial contributions, and the disinterested labor and tenacious loyalty that have been the mainstay of most colleges to this day. Even today the average man is likely to look upon university professors and experts with a mixture of respect, envy, suspicion, and contempt, yet is pleased and proud when his son and daughter come home with a university degree. He is ready to believe his favorite college guilty of all the black arts and a hotbed of every subversion, but when he has made his fortune, is just as likely to leave half of it to that self-same college for a building or a fund to raise professors' salaries. It has always been so. The schizophrenic attitude toward higher education in America has an ancient, if not always honorable, history.

Tappan at Michigan had succumbed to nationalism and anti-intellectualism. Wayland's experiment at Brown collapsed for precisely the opposite reason. Wayland had tried, on the broadest democratic principles, to make equal educational opportunity a reality and to open the college doors to Tom, Dick, and Harry. But the intellectual elite of New England ganged up on him. From the time his program got under way, while popular newspapers generally applauded, the magazines with a highbrow clientele expressed doubts. Brown, like Union, was accused by other college leaders of debasing the educational currency, and a degree from Brown acquired in less than four years or without benefit of Greek or Latin came to be considered shoddy and second-rate. Brown's prestige withered, its enrollment slumped. When Wayland retired, his successor persuaded the trustees to give up the "cheap" A.B. and A.M. programs entirely and to return to the old ways.[35]

Elsewhere, too, educational experimentation was losing momentum. Lindsley in Tennessee was kept from his goal by lack of funds, popular indifference, and the competition of church colleges. The parallel course at Union was retained but did not draw many students. The Amherst plan, after a three-year trial, succumbed to the hostility of the majority of the faculty. Loss of prestige and poor teaching in the new subjects were the assigned reasons for abandoning it. Even at Harvard, where George Ticknor, first American to study in German universities, had brought fresh intellectual stimulus and where President Quincy had introduced limited electives, this freedom was again restricted under later presidents. Of the nonconforming institutions only the University of Virginia was flourishing. But its popularity was due not so much to any widespread approval of its liberal program of studies as to the rising tide of southern nationalism. Its sister state university at Chapel Hill was almost as large as Virginia, yet there the classical curriculum was in full force. The catalogue of North Carolina in the mid-century period shows the customary near-monopoly of the ancient as compared to modern languages; the figures represent the number of class periods per semester in each of the four college years beginning with the freshman: Latin, 83, 65, 57, 30; Greek, 83, 74, 54, 38; French, 0, 18, 47, 18. At Columbia, another institution that had dabbled in reform, a trustees' committee reported that a literary and scientific course established in 1830 had "rolled in on a tide of public excitement," but had attracted few students and "after dragging out a feeble existence" was abolished in 1843. The low regard in which science was held at Columbia appears in another trustees' resolution, in 1862, permitting Professor Torrey, the famous naturalist, to give a series of lectures in botany "at such hours as will not interfere with the regular studies of the undergraduates." [36]

Some of the innovations did become permanent fixtures. The parallel course leading to a diploma or a separate degree was widely adopted, and by the third quarter of the century most college catalogues were listing, in addition to the standard classical course, a modern language course leading to the degree of bachelor of philosophy, Ph.B., and a science course leading to the bachelor of science, B.S. But these remained sideshows and did not admit the student to the main tent. As late as 1880 classical students at Yale could casually dismiss one of the best of them, Sheffield Scientific School, with the words, "Sheff did not count." [37]

When in 1854 John McLean, newly elected president of Princeton, announced the principles that were to guide him, he was expressing the prevailing views of responsible educators of his time. "We shall not aim at innovation," said McLean; "no chimerical experiments in education have ever had the least countenance here." It was not his intention to make Princeton College a collection of separate schools or to permit its students to decide for themselves which branches to study and which to neglect. Aiming, as always, at mental discipline, Princeton would adhere to the tested curriculum and require all its students to take all of it. To modern languages, political economy, and the sciences "sufficient attention will be given to impart a definite idea of the matters of which they treat." Princeton would remain conservative and safe. Even safer and more conservative was the Princeton theological seminary. There, on the occasion of the semicentennial of the revered Professor Charles Hodge, noted Biblical scholar and ardent anti-evolutionist, the latter expressed his fervent satisfaction that in all his fifty years not a single new idea had come out of Princton.[38] Academic and theological orthodoxy went hand in hand. The old guard was still in the saddle. Three decades of agitation had apparently availed little. The nineteenth century was two thirds over, and the traditional college was still pretty much what it had been at its opening. The idea of a university, serving the needs of a changing social order with freedom of choice and encouragement of research, had not yet been realized. Neither Wayland nor Tappan had found much support, and the day of Eliot and Gilman had not dawned.

To describe a formal course of study and its historic development is one thing, to find out what the students subjected to it actually learned quite another. What kind of factual information was accumulated and in what amount? How much intellectual activity went on, how much independent thinking, and of what quality? Questions like these, dealing as they do with the end product of education, are the most important to ask and the most difficult to answer. Today, with the most modern statistical devices at our command, we still can measure only quantitatively, in terms of percentiles, the position

of our students when compared to that of the generality of their contemporaries. The quality and flavor of the individual intelligence and
achievement of each still elude us. We have not accounted for the
wide intangible field of mutual education arising out of the informal
day-by-day contacts of students with each other and with their professors; how can you assign grades to bull sessions and the long, long
thoughts of youth? A century ago even such bookkeeping devices as
we have now were unavailable except in simpler cruder forms. For
another reason, too, comparisons between our time and an earlier
day are not very enlightening. The body of organized knowledge
available to the generations before us was vastly smaller, and the
physical conditions and climate of opinion under which they worked
quite different. Aims and objectives have shifted in the last hundred
years. The best that can be done is to bring into focus bits and samples of information about individual students and colleges and thus
to shed a little light on the nature and quality of the work done.

Who could get into college in the first place? Harvard answered
that question in the very beginning. "When any schollar is able to
understand Tully, or such like classicall Latine Author *extempore,*
and make and speake true Latine in Verse and Prose. . . . And decline perfectly the Paradigm's of Nounes and Verbes in the Greek
tongue: Let him then and not before be capable of admission into
the Colledge." [39] This prescription, somewhat increased as to the
amount read, and reduced as to the facility of speaking Latin, and
with arithmetic added, might have fitted almost any college down to
the invention of entrance units and graduation credits near the end
of the nineteenth century. We might choose one at random. To be
admitted to Rutgers in 1845 a boy had to have "a knowledge of Latin
and Greek grammar, including so much of the Prosody as is necessary for scanning Hexameters: six books of Virgil's Aeneid; Cicero's
Oration against Catiline; Sallust; the Greek Gospels and Acts of the
Apostles; Jacob's or Clark's Greek Reader; and Arithmetic at least
as far as the rule of Proportion—decimal and vulgar fractions inclu-
sive." This had been the catalogue statement, with minor changes,
for the past twenty years; it continued virtually unchanged for
another twenty, when ancient and modern geography and algebra
to quadratic equations were added. Plane geometry and English
grammar and spelling came in 1868, United States history in 1869. [40]

It is significant that until the inclusion of history, admission requirements were limited to "tool" subjects. Facts were secondary.

The classics chosen were read not for the information they conveyed but for the training they gave. The same of course was true of mathematics. The emphasis was not on "what," but on "how to." In an age when the chief end of higher education was discipline, this was only natural.

When a boy had demonstrated to the president, or to a professor designated by the president, that he could handle the tools, he was admitted to college. There was no set time for this such as graduation from high school. There were no high schools as we know them today. Secondary education was the last to be standardized; both the college and the elementary school preceded it. If an entering student was fortunate enough to have attended one of the excellent Latin schools on the Atlantic seaboard, he had an advantage over his classmates. He might have had a few haphazard years at one of the many academies. Or he might have studied Latin and Greek privately with the local minister until the latter thought he was ready. Examining the entering student was a casual matter in the early days, consisting often of nothing more than a sample of oral translation, though gradually the size of the entering classes made more formal arrangements necessary. Even then irregularities in admission procedures were widespread. Ohio University in Athens was not unique in permitting students to enter at any time during the school year, even though the catalogue "earnestly recommended, both for the advantage of the students and the convenience of the Professors, that they should enter at the beginning of the term." The many students who transferred from other colleges to Union to take advantage of the relaxation of the classics requirement were allowed to enter as late as the third term of the senior year without losing time or class standing. A Yale student who urged a friend to join him there rather than go to Harvard cited as inducement his experience with admission standards. When he arrived, with rather better preparation than the average entrant, President Dwight (the elder) "advised me, on making more particular inquiries into my studies, to enter the junior class if my circumstances were easy, if not, to enter the senior class." [41] This case was perhaps not typical, for Dwight and his successor Jeremiah Day did much to improve standards and raise entrance requirements at Yale.

On the whole, though, it was sloppy business, any efficient university admissions officer would say—no entrance units, no quality grades, no prerequisites checked off, no mathematical equalization of transfer credits, none of the legerdemain of present-day high priests of educational efficiency. Yet one hesitates to say that the old easy-going ways were completely ineffectual. They did provide a measure of flexibility and gave some opportunity to the understanding college officer to deal with each student according to his needs and capacities. It is just possible that Timothy Dwight and Eliphalet Nott and Mark Hopkins and others like them knew what they were doing when they made their exceptions seemingly on the spur of the moment. They had a much simpler problem of course in the uncomplicated little colleges over which they presided. Today we are again searching for flexibility and trying to recover the human touch, for we have escaped the old classical rigidities only to be caught in the modern strait jacket of a hundred and twenty points for a degree. It is debatable whether the electronic computers of our day come up with a more honest answer than the old-time college to that disturbing question which keeps the seniors uneasy as graduation time approaches: A.B. or no A.B.?

We do know that even though the wise president did his best to place incoming students where they belonged, the freshman classes that assembled on American campuses a hundred years ago were in most cases an ill-assorted lot. The professors thought so at any rate. But they usually do. Great plans for high achievement often had to be deflated because the material was not there. College after college had to lower its sights to more realistic levels. At Virginia, Jefferson's high-flown ideas were stepped down, and his university was reduced to the ordinary college work of that day because of the poor quality of the secondary feeder schools. Even the classical department of the university had to accept "shameful Latinists." And the Hobart faculty published a strangely modern-sounding complaint that all its efforts to maintain high standards were being frustrated by "the inadequate manner in which young men are generally prepared for college." They were especially weak in grammar and mathematics, said the professors at Hobart. That was in 1840. We are still saying it today.[42]

The students, had they been a little older, might have turned that argument around and asked the professors how well *they* were prepared for the specialties they were professing. As a rule, not very well, for most professors were ministers whose formal training had not gone beyond the classical course of undergraduate studies they had completed at Yale or Princeton and who set up at Knox, or

Wabash, or Tusculum, or Oglethorpe pale reproductions of that. Although there was always the gifted and conscientious teacher who outgrew the leading-strings of his alma mater and continued to advance in his field, the offerings of the average professor were more likely to be seconds and retreads of eastern originals which were themselves not too original. Specialization in any modern sense was nonexistent. There was a rough fourfold division of the curriculum, and the better schools had at least one professor each in the classics, mathematics and science, rhetoric and belles-lettres, logic and philosophy. But these men occupied settees not chairs.[43] Furthermore the president might at any time ask the professor of chemistry, mineralogy, and geology to take on sophomore Greek for a year, and similarly the classics professor would think nothing of spelling the president in his moral and political philosophy course when the latter was away from campus preaching or raising funds. The theological interests or religious motivations of presidents and professors sometimes got in the way of scientific specialization. To call this anti-intellectualism would be too harsh a criticism, yet on many a campus there was continual skirmishing in the no man's land between piety and intellect.

Professional degrees did not mean what they do today. Every professor had the A.B. degree, and some had a theological degree besides, which might be earned or honorary. The Ph.D. as a degree testifying to productive research was a German importation, rare before the last quarter of the century. The A.M. was common; it was easy to obtain and in fact could hardly be avoided. Almost any college graduate who remained alive and kept out of jail could have it. As one college catalogue put it, "Every graduate of the college shall after five years and the payment of ten dollars, be granted an A.M. provided he has been continually of exemplary and virtuous character." [44]

Libraries were not the tool they have become today. Although the older institutions had some very respectable collections, their holdings were uneven and full of serious gaps. What is more, they were not for the undergraduate but intended for faculty use, just as the chained volumes in medieval libraries were for scholars and masters. Most colleges had two collections: one for faculty and one for students, the second usually much smaller. In time the two libraries were merged. At William and Mary this was done as early as 1839, and the combined collections then totaled 6,000 volumes. By way of contrast the undergraduate college of Fordham University announced as late as 1913 that "the library contains 50,000 volumes, of which 10,000 have been carefully selected for the use of students." [45] When students were finally admitted to the whole collections, it was only at stated times and under rigorous safeguards. The limitations as announced in the catalogues were of various kinds. The library might for example be open every Wednesday and Saturday from twelve to one; or every Wednesday after dinner; or five days a week for a half-hour at noon. One institution allowed students to draw either two octavo volumes, or one quarto or folio, at a time. The College of South Carolina was the first to have a library building. This was erected in 1840, one year before the Harvard library of 41,000 volumes was housed in newly erected Gore Hall. Yet even South Carolina had no trained library staff; a professor doubled as librarian for $100 a year.[46]

How much reading students actually did, in or out of the library, is difficult to determine. No doubt many, then as now, covered the class assignments and called it a day. But bits of information from scattered diaries and biographies suggest that there was a considerable minority which read beyond the call of duty. Very few, one can be sure, measured up to the counsel of perfection offered by Thomas Jefferson to his nephew: from dawn to eight—physical studies, ethics, religion, and natural law; from eight to twelve—reading law; from twelve to one—politics; in the afternoon—history; from dark to bedtime—belles-lettres, criticism, rhetoric, and oratory.[47] A Williams man of the class of 1806 had read, besides all the studies and exercises of the course, Bacon's essays, Newton, Locke on *Human Understanding,* Robinson's life of Charles V, Marshall's life of Washington, Gibbon's *Decline and Fall of the Roman Empire,* Hume, the Scottish realists Reid and Stewart, Paley, Jonathan Edwards, Voltaire, and Montesquieu. The published diaries of two students of the 1840's, one at Amherst and the other at South Carolina, make frequent references to the reading they were doing. In his winter vacations of about five weeks William G. Hammond of Amherst read three books of Euclid, fifteen sections of Tacitus, Hazlitt's *Table Talk,* a life of Aaron Burr, *The Merchant of Venice,* Pascal, Bossuet, and Molière in the French original, along with such current bestsellers as Macaulay's *Lays of Ancient Rome* and Carlyle's *Heroes and Hero-Worship.* He was also a regular reader of the *North American Review.* Hammond's contemporary at South Carolina, Giles Patter-

son, was a back-country boy and a serious student. He spoke highly
of the remarkable course given by Francis Lieber, refugee German
scholar, which was a mixture of institutional history and comparative government. No other professor apparently left so favorable an
impression. Patterson complained, however, that the faculty cut
classes too much and hoped the trustees would take them in hand.
His diary indicates that Patterson read De Tocqueville's *Democracy
in America,* Bancroft's *History of the United States,* Homer, Milton,
Plutarch, Gibbon, Hume, Burke, and Adam Smith.[48] Now this was
solid reading. Whatever the limitations of breadth and scope, one
thing seems certain: When college students in those days did read,
they read the great authors themselves and not diluted textbooks
about them or samples of "readings" from their works.

Hammond and Patterson were probably exceptional students. A
more accurate picture of the routine demands on the time of the
average student could be obtained if data were available listing the
work done and ground covered by a given class in a given term. We
have such a glimpse of what went on in one college in an "Abstract
of Studies" reported by the faculty of Hobart in 1840.[49] Here is a
down-to-earth account, not inflated or prettified, of work completed
in that year by the four classes of Hobart. There we read, for example, that the freshmen read *"The Odyssey,* Books VII, VIII, and IX,
entire, and X, to 245th line, and reviewed." The complete senior
program was as follows: "Cousin's Psychology, entire and reviewed.
History of Philosophy . . . dissertations by all members of the class;
thirteen exercises. Chronology of the Old Testament; Genesis and
Exodus. Butler's Analogy, entire and reviewed. De Tocqueville's Democracy, Volume I, entire. Wayland's Political Economy, entire and
reviewed. Boucharlat's Mechanics, 25 pages (left from the preceding
year). Electricity and Magnetism, by lectures, twelve. Bartlett's Op-
tics, entire and reviewed. Norton's Astronomy, 212 pages, and reviewed. Chemistry, 79 lectures and examinations. Mineralogy and
Geology, twenty lectures. Demosthenes, Oration 'On the Crown,'
eighty pages. Aeschylus, 'Prometheus Vinctus,' and 'Septem contra
Thebas,' entire. Greek Testament, I and II Timothy, I and II Peter,
entire. Don Juan d'Autriche, 170 pages."

It is difficult to recognize this studious institution as the carousing
college of Andrew Dickson White's *Autobiography,* where students
threw beer bottles at the president, and White learned nothing. The
Hobart faculty's own comment on its abstract of studies: "This

shows what a high standard we try to maintain against great obstacles, chief of which are narrow financial resources and the [already mentioned] inadequate manner in which young men are generally prepared for college."

An even better measure of the range and character of the old classical education at its best is found in a set of examination questions given to the senior class at Princeton in 1870.⁵⁰ This was the first year of Eliot's regime at Harvard, where the epoch-making reforms that were to convert the college into a university were about to begin. Here then, at Princeton, was the classical college at the summit of its career. All the seniors at Princeton that year were examined in Latin, Greek, chemistry, ethics, political economy, modern history, science and religion. There were from eight to ten questions in each of these subjects, and all had to be answered. A sampling will give the flavor. In Latin the *pièce de résistance* was a passage from Quintilian which first had to be translated into idiomatic English. It was then to be analyzed for syntax, derivation, subjunctives, and kinds of clauses. Then the student had to give the year and place of Quintilian's birth, "with proof," name his works, and characterize the Silver Age of literature. An essay on the history of the Greek and Latin verb, with derivations from the Sanskrit, completed the examination in the ancient languages.

Some of the questions in the other fields were as follows:

In chemistry: "A pound of marble contains how much oxygen?" "Explain the preparation and uses of H_2S." "If ten grams of iron rust, it is then what and how much?"

In ethics: "Define conscience, how far it is cognitive and emotional, and what light it sheds on the Nature of Virtue. Define truth, and our various obligations in reference to promoting, stating, and keeping it." "Explain professional ethics, especially as related to the various obligations of lawyers."

In political economy: "Explain value, utility, price, wealth, the rise and fall of prices and values in relation to supply and demand." "State the various modes of restricting the freedom of labor, and explain the effects of bounties, special taxes, trade unions, and other forms of such restriction."

In history: "How is history treated by Political, Ecclesiastical, Scientific, and Speculative historians?" "Define Civilization as a subject of history." "What were the causes of the fall of the Roman Empire?" "What was the origin of the Feudal System?" "What were the causes of the Reformation?" "What was the effect of the Treaty of Westphalia on the international system of Europe?" "How did American civilization differ in its origin from European?"

In science and religion: "How does physical science show that there is an intelligent Author of Nature?" "How does physiology and psychology show the probability of a future life?" "Define metaphysics." "State the logical and chronological order of ideas. Distinguish between Realism and Nominalism."

Those were the results expected of students who had spent four years pursuing a linguistic, mathematical, and philosophical program by way of sharpening their intelligence and who had also, in the language of Princeton's president, given sufficient attention to modern languages, political economy, and the sciences "to impart a definite idea of the matters of which they treat." Any judgment of the quality of this examination in terms of present-day requirements would be difficult and also unfair in view of new presuppositions that prevail today. Nevertheless certain comparisons can profitably be made. One is struck by the complete absence of English literature, which apparently was not yet taught as such.[51] There was no examination in mathematics, probably because it had been taken care of in the three lower years. The chemistry questions seem a bit elementary; still, a senior of today, having taken introductory chemistry in his freshman year, might not find them so. Political economy was straight Manchester *laissez faire* theory with a probably unconscious antilabor bias. History was no longer chronology but dealt with causes, origins, and results. "Trends" had not yet been discovered, but the questions include some old chestnuts which are still around. Ethics was quite theoretical except for that reference to lawyers. Metaphysics too was formal and antiquated and had an eighteenth century if not Aristotelian flavor. Science and religion, with its loaded questions, was based on the president's lectures in evidences of Christianity. Latin and Greek are harder to compare because no comparison is possible with what no longer exists. Not a senior in a thousand could tackle those questions today. In sum, this examination mirrors the achievements and the limitations of the classical college of our great-grandfathers.

Chapter Four

Portrait of the Residential College

~~~~~~

The very first entry on the faculty records of Bowdoin College was an admonition to John O'Brien and Moses Quinby for fighting.[1] This was symptomatic. Faculty members and administrators in virtually all American colleges spent almost as much time trying to cope with the behavior of the adolescents entrusted to them as with their studies. Campus life in all its aspects profoundly affected the intellectual product.

The classical college flourished for more than a century, from about the middle of the eighteenth to the late nineteenth. This was a period of growth and expansion for colleges as well as for the nation as a whole; however, the growth of colleges was largely external. Internal changes were so small that it is possible without much distortion to speak of the typical college of the nineteenth century. It was only in the last three decades of that century that any substantial changes occurred either in the aims or the methods of higher education. By the time of the accession of President Eliot at Harvard, which might be considered the beginning of the end of the "college era," there were some two hundred such institutions covering the United States from the Atlantic to the Pacific, the survivors of a precarious and often intensely competitive infancy. The exact number is difficult to determine, since "college" as well as "university" was then a term of hopeful ambition rather than of precise definition. By the opening of the Civil War, however, perhaps twenty to twenty-five thousand young men and a few hundred young women were being given the current version of a liberal education. On the whole college growth had not been very rapid, certainly not even. In the populous northeastern states, for example, college enrollments between 1840 and 1860 had not kept pace with the population. The largest in terms of student enrollment in 1860 were Yale, the University of Virginia, and the University of North Carolina, each with five hundred or more undergraduates. If such factors as the size of the faculty and the library are taken as the standard of measurement, Harvard led all the rest with a faculty of twenty-four scholars and gentlemen in its college of arts and a library of 123,000 volumes. At the other end of the scale were dozens of little establishments where half a hundred students together with a president, a couple of tutors, a shelf of Latin and Greek classics, and a dingy philosophical cabinet constituted the enterprise. But all of them, large or small, would have understood one another's courses of study and campus problems.[2]

The cost of a college education varied considerably, according to the character of the institution. Lowest in cost were the smaller institutions of the frontier or up-country, where local community and church support, as well as the desire to cater to ministerial students, kept expenses down. In places like Bowdoin, Hamilton, Oberlin, and Davidson, at the middle of the century and for some time before and after, a thrifty student could keep expenses for tuition, room, board, fuel, and washing within $100 a year. It was a different story in the older seaboard colleges with a national reputation. At Harvard tuition alone was $75, and the total annual bill was likely to run up to at least $250. Some students, of course, spent much more. Early in the century John Rutledge, wealthy South Carolina planter, estimated that his son, a student at Harvard, ought to be able to get along on $600 a year. A commencement spread for a hundred guests given by a Harvard senior in 1817 cost his parents $780, of which $79 was for wine, and the ice cream cost $2 a quart. Princeton too got a reputation quite early as a place for well-to-do young gentlemen, and its presidents throughout the nineteenth century felt it necessary to reassure the Presbyterian brethren that a poor boy could make out quite well at Old Nassau. In 1804 President Smith estimated the average annual expense there at $171.23, yet it was known that many students spent $500 and more. An experiment in 1831 of a poor students' table in the dining hall only emphasized the class distinctions it was designed to minimize. And in 1883 President McCosh, once again compelled to defend the college against the charge of conspicuous consumption, insisted that it was possible to go through on as little as $200 a year.

Matching these northern schools in costs were the state-supported institutions of the South. The most expensive college in the country next to Harvard was the University of Virginia. At South Carolina College in 1840 tuition was one third higher than at Oberlin as late as 1890. In general, southern state universities charged higher rates than the private and denominational colleges of the section and were widely criticized by the church people as the exclusive preserves of the rich and socially elite. Something of the same thing happened in time at the older inland colleges of the North. Amherst began to undergo a transformation after the middle of the century, when sons of well-to-do businessmen displaced the poor farm boys and ministers' sons of the early years. Andrew Dickson White felt uncomfortable among his wealthy and dissipated classmates at Hobart.[3]

With some exceptions, then, the colleges had not remained what most of them had set out to be: institutions for all the people. This condition was to be remedied in the last third of the century by the new type of state university in the West and Midwest, entirely tax-supported and state-controlled, and with tuition costs low or entirely free.

Rich or poor, all students at first lived in one building surrounded by as much land as had been donated, or as the trustees had had the vision and the cash to acquire. Harvard called it the Yard because it was cut out of one of the cowyards at the edge of Cambridge; William and Mary and Yale, too, used the term to designate their properties. But Princeton in 1774 adopted the Latin "campus," and one by one the other colleges, except Harvard, followed suit. In its one building the college lived and worked and played, until such a time as its fortunes permitted the erection of more. On many a campus the original college hall still stands, overshadowed by larger and more modern structures, a chaste reminder of a simpler but glorious past. When new, it housed all the students, the unmarried tutors, all the classrooms, and the assembly room for morning and evening prayers. And all without benefit of plumbing or central heating.

On a typical school day—and this is a composite picture drawn from many sets of college rules—the boys were routed out by the college bell at five or five-thirty, filed into an unheated chapel for fifteen minutes of morning prayer, then returned to their rooms for an hour of study. Breakfast at seven-thirty or thereabouts was followed by the first class at eight. Classes continued to noon, resumed at two and ran to four-thirty or five. On days when his class was not reciting at these hours the student was expected to spend his time usefully in his room. Prayers again at five were followed by supper at six. There was an evening study period of two hours or so, and lights were out at ten. To facilitate the smooth functioning of such a tight schedule and to make life endurable under such cramped conditions, an elaborate set of rules seemed indicated. Every college had them. Nothing makes the contrast between then and now stand out more vividly than a glance at these rules. To understand them, one must remember that the patriarchal regime they reflect was fashioned by a generation which believed in discipline, and, what is more important, that the age of the students corresponded rather to that of senior high school students and college freshmen of today. A boy entered college at fourteen or fifteen and graduated four years later, still not full-grown.[4] This alone was enough to make any attempt at student self-government a dubious experiment, especially in view of a home and school training that made much of honoring father and mother but said little about self-realization or education for democracy. These facts led inevitably to a regime that resembled nothing so much as a benevolent parental despotism, with overtones of a military barracks. Quite unconsciously, it seems, President Willard of Harvard addressed every student who came to him with the same words: "Well, child, what do you want?" [5]

But let us take another look at the rules. The laws of Union College in 1802 consisted of eleven chapters of from seven to twenty-three sections each. Every student was required to have a copy and to familiarize himself with its contents. Besides prescribing entrance requirements, fees, and the course of study, very much as college catalogues do today, the laws called for compulsory attendance at all classes, morning and evening prayers, and church on Sundays. On the index of prohibited activities were card-playing, swearing, drunkenness, striking instructors or locking them in their rooms. "Perhaps no college"—that was the verdict of Eliphalet Nott, its president—"has ever furnished such complete security to the manners and morals of youth." Union was typical. A similar regime prevailed everywhere. Joint meals in the "commons," when the college provided them, were often an additional regulated feature and the source of many complaints and disorders. Dancing, theater, and games of chance were almost universally taboo. So was liquor and, in some cases, tobacco. William and Mary permitted drinking "in that moderation which becomes the prudent and industrious student." But frequenting taverns was frowned upon, as were all unauthorized out-of-bounds expeditions. "Nocturnal disorders and revelling" were under the same condemnation. Swarthmore stated categorically that any prospective student not prepared to renounce tobacco entirely should not even apply for admission. Mercer forbade smoking but permitted chewing. Colleges near the frontier found it expedient to require pledges from students that they were not carrying guns or bowie knives. The lesser virtues of courtesy and good manners were not overlooked. Princeton students, at any rate before the Revolution, were instructed to raise their hats to the president at a distance of ten rods and to tutors at five; and the trustees of Transylvania University passed a resolution that students should not lean on one another during recitations. The University of Georgia, lest anything essential be omitted, concluded its pages of rules with an elastic clause: "Since these laws are few and general, the faculty shall use discretion in all cases not covered." [6]

In some southern colleges the gentleman's code was basic. At the University of Virginia the cornerstone of behavior was the student's personal honor. Or, as it was put by the authorities of William and Mary, "the student comes to us as a gentleman. As such we receive and treat him. . . . He is not harassed with petty regulations; he is not insulted and annoyed by impertinent surveillance." But few college governors agreed with this view. It was taking too much of a chance. On more than one campus the detailed code of regulations remained virtually unchanged for seventy-five to a hundred years. Only toward the end of the nineteenth century was there any considerable relaxation. By that time references to bowie knives and desecration of the Sabbath were replaced by cushioned phrases about responsible conduct and courteous behavior. But only toward the end. Princeton in 1870 was no longer a naïve school of the prophets, yet the old rules, pretty much intact, were still on the statute books, and professors and tutors in quest of evildoers still had the right to enter the room of any student at their pleasure.[7]

Somehow the students survived, and so did the professors. Morale in the young is a wonderful thing and seems to thrive, in schools as in armies, in direct proportion to the weight of adversity. Then too there were bright spots to relieve the drab monotony of daily routine. They grew brighter in retrospect, as the memoirs of nostalgic old grads eloquently testify. Incidents like the following, picked at ran-

dom, have a universal flavor. In the early days of the College of Philadelphia, in the cultural capital of America, dancing was permitted
under careful restrictions. Benjamin Franklin's grandson, finding the
way clear to a Saturday afternoon dancing class on condition that
he make up the Latin he would be missing, reflected ruefully: "I
don't think I shall be able to dance with so much spirit when the
thought of making a Latin theme before I go to bed is sticking in
my stomach." A half-century later a senior at South Carolina College
was invited with his class to a party given by the president for
Daniel Webster, who was on campus for a speech. The senior did
not think much of Webster's oratory but willingly pitched into the
cake, claret, ice cream, lemonade, and strawberries served at the
reception. At about this same time an Amherst student was con-
fiding to his diary at the end of a perfect day: "Had a letter from
Nelly, full of love, and one from Father, full of money." [8]

The daily routine with its disciplinary machinery was nonetheless
an ever-present reality. That the machinery creaked goes without
saying. The cold formality of it all had no appeal for adolescents
craving understanding and sympathy. The pomp and solemnity of
a faculty hearing might overawe the guilty but was not calculated
to win their confidence. If conscientious observance of every regu-
lation makes one a model student, Yale undergraduate Julian Sturtevant was one, for during his whole four years he never intentionally
transgressed a rule; yet even he was forced to confess that such rigors
as early morning chapel were a burden rather than an inspiration:
"I was always punctual in attendance upon these early exercises, but
it was impossible for me to derive any benefit from them. It was
simply a matter of endurance." [9] Sturtevant's characterization of the
Yale student body of his time—the 1820's—would probably have
been true for most campuses. They were decent in the main, but
always there was a sprinkling of rowdies stirring up trouble. One
did not have to be an incorrigible rowdy, however, to chafe under
the regime, for it was so confining that smoldering resentment became endemic. Violations of the rules were the order of the day.
Often they were no more than a letting-off of steam: horseplay and
pranks of the kind that old grads like to recall and embellish. All
too frequently, though, they took the form of open insubordination
and concerted uprising against constituted authority. They were not
the town-and-gown riots of the medieval university, though these
also occurred, but tensions and conflicts within the college family

itself. So numerous and widespread are the accounts of such occurrences that even when taken with a considerable grain of salt they
indicate a condition of affairs in most colleges that approached
chronic anarchy. It was autocracy tempered by rebellion.

Painting the president's horse, tying his cow in chapel, smoking
tutors out of their rooms, and similar adolescent inanities date back
no one knows how far. These, and more serious rowdyism, occurred
in all colleges, large and small, in sophisticated Harvard and bucolic
Miami, in the saintly College of New Jersey and the godless University of Virginia. In the remoter seats of learning these "extra-curricu-
lar activities" were more lurid and spectacular. During Andrew Dickson White's student days at Hobart, professors were buried under
mattresses and tutors badly burned by red-hot cannon balls rolling
down the corridors. The president at one time escaped from his
classroom through a window and on another occasion was kept at
bay by a shower of beer bottles. White transferred to Yale, having
become skeptical of the "direct Christian influence" of small church
colleges. Students at Miami, in Ohio, blockaded lecture halls and
professors' houses after a heavy snowfall and brought college activities to a complete standstill. At Chapel Hill they rode horses
through the dormitory and shot up the place generally. The blocking of stagecoaches, the whipping and shooting of professors, and
the singing of ribald songs in front of churches are reported from
the University of Virginia.[10]

The common dining room was the source of many disorders. A
crockery battle at Harvard when the door between sophomore and
freshman commons had accidentally been left open, ended only when
all the dishes had been smashed. That happened in 1817. A Yale
student at about the same time was so disgusted at the rapaciousness
displayed in commons that he transferred to a private boarding
house. The young gentlemen of South Carolina College made a fine
art of rushing into the dining hall the minute the doors were opened
and spearing the largest piece of meat in sight. On one occasion two
of them got themselves anchored to the same piece of fish, and since
each felt that his honor was involved, they ended by fighting a duel
to decide the issue. J. Marion Sims, a student at the time, vouches
for this fish story.

Those colleges were rare that did not boast at least one first-class
rebellion. The students at Davidson, where professors were authorized to visit rooms at any hour of the day or night, rioted in 1855

because their mathematics problems were too difficult and threw rocks at the faculty members who came to investigate. One of the latter, a West Pointer, drew a sword, and following his lead, the professors advanced on the dormitory, battered down the door with an ax, and suppressed the rebellion. When three Princeton students were expelled in 1807 for drunkenness and insolence to professors, the student body protested in a manner that seemed to presage organized rebellion. The faculty met and, to an obbligato of crashing windows and ripping stair-rails, suspended one hundred and twenty-five of a student body of less than two hundred. Similarly Yale expelled forty-four sophomores in 1830, and Harvard threw out forty-three of a class of seventy-three seniors, including a son of John Quincy Adams, on the eve of commencement. Usually in such cases of wholesale expulsion the names of the expellees were circulated among the other colleges, and blacklisted.

Penalties were as mechanical as the rules and everywhere the same. The ordinary sequence, proportioned to the gravity of the offense, was private admonition, public admonition, suspension, and expulsion. Between the last two some institutions inserted a device known as rustication. This was a limited suspension during which the culprit was relegated to a remote village with his books and committed to the chaperonage of the village minister, who supervised his studies so that he would not lose ground or get into mischief, and who informed the college authorities when the boy was duly penitent and ready to return. James Russell Lowell was rusticated for two months during his senior year at Harvard; when on his return he successfully passed an examination in the studies he had missed, he was allowed to continue with his class.[11]

Accompanying these penalties were money fines, also graded. The Harvard laws of 1734 reflect current ideas on degrees of sinfulness and, for that matter, the ethical concepts that governed most campuses during the entire period of the ascendancy of the college. The laws built up in a steady crescendo to a financial and moral climax.

Tardiness to prayers or lectures	2*d.*
Absence from prayers or lectures	4*d.*
Tarrying after vacation, per day	8*d.*
Tarrying after chamber in study hours; going outside the Yard without coat or gown; entering meetinghouse before the bell	2*s.*

Absence from divine worship on the Sabbath; failure to
repeat sermons; keeping a gun or pistol; going gunning,
fishing, or "scating over deep waters" without leave   3*s.*

Fighting; lying; drunkenness; neglecting declamations;
cutting classes; frequenting forbidden houses in Cambridge; gambling for money; swapping books or cloth-
ing; "Tumultuous and Indecent Noises"; using or sending for distilled spirits, punch, or flip; going on roof of
Old Harvard, or cutting lead from same   5*s.*

Profane cursing and swearing; playing cards or dice;
neglecting analysis of Scripture; walking or other diversions on the Sabbath; firing gun or pistol in Yard   10*s.*

Breaking open doors or picking locks   20*s.*

Blasphemy, fornication, robbery, forgery, "or any other
atrocious crime"   Expulsion

A similar scale, with cents and dollars gradually replacing shillings
and pence, prevailed in most places. The laws of Union College provided an elaborate series of fines ranging from four cents for cutting
chapel to $3 for drunkenness. Going to the theater and beating up
instructors were costly diversions too. At Harvard in President Kirkland's day a student who went to a party in Boston was fined $5,
and a visit to the theater set the offender back $10. Dartmouth in
the 1820's established a $6 ceiling. Writing to his mother from
Bowdoin while a student there, Nathaniel Hawthorne confessed that
he had been caught playing cards and fined fifty cents; a repetition
of the offense, he had been warned, would bring suspension.[12]

On close examination, campus crime and punishment turned out
to be not quite the automatic process that college laws would seem
to have made it. After all, both students and professors were human
—though each group had its moments of doubt about the other;
there were variations in practice and many exceptions in individual
cases. One of these, the idea of personal honor, has been mentioned.
Where this prevailed, picayune regulations were less frequent and
the faculty did less detective work. It also stirred up a lot of trouble.
Under the gentleman's code a student's statement was assumed to
be the truth, and the president and faculty were not expected to
probe behind this prima-facie evidence. From these principles undergraduate logic deduced certain corollaries: A student should

under no circumstances be expected to report the misdeeds of another; and the faculty should be sporting enough not to ask direct questions whereby the suspect, under honor to answer truthfully, might incriminate himself. This Fifth-Amendment-like dilemma was widely discussed in academic circles and had a thorough airing at the University of Alabama, among others, in the fifties. Alabama had not adopted the full honor plan as it was practiced at Virginia or William and Mary, and public pressure was building up in the state against the university's practice of requiring students to give evidence in discipline cases. A faculty committee was set up under Professor Barnard, later president of Columbia, to answer the public complaints. In its report the committee upheld the university's practice at every point. Alabama, so Barnard and his colleagues pointed out, was not unique in the South in its stand, for its laws had been copied verbatim from those of the College of South Carolina. Requiring students to give evidence, the committee went on, was admittedly distasteful, but it did not happen often. Life on a small-town campus had a way of intensifying situations and incidents which would not even arise if the university were in a larger city. The issue to be kept in sight was simply this: "Shall law prevail or shall misrule be triumphant and all the operations of college come to an end?" So said Barnard, Connecticut Yankee and graduate of Yale, the fountainhead of the philosophy of discipline.[13]

The problem that troubled Alabama a hundred years ago has not disappeared from American college life. Under different circumstances and with vastly more student participation, so-called "honor systems" have been tried out in recent years on many campuses, with the intention of eliminating, in classrooms and at times in general campus situations, the faculty's disagreeable role of proctor, prosecutor, and judge. Where such attempts have failed, it has usually been for one of the following reasons: extreme heterogeneity of the student body with resulting absence of any esprit de corps; lack of sustained effort; an oversentimentalized notion of personal honor coupled with failure to appreciate the importance of the general welfare. But where these systems have been solidly built on the overwhelming and continuous support of students, faculty, and administration, and where they have squarely faced the need for collective responsibility for the intellectual standards and moral integrity of campus life as a whole, they have been one of the most conspicuous successes of American higher education, heartening to students and teachers alike.

The patriarchal college of an earlier day was not up to this. There were, however, degrees of law enforcement. Most dismal was the failure of those administrators who, in adhering to the letter of the law, went to the extreme of bringing in the public authority. At Harvard, to mention only one, this was the unpardonable sin. When Harvard's President Josiah Quincy, exasperated by campus rowdyism, took refuge in a grand jury investigation, he failed completely. The college turned solidly against him, rioting grew worse, the grand jury found out nothing of consequence from the tight-lipped students, and Quincy never regained face.[14]

Quincy found few imitators. More promising was the ability of an occasional officer with humanitarian leanings, usually the president, to rise above the letter of the law. It was the president's interpretation of the rules that determined not only the outward order and discipline but also the life and spirit of the college. The president could not of course do it alone but needed the support of the faculty and the trustees. In advocating, and practicing, a form of government characterized by leniency, few rules, and attention to the individual student, President Leonard Woods of Bowdoin lost the support of his faculty, who insisted on rigid observance of the letter of the law. Woods was not altogether unacquainted with the problem of human behavior, at least on the theoretical side, for a few years before he had won a $300 prize for his *Essay on Native Depravity*. The trustees eventually restored harmony at Bowdoin, and from then on student punishments usually represented a compromise between the human sympathies of the president and the holy indignation of the professors. Elsewhere it was the president who held the reins tight and individual professors who preferred to appeal to the students' better nature. In their role as moral guardians of youth, college officers vacillated between an optimistic perfectionism and the more easily verifiable doctrine of total human depravity.[15]

Depraved or not, students needed an outlet for their animal energies. The more enlightened pedagogues were aware of this and tried by various schemes to supply the need. Some thought they had found a satisfactory one in the manual labor school, a European importation which enjoyed wide popularity in the second quarter of the nineteenth century. This was a device for killing two birds with one stone, for it helped the student finance his college career while at the same time it was useful in solving the vexing problem of discipline. The student in a manual labor college was customarily required to spend two hours or more a day working on the college farm or in specially constructed shops, and was paid for his labor. It was in its compulsory feature, primarily, that manual labor differed from the familiar self-help programs of modern campuses. Besides enabling poor boys to earn at least part of their tuition, the plan was welcomed as a way out of most of the president's difficulties with discipline, for on the principle that the devil finds work for idle hands, steady occupation ought to be the best deterrent against mischief and insubordination. Manual labor programs were numerous in rural and newly settled areas. Mercer in Georgia, Davidson in North Carolina, Randolph-Macon in Virginia, Marietta and Oberlin in Ohio, and Knox in Illinois were among the colleges which experimented with them. But they did not fulfill their promise. The system was uneconomical for one thing, since jobs could not be manufactured and students could not be paid, except in a limited way in lieu of hired help, unless there was a demand for the products of their labor. And that was not the only weakness. The hours spent in shop and field cut into study time and thereby tended to debase standards of scholarship. An alumnus of a manual labor school stated the case bluntly: He and his fellow students had come to college to study and were not at all anxious "to make brooms and barrels for the salvation of their souls." [16]

Both as a financial and a disciplinary measure manual labor was a passing phenomenon in that period. Far more widespread and persistent was the use of the traditional and obvious disciplinary device of religious restraint. After all, the moral and religious foundations of the college were as deep as the intellectual, being grounded in a metaphysic of supernaturalism as interpreted by an authoritative Christian revelation. Even liberal institutions paid more than lip-service to this tenet, and the orthodox, Protestant or Catholic, never dreamed of questioning it. Opportunities abounded for bringing theological abstractions home to the student. All seniors listened to lectures on the evidences of Christianity. Standing *in loco parentis* and, by inference, *in loco dei*, presidents and faculties could make impressive use of morning and evening prayers to appeal to the better instincts of their captive audience, or to threaten them with the wrath of God. Church attendance Sunday mornings was compulsory,

and in the afternoon the student body was herded into chapel for a
religious lecture by the president. Some colleges, as for example Ohio
Wesleyan, topped this off with an early Sunday morning Bible class
by members of the faculty, which "all have the privilege of attending." [17]

Such a regime undoubtedly created a campus climate of opinion
that encouraged submission to constituted authority, but it also made
for psychological security and philosophical serenity. One might protest against concrete injustices and kick over the traces in adolescent
irritation, but one did not question the authority itself. And as long
as its major premises remained unquestioned, the college, for all its
turbulence, had inner unity. One can well believe the Dartmouth
student, not noted for his piety, who recalled that whenever President Lord closed morning prayers with "God bless these boys, every
one of them," he felt secure for the rest of the day.[18] This inner
unity endured until after the turn of the century, when the triple
assault of the evolutionary hypothesis, the popularizers of Freud, and
the temptations of uncontrolled material wealth smashed it to pieces.
The colleges have been trying ever since to put the pieces together
again, reshaping them in closer harmony with twentieth century facts
of life.

Whenever religion became routine, it was revived by a "season
of refreshing." The revival, that peculiarly American religious phenomenon, hit the campuses, as it did the nation at large, with considerable regularity and spread with epidemic speed. A potent
weapon in the hands of religious orthodoxy in its conquest of
"French" deism in the nation at large, the revival was used for the
same purpose by college officials, many of whom believed that student misbehavior and campus radicalism were close kin of religious
and political liberalism. Timothy Dwight of Yale announced in 1800
that "in New England the name infidel proverbially denotes an immoral character," and fifty years later President Thornwell of South
Carolina College echoed the same sentiment when he denounced
atheism, jacobinism, and communism as all of a piece and all designed to undermine the security of the American college and American life.[19] To suspect the student who utters unpopular opinions
of subversive leanings is nothing new in the history of American
higher education. But in our day, as in Dwight's and Thornwell's, the
real causes of such perverse behavior are likely to be more complex.
The embattled undergraduate whose published letter sternly de-

nouncing the most hallowed traditions of college and country has set the campus by its ears may be caught in the toils of a subversive conspiracy, but probably not. More likely he has produced an independent critical thought for the first time in his life and it has dazzled him; or he has just been defeated in a campus election, or drawn a C— in a history test, or lost out on a date for Junior Prom. And then again, his critical comments may be justified.

Opinions varied as to the effectiveness of revivals. Those who believed in the technique to begin with saw showers of blessings. When Timothy Dwight moved in on the deists and infidels that infested Yale, "all infidelity skulked and hid its head" according to Lyman Beecher, who wanted it to happen that way. But Beecher was not alone in this sentiment. Benjamin Silliman, soon to become Yale's foremost scientist, agreed: "Yale College," he said at that time, "is a little temple; prayer and praise seem to be the delight of the greater part of the students while those who are still unfeeling are awed into respectful silence." Similar expressions came from many other campuses. After one such revival season, in 1831, a survey article in a contemporary journal exulted over the beneficial results in institutions as far apart as Bowdoin, Williams, Yale, Western Reserve, Washington and Jefferson, Kenyon, Hampden-Sydney, North Carolina, and Georgia. All spoke of seasons of refreshing, outpourings of the spirit, and a higher tone of piety among the students. The same journal produced statistics in the following year showing that 683 of 3,582 students in fifty-nine colleges were now "hopefully pious." [20]

These were of course official views. Not all comments were so favorable. There were critics too, and their complaints grew more frequent. They chiefly objected to the inevitable subordination of intellectual interests to emotional orgies. Already in the Great Awakening of colonial days, the first American revival, the faculties of Harvard and Yale had had reservations over the extravagances of George Whitefield, traveling evangelist from England, and some of his more bizarre followers. The elements in the situation were essentially the same in the seasons of awakening and refreshing of the nineteenth century. Revival meetings always carried a high emotional charge, in college towns as in the remoter frontier camp meetings; and spellbinding eloquence had unpredictable consequences. When a student burst into a classroom at DePauw in 1847, with the news that President Simpson was about to preach in the camp grounds, the class promptly broke up. While recognizing the possibility of mixed motives on the part of the students, one is impressed with the confession of a professor, who was there too, that if the sermon had lasted fifteen minutes longer, he himself would have died of excitement. With such disruptive forces at work, normal intellectual processes had little chance. At DePauw, on the occasion mentioned, classes and recitations were virtually suspended for two weeks. At a Williams revival in 1825, prayer meetings made all study impossible for several days. Oberlin, "God's college," wallowed in almost continuous revivals from 1836 to 1842 with all the camp meeting symptoms of shouting, clapping of hands, and swooning. In fairness to the Oberlin authorities it must be said that they did not encourage the more picturesque hysterics.[21]

An unanticipated result of the Oberlin revivals was the formation of a student group of freethinkers who completely disavowed Christianity and "priestcraft"—and promptly got themselves expelled. Similar negative results were felt elsewhere when the emotional effects wore off and the inevitable reaction set in. A Davidson student estimated the probable results of a season of twice-a-day religious exhortations: "We will either grow in grace or increase fearfully in wickedness." In Illinois College, where on one occasion zealous students had petitioned to have morning prayers moved up from five to four-thirty, there were about as many students disciplined for intoxication, swearing, and carrying knives as in less self-consciously pious institutions. But it was left for the Amherst student who had regularly recorded in his diary, "Sunday, professor X preached. Slept," to speak the sentiments of nonviolent resisters of all ages with the entry: "A day of fasting and prayer for colleges. I neither fasted nor prayed." [22]

In view of such equivocal results, more and more educational leaders came to doubt the wisdom of high-pressure religious methods. Julian Sturtevant, who as an undergraduate had objected to the rigors of early morning chapel, later became president of Illinois College. There he found the sectarian bickering which often accompanied emotional religion particularly obnoxious. In Jacksonville he had encountered the formidable Peter Cartwright, circuit rider and revivalist, who made it plain in rousing sermons in the courthouse that he had no use for educated preachers. Sturtevant, who had been trained at Yale to write sermons that were logical and coherent expositions of a text and to read them from the pulpit, came off second-best in the encounter with the flaming evangelist. And so, though an original member of the mission-inspired "Yale Band," he came to think of college more and more as an intellectual enterprise, in a moral and religious framework to be sure, but nevertheless essentially an affair of the mind.[23] In time his view was to prevail. But as long as colleges were still considered agencies of the church, Cartwright had a point too. His set-to with Sturtevant was a chapter in the age-old feud between the worker and the thinker, the activist and the intellectual. The latter, secure and unruffled in his ivory tower, can plan and theorize for the world of scholarship or politics or business. And he does so with a good conscience because he is rationally persuaded that all action that does not proceed from a reasoned plan is futile if not dangerous. But in the eyes of the practical worker in the field, the theorist is a shirker who is unwilling or unable to bear the heat and burden of the day. In the world of higher education, though the terms and the specific issues have changed, the conflict between theorists and practitioners is still very much alive.

However insistent the problem of discipline, however pervasive the influence of religion, the main business of the college was teaching. What then was the actual teaching and classroom procedure? When Western man thinks of education, he almost automatically visualizes it in terms of a class—a collective abstraction—going through a drill, or receiving information or instruction in techniques from a specialist, a professor, at a given place for a given length of time. This is one way of doing it but by no means the only way. The classroom was not, in fact, a part of ancient civilization. The Greeks did not use it, and it was certainly not a part of the Oriental tradition. The wise man imparted wisdom to his followers, at odd times and places, when the spirit moved him; a peripatetic saint or prophet gathered a handful of disciples and imparted his views to them in close personal contact. This was the method of Buddha, of Socrates, and of Jesus. It is the ideal of Mark Hopkins and the log, which no American college, not even that of Mark Hopkins, has ever realized. We have not discarded the ideal entirely but still pay it wistful tribute hoping that somehow, some day, it may distill out of the efficiency of our business civilization.

The modern classroom is a product of the Middle Ages, a time of weak central government when every civilized activity had to organize and institutionalize itself for its own protection. Scholars were no exception. They too soon discovered that their craft had a better chance of survival if they banded together and made definite agreements with their followers as to times and places of meeting, subject matter to be covered in their lectures, and fees to be paid. The end-product of all this was the classroom and the school, where the professor dispensed learning and the student body, itself an institutional abstraction, took in what it could. The emerging system had a certain rough efficiency which commended itself to everyone who tried it, and we have had it with us ever since.

The actual arrangement of class time in the colonial and early national college is difficult to reconstruct from the meager evidence. The most common pattern seems to have been two class periods before noon, each an hour or more in length, and one such period in the afternoon. Saturday classes were not uncommon. As course offerings multiplied, after the middle of the nineteenth century, the number of class hours tended to increase and spread over the day. The currently standard fifty-minute class with a ten-minute break apparently came in with the credit-point system at the end of the century.[24]

As to classroom procedure and teaching methods, the evidence, too, is scattered and indirect. The catalogues and college laws did not give precise information any more than they do today. But from casual comments of many professors and recollections of many former students we can fit the pieces together and re-create the scene. What emerges is a procedure many of whose aspects would be recognized by university and high school graduates of today as something that had happened to them. Modern educational specialists would frown on much of it as outdated and unscientific, but of course things were less complicated then. Laboratories were unknown, case methods and source studies had to await the influx of German-trained scholars, and problem-solving was still in the mists of the future. Teaching then was of classic simplicity. On one day the professor handed out a quantity of information, on the next the students handed it back, reciting in alphabetical order or in any other sequence that the instructor might devise. For his recitation the student got a mark which fitted into a system of grades that was again left to the instructor's ingenuity, unless a general college standard had been prescribed. If a text was used, the professor enlarged on that, the class being held responsible both for the material in the book and the professor's comments. In the absence of a suitable text the professor might dictate his lectures and perhaps eventually bring them out as his own text. Timothy Dwight described his method of procedure at Yale, which was standard for so much of the country, as follows: "The senior class recites once a day to the president. All the classes are made responsible for the manner in which they hear, and remember the lectures; being examined at every lecture concerning their knowledge of the preceding; and accordingly are furnished with note books, in which they take down at the time the principal subjects of every lecture." [25]

This was the method in the philosophical subjects; instruction in the languages was even more mechanical. Here each student in turn translated a sentence or a paragraph in a previously assigned passage of a Latin or Greek author, answered probing questions on its grammatical forms and syntactic peculiarities, and received a grade, after which a second young gentleman answered the call and worked over the next paragraph.

There were infinite variations on this standard procedure, depending on the training, the interests, and the temperament of the individual instructor. As a class, college faculties were recruited largely from the ministry. Those in the newer institutions were graduates of the older, with Yale and Princeton furnishing the lion's share. Most colleges in the first struggling years had to pick their teachers where they could find them, though few resorted to the heroic extremes of the University of North Carolina, where the first faculty consisted of the twenty-four-year-old president, Joseph Caldwell, a Frenchman who had been a monk, a strolling player, and a deserter from the British navy.[26] Apart from professional training, the personality factor loomed large. If the teacher was a time-server, who kept one lesson ahead of his class and whose real interests were preaching or gardening or fishing, nothing much came of his efforts; if he was a martinet and a literalist, his students might acquire a useful technical competence without much perspective or understanding. But let the teacher be that rare individual who combines deep scholarship with a gift of expression and genuine human sympathies and the drab classroom was transformed into a dwelling-place of light. Such a man could enliven even the dullest material, for he had the wisdom and the versatility to use his subject, whatever it might be, as a means for achieving that most exhilarating of experiences: a genuine meeting of minds.

Every college has had its Mr. Chips. He is a protean Mr. Chips, who stalks through the pages of the college annals in many guises. Sometimes his learning was meager, but, diluted with the milk of human kindness, it went a long way. He might be remembered for his wit and humor, good-natured or bitter. If that was all he had to offer, he soon flickered out like a straw fire; though impressive to the sophomores, he shrank in reputation as the student grew in wisdom and stature. The professor longest remembered might even have been an austere, forbidding figure who never yielded to the popular cry, whose solidly reasoned discourses were always just beyond the grasp of his students, but whose classes, for this tantalizing reason, remained in retrospect the most invigorating intellectual experience of a lifetime. Legends clustered about such figures, blown up bigger than life by the well-intentioned but not always accurate recollections of hundreds of alumni. If such a remembered teacher spent his life at a small college, he was forever being credited with refusing offers from the big schools. "Professor X could have gone to Michigan; Harvard made him an offer; but he loyally stayed on at good old Siwash." Though probably untrue nine times out of ten, the Cinderella careers suggested in these legends became realities just often enough to keep the rumors alive.

All colleges had such teachers but they did not have many. Most professors of the nineteenth century, it is safe to say, were uninspired pedants, well-meaning and conscientious, but neither masters of their subject nor psychologically equipped to communicate it to others. Besides regular professors, most institutions also had tutors, who did not add to the strength of the faculty. They resembled the tutors of Oxford and Cambridge in name only, and were nothing like the specialists who conduct tutorials at Harvard and preceptorials at Princeton today, and who may be full professors in their own right. These old-time tutors were recent graduates who were favorably known to the president and the faculty and who were appointed, for a year or two at a time, to provide flexibility of the teaching staff. Furthermore they taught classes not subjects. One tutor might teach the freshmen, another the sophomores, in *all* subjects. Harvard, to be sure, had introduced subject specialization for tutors as early as 1767, but few had followed its example. In addition to teaching, the tutors had the thankless job of policing the dormitories and reporting student misdeeds, a role for which they had no experience and often no aptitude. The historian of Princeton has this to say about them: "Selected for their piety and scholarly ability, egged on by the faculty and trustees, often inexperienced and tactless, they were resented and sometimes hated by the students." The best that can be said for the system is that it formed a reservoir of new blood for the faculty and that occasionally a good professor emerged from the ranks. But not often. Some colleges recognized these evils and tried to do without tutors. Thus the catalogues of Rutgers in the 1840's boasted that there were no tutors but that instruction was given entirely by full professors.[27]

Faculties in general labored under considerable handicaps. They had no security of tenure. The president or the trustees could discharge them individually or collectively, without notice and on the flimsiest pretexts. They had no guild organization as they had had in the medieval universities and have again today. The proud scholars' guilds of the Middle Ages had given way to the American system of government by external trustees, and though professors were still at times referred to as officers of the institution, this meant little in practice. With some notable exceptions their share in management was negligible. Though held responsible when things went wrong, they rarely wielded enough authority to keep things from going wrong. Economically, they were none too secure. Generalization in this area is difficult because salaries varied widely. Following at a respectful distance any general rise in the price level, but collapsing most promptly in any budget crisis, a professor's salary in terms of actual purchasing power at any given time was a most unpredictable thing. In this the professors were more like day laborers than professional people. Sometimes salary was supplemented by free lodging in dormitories or faculty residences, as was the case with ministers of settled congregations. Often it was delayed, sometimes not paid at all. In country colleges it might be eked out with potatoes and beans. There are numerous instances when faculties, faced by a bankrupt treasury, heroically resolved—they had no other choice— to divide the net revenues among themselves in lieu of salary. This always meant a considerable sacrifice of income.

A further complicating factor was the occasional practice of allowing professors to keep the tuition fees paid by the students in their classes in lieu of, or sometimes in addition to, their salaries. This vestige of the profit system was done away with in time, for it merely added another element of uncertainty to the already shaky financial structure of most colleges, and it did not make for harmony among the faculty. In general, it seems fair to say that the economic level of college professors until the late nineteenth century was about that of the clergy from which they stemmed, without however the relative security of the clergy, and far below that of doctors and lawyers.[28]

Trustees, and in state institutions the legislature, sometimes bedeviled the faculty with minor regulations and picayune criticisms. Princeton trustees in the early days insisted on examining the minutes of faculty meetings and on one occasion voted formal censure because the pages were not properly numbered. In the first years of the University of Missouri the state legislature pointedly asked the president for information as to the number of hours a day the faculty was actually working. The chairman of the faculty of the University of Virginia was required to report regularly to the trustees on the work and behavior of his colleagues as well as of the students. And at Columbia the trustees, up to the time of President Barnard's accession in 1864, were still requiring faculty as well as students to attend daily chapel.[29]

With their work circumscribed by such limitations, it is not surprising that many professors turned into starchy pedants or that most students left their classes with a yawn. The pedantic type is not identified as frequently in memoirs and letters, probably because he was a type. The reminiscent alumnus was more likely to single out by name the exceptional professor who excited him and then to lump all the rest as boring, uninspiring, and insignificant. Nor can one distinguish here between large and small, old and new, institutions. Exciting teaching went on in the prairies and cornfields, while the ivy colleges had their share of bores. Andrew Dickson White found the teaching at Yale, for all its shortcomings, superior to that of Hobart from which he had transferred; on the other hand, some students who left Yale to come to Rutgers preferred the professors of their new alma mater to the "haughty authority" of the school they had left.[30] Subjective experiences like these obviously do not offer enough evidence for definitive judgments about the quality of teaching at one college or another. Such things fluctuated.

Trustees on their part also found reasons for complaint. Faculties, they sometimes charged, were so immersed in the details and mechanics of their profession that they lost touch with the world and were even unresponsive to newer developments in their own fields. When Bishop Alonzo Potter of the trustees of the University of Pennsylvania submitted a comprehensive plan in 1854 designed to raise the college out of its rut of mediocrity, and set it on the road to real university eminence, he was flatly opposed by the faculty because, so the bishop thought, it was beyond their depth. They did not understand the plan and did not want to be bothered. Pennsylvania had to wait another generation to become a real university. In that same year, 1854, a trustees' committee at Columbia brought in a report on a number of important matters of broad college policy. In its preparation they had asked the faculty for opinions and suggestions with not very satisfying results. "The faculty," said the chairman of the committee sadly, "with one exception, mostly confine themselves to the subject of discipline and modes of instruction . . . and although their suggestions are valuable in themselves, they have not much reference to the matter immediately in hand." To put it bluntly, the faculty were out of touch with reality. If professors in New York and Philadelphia were so absorbed in the mechanics of their craft as to be unaware of the larger developments around them, one cannot blame the faculty of Kenyon, twenty-four miles from a railroad and six miles from the national pike, for displaying an equal degree of pedantry. There the faculty in the 1840's determined by resolution the proper pronunciation of Latin, reversed themselves, referred the question to the trustees who were no help, rescinded this motion, and finally resolved: "That the Faculty do possess entire control over the pronunciation of the Greek and Latin languages." It was about at this same time that a secretary of the faculty, apparently not with tongue in cheek, concluded his minutes with the words: "Thus ended a delightful session. During its swift passage very little occurred to mar pleasure—everything contributed to enhance the joy of all dwelling within Kenyon's walls." [31]

In general all educational devices and programs were handed down from above. An unquestioned authority decided what was good and imposed it on the students without asking their consent. There was one program, however, broadly intellectual and social, that the boys managed themselves and which, perhaps for that reason, enlisted their spontaneous support more than any other campus activity. This was the debating society. In a sense it too grew out of the prescribed course of study, for public speaking in one form or another, forensics, was a standard feature of every college curriculum. But though the faculty encouraged the activity, it was the students who organized the clubs and planned and executed their programs. Variously known as speaking clubs or debating or literary societies, and endowed with mellifluous Greek names, these organizations all served about the same purpose and were, before the days of football and fraternities, the shining center of college days, as reminiscent letters and memoirs of many an alumnus testify. The colonial colleges had them. Some were the outgrowth of the political ferment that preceded the Revolution and were maintained by concerned and serious students. The founder of the first Harvard Speaking Club was so engrossed in the college library one June day in 1775 that he did not even hear the guns of Bunker Hill. Princeton's Cliosophic and Whig—or as they were first known, the Well Meaning and the Plain Dealing Club— date from 1769 and 1770, respectively. Princeton's president at that time, John Witherspoon, one of the Signers of the Declaration of Independence, encouraged debates on public issues, to the chagrin of at least one critic of Tory tendencies who expressed his astonishment at hearing the graduating class of 1772, instead of behaving like "the meek disciples of wisdom they were," discuss burning political issues, which they solved "with a jerk." [32]

The intellectual fare of the student societies was varied. Formal orations, expository essays, literary criticism, and poetry appeared on their programs; but the favorite activity was the formal debate, for here interest in content was heightened by the spirit of competition and loyalty to the team. The subjects of the debates ranged widely through time and space. They included sweeping philosophical puzzlers which would have sounded familiar to the hungry scholars who sat at the feet of Peter Abelard in eleventh century Paris: Is man by nature formed to be virtuous? Is human reason competent to discuss the immortality of the soul? Social and ethical questions were settled with ease and finality: Are early marriages beneficial? Are theatrical entertainments helpful to mankind? History furnished endless topics, and Caesar and Napoleon were bound to appear sooner or later on all the programs: Was the murder of Caesar justified? Was the career of Napoleon beneficial to civilization? But with equal facility they would shift to a burning contemporary problem: Is the war with Mexico justified? Would it be expedient to change the present tariff of the United States? Slavery was widely debated on northern and southern campuses until it became too much of a hot potato and was barred by the faculty, as at Amherst, or until public opinion had moved overwhelmingly to one side or the other so that it was no longer an issue, as at South Carolina and Oberlin. Secession was debated in southern institutions, in Georgia, South Carolina, Missouri, almost through 1860. Leaving politics, the debates sometimes came close to home to ask whether a liberal education had any value for persons intended for mechanical and mercantile pursuits, whether the study of Latin and Greek was worth the time spent, and whether the morals of youth were likely to be corrupted by the study of ancient literature and mythology.

The student literary societies, with their persistent if fumbling search for truth and their Cook's tour of the issues of the day, were probably the most liberal part of the "liberal" education of the nineteenth century. They were much more than that. They taught the art of public speaking which, though turgid and bombastic in the style of the day, was yet so necessary for any American contemplating a public or professional career. President Maxcy of South Carolina, himself no mean orator, put it plainly: "Whatever the test in other lands, here a man must speak and speak well if he expects to acquire and maintain a permanent influence in society." [33] Membership in the clubs, though voluntary, was widespread, and it was not unusual for almost the entire student body to belong to one or another. Occasionally a faculty, to make sure that a good thing was kept alive, would make membership compulsory, only to find that they had weakened not strengthened the institution.

Finally the clubs filled a social vacuum, were an outlet for joiners, and aided in solving the problem of discipline. When the student body remained in session all day Saturday listening to their champions, and when the debate even spilled over into the next week, there was less hooliganism. Nothing in the regular curriculum of lectures and recitations evoked such enthusiasm. Nor did the regular courses provide better sources of information. The societies subscribed to newspapers and periodicals and accumulated their own libraries, which in time rivaled the official college library in size and diversity. The two society libraries at Columbia in 1831 contained six thousand volumes, as compared with eight thousand in that of the college itself.[34]

The societies were well housed, often occupying the best quarters the college could afford. Princeton's Whig and Clio were proud of their twin Ionic temples. The halls of the literary clubs at South Carolina were splendid beyond anything in the state except the chambers of the legislature in the capital. To live up to their surroundings the societies made an attempt at least to polish student behavior. Thus the Athenaeum Literary Society of the University of Missouri prohibited spitting (after it had bought a floor carpet), placing feet on furniture, loud laughing, and disorderly language. (Swearing in a whisper was not considered disorderly.) Similar curbs were in force elsewhere.

The prestige of the literary societies continued until the late nineteenth century, when secret fraternities and intercollegiate athletics began to dim their luster. Their success in the days of their prime is to be accounted for primarily by two factors. One, of course, was that the students themselves planned and managed the enterprise. But there was another reason, and that was their public character. The programs were usually open to all students and faculty, and on special occasions the general public was invited. Such affairs were attended by prominent citizens as well as the young ladies of the community. At the University of Pennsylvania, for example, they drew a "learned, polite and brilliant assembly," a "vast concourse of people of all ranks." [35] The incentive for special effort and letter-perfect performance in such circumstances was immeasurably greater than it was to produce a creditable translation of a period of Demosthenes in the presence of nobody but bored classmates and the professor who marked the effort for syntax. Young ladies did not visit Greek classes. Questions of motivation are pertinent on our campuses today. How much more exciting to work your head off for even a minor role in a play offered by the drama department, or to have that sonata well polished in time for the public recital of the music department, or, of course, to "die for dear old alma mater" in the football stadium to the howling approval of thousands, than to grind out an English theme or a history term paper which will be appreciated by nobody but the professor who assigned it, and perhaps not even by him!

In the old days publicity attended examinations too. Up to about the middle of the nineteenth century final examinations were usually oral, and open to the ladies and gentlemen of the community. College graduates in the audience, like the masters of arts in the medieval universities, were privileged to inject questions of their own or to criticize the answers of the candidates. It was a privilege of which estimable gentlemen, especially if they had been out of college a long time, did not often avail themselves. Public final examinations were discarded later in the century on the ground that they did not give the student a chance to display his true ability. Confident extroverts might perform over their heads, while self-conscious and timid youths might do less well than they could if left to write in private.

Yet even to flunk in public must have had some gaudy satisfactions. It was better to go out with a bang than a whimper, and nothing was so annoying as to be obscurely hanged.

Final examinations came, naturally, near the end of the school year. The latter by the way was not divided as is now customary into two semesters, from September through January and from February to June. Far more common until late in the century was the three-term calendar: the Michaelmas, Hilary, and Easter terms inherited from the British universities and adapted to American conditions. This meant, with minor variations, a fall term from about mid-September to mid-December, followed by a month's vacation; a winter term to early April, with perhaps a two-week holiday following; and the third term running to late July. Such a division of the year had certain practical advantages. The break in midwinter saved the college fuel and also enabled indigent seniors to earn a little money teaching a term of district school; the spring vacation was handy for help with the plowing. The University of Virginia, however, broke precedent with one continuous term from October to June, and a number of southern colleges followed its lead.

The crowning glory of the year was the public commencement, usually in midsummer.[36] On a hot morning in late July the exercises would get under way with a procession made up of the student body, the faculty, the governor, and the legislature (if the college rated this honor), the neighboring clergy, visiting dignitaries, and citizens of the town. Led by the trustees, or the band, or even the janitor, the assemblage moved to the largest church in town and settled down to be edified, as the humidity mounted, by the young gentlemen of the graduating class. Sandwiched in between the salutatorian, who spoke in Latin, and the valedictorian, who was either the best scholar or the most important man on campus, every candidate for a degree delivered an oration or read a poem or an essay or took part in a disputation. *Labor omnia vincit,* Intellectual Pride, The Immortality of Literature, The Last Hours of Copernicus (Charles W. Eliot's graduation speech at Harvard), The Sabbath Necessary for National Prosperity, The Poet's Dream, The Deterioration of the Fashions, The Honest Skeptic, The Glaring Stupidity of Skepticism—these give the flavor. In time, as graduation classes grew in size, these occasions became unmanageable. When Eliot graduated in 1853, there were forty-four speeches and five musical interludes. Various devices were employed to reduce the congestion. At Georgia, for example, a ten-minute limit was placed on each speech with a fifty-cent fine for each minute overtime; and Wesleyan decided, in 1850, to hold two sessions to accommodate the traffic. Eventually of course the speeches had to go.[37]

Commencement was a community festival as well as an academic rite, and at times took on the aspect of a carnival or a county fair, with hawkers of novelties on the fringes, and food and drink for everybody. An Amherst graduation in the 1830's, with twenty-three orations of fifteen minutes each, lasted from nine to three and was followed by a dinner for three hundred, mostly clergy, at which one of the brethren "was seized by death while partaking of a watermelon." [38] Later in the century, public participation fell off, and the noisy and bibulous part of the celebration was taken over by nostalgic alumni. Commencement over, the academic community scattered to their various homes, though not to take summer jobs except perhaps on the parental farm. The deserted college town settled into late summer somnolence, waiting for the first fresh breezes of autumn, when the young gentlemen would reassemble for another season of communion with the muses.

Chapter Five

The Old-Time College President

The most important individual in the early college was the president. He was the leader of a comparatively uncomplicated institution. Unlike the modern university, which approaches a metropolitan department store in variety of offerings and the federal Department of Defense in complexity of organization, the classical college was a simple establishment which rather resembled the old-time general store. Its wares were few and accessible. And just as the storekeeper met his customers informally and often, so the college president was a familiar figure to students and faculty alike. He was not, like the executive heads of some modern universities, a half-mythical personality, in whose existence the undergraduates have been taught to believe but whom they never expect to see in the flesh. He was a real presence, very much in evidence and in continuous contact with all members of the college community; he was the kingpin, without whom the enterprise fell apart. Unlike the impersonal multiheaded university of today, the old American college was the lengthened shadow of the president. For a better understanding of his function, several of the more conspicuous presidents will be examined here. They were chosen not because they were the greatest—that would be hard to prove—but because they represent certain qualities of college leaders in general and because the problems they faced were typical.

The office itself was uniquely American. Modeled on English precedents, it evolved, like American society in general, into something quite different. Beginning with Dunster at Harvard, the first to hold the title, the president was a more important figure than the presidents or principals of the colleges of Oxford and Cambridge, who, though their powers were expanding, were primarily the senior teaching fellows; and his functions were much broader and more varied than those of the rectors and chancellors of the large European universities.[1] The office was usually established in the college charter and its duties explicitly stated in the laws enacted by the trustees. Since the younger institutions to the west generally copied the practices of the colonial colleges, the presidential function varied little from one school to the next. At Harvard early in the nineteenth century the duties of the president were to reside in Cambridge; exercise general superintendence; see that the course of instruction and the discipline were executed; call and preside over meetings of the faculty, at which he also had a vote; preside at examinations, exhibitions, and commencements; teach classes; counsel students as occasion arose; make rules for the government of the students subject to veto by the Corporation; with the faculty maintain discipline, punish offenses, promote "virtue, piety, and good learning." Descriptions like this recur, sometimes in identical phrases, whether the place was Harvard, Princeton, Columbia, Oberlin, or the University of Nashville, out in Andrew Jackson's Tennessee.[2]

When the instructions are analyzed, several functions stand out. First of all the president was the chief executive, responsible for the general maintenance of the college including its financial solvency. He enforced the observance of the rules by all members and was, under the trustees, the court of last appeal. He was a teacher, usually taking the philosophical and theological subjects as his field; and in connection with his classroom duties he was the counselor and spiritual guide of all students, collectively and individually. Finally, as ceremonial head, he presided at all formal and traditional functions and handed out diplomas. The first campus experience of the incoming freshman was the personal greeting by the president, and the last campus memory of the departing senior was the magic Latin phrase in which the president declared him a *baccalaureus artium*. The old-time president combined, on a smaller scale to be sure, the present-day offices of the president, the dean of students, the bursar, the chaplain, the department of philosophy, and the office of public relations.

And that was not all. After assuming office, the president was likely to discover that all kinds of fringe activities were expected of him, not covered by the laws. Not every president had his ingenuity taxed as severely as Josiah Meigs, who went down from New Haven to Athens, Georgia, to open the state university, and found a town of two houses and a university without funds or buildings, and who started his educational activities, as he himself said, by making bricks and teaching his first classes under an oak tree. Eleazar Wheelock had to do similar yeoman service at Dartmouth. Less primitive but equally exacting were the demands on the time of President James Manning of Brown. Through most of his administration he was full-time pastor of a local church (not an uncommon practice), listened to the complaints of the undergraduates and of their fathers and mothers, cultivated a garden, did the family marketing, and attended the funeral of every baby that died in Providence.[3]

Clearly this was not a profession for which one could be trained, as one could for law or engineering. It was an art, and was learned by doing. The president's theological background was an asset in that it enabled the college to maintain good relations with the denominational leaders of the community on whose support it had to depend. Above all the office was, as it has remained, a public relations job. The successful president was not, as a rule, the great scholar or the super-efficient administrator. Nor was he the man who bulled his way through by the exercise of arbitrary power. Some tried this, only to reinforce the observation that power corrupts and absolute power corrupts absolutely. The successful president was the man who managed, largely by personal contact, to reconcile the conflicting interests of the various participating groups into that harmonious cooperation without which no college could exist. He created and maintained friendly relations, on different levels, with the students, their parents, the faculty, the trustees, the general public, and the angels who could be tapped for donations. He had to give special attention to the last.

With monotonous regularity the college histories tell the same story. That institution was rare which did not record at least one period of crisis when the president, through some legerdemain known only to himself, produced the necessary funds just in the nick of time and kept the enterprise alive. President Edward Griffin saved Williams from extinction by raising $25,000, of which he contributed $1,000 himself. A similar service was performed by Edward Hitchcock for Williams' neighbor, Amherst. Jasper Adams took over the moribund College of Charleston in 1824, worked like a galley slave to restore confidence in the school, succeeded in converting its deficit into a surplus, and left it one of the largest and most flourishing institutions in the South. Adams, incidentally, was also an outstanding scholar and philosopher of education. President Edward Beecher and other members of the rather impecunious "Yale Band" raised $80,000 for Illinois College, only to see most of it swept away in the panic of 1837. Jonathan Blanchard summarized his regime at Knox as follows: "I had found the college $5,000 in debt and running behind five dollars a day. I credited the treasury with more than $6,000 given me for my personal support. . . . I wrote the college diploma, procured the college seal; a library; graduated thirteen classes; and left Knox College free from debt, and worth $400,000." When he was a professor at the University of Mississippi, Frederick A. P. Barnard unearthed records to show that the state owed the university $900,000; the next year he was chosen president. The chronicler of Miami University in Ohio records with satisfaction that President Robert Bishop accomplished the unheard-of feat of closing nearly every year of his administration with a surplus. Bishop was a versatile individual; one wonders whether his methods of persuasion with prospective benefactors were similar to those he used on campus. An exponent of muscular Christianity, he combined a keen sense of propriety with a fiery temper. In chapel he prayed "with one eye open," and when he saw a disturbance, he would make a flying leap off the platform and onto the back of the luckless offender, reduce him to submission, then return to the pulpit and calmly resume praying.[4]

Under pressure from so many conflicting interests, the presidents were likely to find the going safest in the middle of the road. Many of them chose it. The great ones did not. But it easily became second nature to reassure the public on every occasion that their college, while overlooking no bets in the way of progressive innovations, would continue to revere the sacred traditions and preserve the eternal values. In doing so, they risked being labeled straddlers, or charged with disingenuousness. This was an occupational hazard which the president learned to take in his stride. There was bound to be criticism, and it would assuredly hit him first. In that respect the office has not changed much. The university president today, though supported by a far more complex organization, is still the most conspicuous target for the critics of higher education. He draws the charges from above and below, from within the university family and from the general public without. In preparing to meet the critics, he cannot fall back on any organization for support. The public calling for his scalp is an anonymous mass, and the trustees can present a solid front. The undergraduates are organized in student governments, and the faculty has its professional association. Even the deans in the larger universities can at least commiserate with one another. The president has no guild, nor has he ever had one. He has always stood alone.

Before the generalizations wear too thin, we had better turn our attention to a few of the actual presidents of the past two hundred years, examine their strengths and weaknesses, and their achievements. Through their experiences we shall discover American attitudes toward higher education and become more vividly aware of the college as a cultural institution. The individuals who have been singled out are John Witherspoon of Princeton, Timothy Dwight of Yale, Charles Nisbet of Dickinson, Eliphalet Nott of Union, Philip Lindsley of the University of Nashville (predecessor of Peabody), Horace Holley of Transylvania, and Mark Hopkins of Williams. Let it be emphasized that these are not necessarily the greatest or the most successful; one or two of them in fact could be considered complete failures. But each represents a type of individual or operated in a type of social situation that was fairly common.

John Witherspoon, president of Princeton from 1769 to 1794, was, in the opinion of the author of the university's bicentennial history, the greatest American educational and ecclesiastical leader of the eighteenth century.[5] A prominent Scottish theologian of liberal leanings, Witherspoon was invited to come to the colonies as president of the struggling College of New Jersey at a critical moment in its history, when the first wave of enthusiasm had begun to ebb and it had unexpectedly lost several of its ablest leaders. He hesitated long before accepting, but once the decision was made he cast his lot wholeheartedly with the New World. Entering the struggle for independence, he immediately took a prominent role. In fact, readers of general American history probably know Witherspoon better as a member of the Continental Congress from New Jersey and a signer of the Declaration of Independence than as a college president. Witherspoon's achievement was precisely the successful combination of a political, pedagogical, and ecclesiastical career. Through his public service his college gained in prestige and

in awareness of the events of the day. Princeton during Witherspoon's administration was no cloistered retreat. It could hardly be
that, what with Washington's Continentals and British regulars
marching and fighting across Jersey for six years, in the course of
which Nassau Hall took a battering that would leave a lasting
memory of the cost of independence. After the war an impressive
number of Witherspoon's former students assumed positions of importance in the new republic.

His post at the College of New Jersey was not an easy one. His
first task on arriving was to heal the rift between the old side and
new light factions of the colonial Presbyterian church. This he succeeded in doing, though at the cost of lowering the temperature
of religious and missionary zeal in the college and the church.
Throughout Witherspoon's regime the number of dedicated candidates for the ministry in the student body steadily declined, while
secular interests like law, business, and politics advanced. Moreover,
immediately upon taking office and frequently thereafter, he had to
give the major share of his attention to that perennial chore of college presidents, the raising of funds. Under his direction agents of
the college traversed the colonies from New England to South Carolina and even planned a fund-raising campaign in the West Indies.
Witherspoon himself covered the territory as far as Boston to the
east and Williamsburg to the south. Over £5,000, a tidy sum for
those days, was garnered in that first campaign, but more important,
the provincial College of New Jersey, school of a dissenting minority,
became nationally known. Wherever the Scotch-Irish Presbyterians
settled thereafter, especially in the South and West, they carried
with them the knowledge of Witherspoon's college. The financial
problem he never solved. His last years, what with the physical
destruction of the war and the loss of college funds in the postwar
inflation, were as full of financial worries as the first. On top of all
this, an eye injury left him blind for the last ten years of his life.

During nearly his entire twenty-five years in office, Witherspoon
carried a full teaching load. He lectured on "eloquence, moral philosophy, chronology, history, and divinity," and conducted the competition in speaking and writing Latin. Under his direction the Scottish philosophy of common sense drove Berkeleyan idealism out of
the classroom at Princeton. In time his philosophy lectures were
published as a guide for his successors. Witherspoon then was all

things to all men, as a good college president should be. His significance in the larger framework of American history was perhaps not his immediate service to his college, but his indirect achievements for his church and nationality. It was President Witherspoon who, more than any other one person, changed the Scottish Presbyterian element in the population from an upstart minority, looked down upon by substantial Anglicans and Quakers alike, to a triumphant group ready to grasp the intellectual and political leadership of the young republic, a leadership disputed only by the already waning tidewater aristocracy and the Puritan forces of New England, who were kin to the Presbyterians in theology and morals.[6]

Turning now to New England, we encounter one of the all-time greats of Yale: Timothy Dwight. Coming into the presidency there in 1795, a year after the death of Witherspoon, Dwight remained in office for twenty-two years; in that time he put the stamp of his personality and ideas on Yale and, through Yale, on the educational thinking and practice of most of the country. Like Witherspoon, Dwight was a theologian, a patriot, an administrator, a teacher and counselor of the young. But the emphasis was not the same. The theologian in Dwight was more prominent; he did not have the distinguished political career of the New Jersey man, and his patriotism had a provincial cast. Unlike Witherspoon again, Dwight ventured into the field of belles-lettres, turning out epic and didactic verse as a member of that earnest if not overly inspired group, the Connecticut Wits.

Dwight's theology was conservative but conciliatory. A Calvinist by birth and only a generation removed from Jonathan Edwards, he was nevertheless engaged in the practical business of making solid citizens out of adolescent boys, and so he eschewed the Edwardian subtleties and as far as possible avoided sectarian bickering. His four-volume dogmatic treatise, *Theology Explained and Defended,* is moderately Calvinistic, and instructive rather than argumentative; at any rate it does not bristle with polemics.

His patriotism was beyond reproach. As a chaplain in the Connecticut forces during the War for Independence, he had no qualms about right of revolution. He was an advocate of manifest destiny long before that term was coined. The theme of his didactic poem, *Greenfield Hill,* was in the lines: "All hail, thou western world! By heaven design'd/ Th'example bright, to renovate mankind." The poem goes on to paint in lurid contrast the depravities of Europe, developing the same theme as Judge Royall Tyler in the first American play, *The Contrast*. But Dwight's patriotism had a provincial quality too, and at times narrowed down to an uncritical glorification of his own section. What America was to Europe, New England was to America, Connecticut to New England, and, presumably, his parish of Greenfield Hill to Connecticut. In close sympathy with his brother Theodore, the Federalist party leader of the state, he was an unswerving supporter of the conservative "standing order," even to the extent of defending the established church which lingered in Connecticut until 1818, the year after his death. His opponents dubbed him "pope Dwight." In his opinion the old order had justified itself, for while European jails and gallows were full, Connecticut had scarcely a criminal; with immorality and unbelief the fashion in the Old World, Connecticut was profoundly religious. Dwight used to hitch up a horse and buggy in his summer vacations and take trips all over Yankeedom, even venturing across the line into New York state. Out of these trips grew four volumes of travels which are still a prime source for the social and cultural history of his time. But the *Travels* betrayed the same restricted vision as *Greenfield Hill*. A New England village, any village, was "one of the most delightful prospects which this world can afford." New England was freer, wealthier, more cultured, and more healthful than any other section of the country. When he crossed into New York, the soil at once grew poorer, the people lazier, the inns dirtier, and the rivers turned so muddy that even the horses refused to drink out of them. In the event of the ultimate dissolution of the Union—this was written in the shadow of the War of 1812 and the Hartford Convention—Dwight believed that a northeastern confederacy would be able to manage quite comfortably without the rest of the country.[7]

These were the religious and political sentiments that Timothy Dwight brought to Yale and through the force of his personality impressed on students and faculty. In a letter in 1811 a Yale student urged a friend to come to Yale rather than go to Harvard, for "the President and Professors are perfectly united in their sentiments with regard to Politics and Religion. These are very nearly the same with those of Calvin and Washington." When on one occasion an instructor got out of line to the extent of blatantly proclaiming French and Jeffersonian sentiments, only a public apology and a profession of love for the Constitution saved him from dismissal. This happened to Josiah Meigs, who soon left Yale anyway for the more hospitable climate of Georgia. Not all students shared the admiration of the lad who set up the trinity of Dwight, Calvin, and Washington. Occasional protests came from below the Mason and Dixon line—the South, by the way, had always sent a sizable contingent to Yale. An undergraduate from Virginia, writing in 1814, commented disparagingly on the prevailing secession sentiment in the land of steady habits, which meant, so he said, steady adherence and attachment to money. "His Excellency Dr. Dwight is most grossly infected by this raging political epidemick and instead of resisting the current of this pestilential malady he is borne willingly along. . . . But what of him? He is nothing to us so I'll let him rest." [8]

Dwight was much more than a conservative politician and theologian. He was an efficient administrator, a humane disciplinarian, and a stimulating teacher. During his term of office the enrollment tripled, rising from 110 to 313. He humanized discipline by abolishing the mechanical and vicious system of fines, providing wider opportunity for personal contact, and treating the students as gentlemen. An exponent of the prevailing disciplinary theory of education, he retained the sparse classical curriculum and set his face against frills. By contrast with the solid course at Yale, the current education of wealthy Bostonians with its novels and poetry and art and music seemed to him trivial. "The sight of a classic author gives him [the Boston young man of fashion] a chill; a lesson in Locke or Euclid, a mental ague." His formula for a sound education was the same as for sound farming: Till little, and that little well. Thus he confirmed the Yale pattern for years to come. Yet he had the good sense to encourage a young instructor like Benjamin Silliman to develop the sciences, which were "solid stuff." His own class lectures on moral philosophy and on rhetoric were lively and full of original comment. Though he used Paley and the Scottish philosophers, he did not hesitate to disagree sharply and substitute his own views. Among other things he warned his students against the theater, which to him was built on insincerity and deception. Besides, actors led such sloppy and un-Yankee-like lives. On novel-reading he was more liberal. At a time when many moralists were condemning this new art form outright, Dwight made distinctions. Fielding was not to be tolerated, but *Robinson Crusoe* was wholesome (the students' notes spelled the author's name "DeFeau"), and Richardson was commended as morally sound and the best novelist in the English language.[9]

All learning, however, was to serve the purpose of morality and religion, and was never an end in itself. One of the first tasks Dwight had set himself on entering the presidency was to clean out "French" skepticism and atheism, which, if the retrospective account of Lyman Beecher is to be believed, was rampant at Yale. This he did in a series of vigorous chapel talks in which he allowed students to present their arguments and met them fairly. While one suspects that in this seemingly balanced debate the cards were stacked in favor of the president, yet, for the times, it was a generous gesture.

The learned man had an obligation to society; of this Dwight was also convinced. For the closet philosopher who lives for his scholarship alone he had nothing but contempt. "In his study he dwells, in his books he passes his life." He has not discovered that science is a means not an end, and does not know that the humblest ploughman is a better member of society than he. He feels no obligation to promote human welfare or share in the life of the community. His talents remain closeted in his mind. And the end result? "After his death, his whole history may be written in this short epitaph: 'Here lies a learned man.'" The admiration that most of his students and contemporaries felt for this man of many parts is well expressed in a student's letter which maintained that virtually nobody could compare with President Dwight "as a private Christian, a polite gentleman, a general scholar, a historian, an extemporaneous lecturer, a politician, or divine." [10]

Crossing from New England into the Mohawk Valley, where Yankees and Yorkers mingled, we encounter that paragon of college patriarchs, the incredible Eliphalet Nott, who presided over the fortunes of Union College for sixty-two years. Taking office in 1804, he lasted through the Civil War. For the last ten years he was president in name only, while the actual administration was carried on by others; yet for better than half a century this resilient pedagogue actively guided and managed his college. Like Witherspoon and Dwight, Nott was a national figure, though in a different way. Before the end of his career he was widely known as a vigorous opponent of slavery and liquor, as a formidable financier, as the inventor of the first anthracite stove and the first steamboat to use coal for fuel, but primarily as the president of the most conspicuous "progressive" college of the first half of the nineteenth century. For much of his time Union was the second largest college in the country in enrollment, and in some years its graduating class was the largest, outstripping even Yale.

A product of the Puritan tradition like so many of his peers, Nott was caught up in the vision of a growing America. The fantastic New World success story of which he and his colleagues were a part was too much for the dour determinism of his Calvinistic upbringing, and he came out of it a confirmed optimist. Without deviating from accepted moral standards—he could devote an entire commencement address to the evils of gambling or strong drink—and without repudiating outright the theology of his fathers, he dressed it up in ever-brighter colors and eventually found himself preaching a gospel of progress and opportunity for all. At his semicentennial in 1854 he summed it up: "I believe that Progression is everywhere apparent . . . that we stand at the mere vestibule of the era of human progress . . . ," and went on to describe the glorious future when democracy, enlightened by science and sanctified by grace, would cause thrones to crumble, armies to disband, and when a bloodless revolution would regenerate the world. He carried this optimism into his teaching and administration. Finding the traditional curriculum inconsistent with progress, he modified it. He had the temerity to attack the sacred cow of Greek and Latin and tried to raise modern languages and modern science to a position of equal dignity with the classical studies—to the horror of his conservative colleagues in neighboring institutions.

But it was in campus government that Nott's unique ideas had fullest expression. Here he emerged as the patriarch and benevolent despot. Like Dwight at Yale, he resented the formalities and legalisms which controlled campus life, but in simplifying and humanizing them he dispensed with faculty help altogether, assuming all authority and accepting all responsibility himself. In his own words, "the college is a family, and its government should be parental. These young students are my children. I am to them in place of a father." He did not believe that true education was furthered by having the faculty sit in their robes as a court, cause offenders to be brought before them, examine witnesses, and pronounce judgment. So he waited until the first faculty resolution expelling a student had been reversed by the trustees, then changed the entire procedure. Determined never again to convene the faculty on a question of discipline, he began to deal with offenders personally and, on the whole, very successfully, by methods best known to himself. Incipient student revolts, that chronic affliction of all campuses, he nipped immediately by sending home the ringleaders, whom he miraculously ferreted out, and then exerting suitable pressure on the others. "He had studied every individual and could readily decide as to the kind of moral artillery that could be brought to bear on each." [11]

With the same confidence in his own powers, Nott managed the college finances. Here his operations were sometimes too jaunty. Lotteries and speculative ventures supplemented the more conventional appeals to the churches and the legislature. In the process of these manipulations the line between college monies and Nott's personal funds was not always kept clear, and an investigating committee of the legislature censured his conduct. Nott denied all charges and cleared himself to the satisfaction of most of his constituents, but ugly rumors continued to circulate, especially when it became known that the president had amassed a personal fortune while the college remained in financial straits.[12]

Nott's system of autocratic paternalism had its weaknesses. In the absence of any official check or audit of funds, one had to accept the president's word and assurance of integrity or else remain suspicious, with or without cause. By shutting out faculty participation and joint responsibility in discipline cases, Nott laid himself open to charges of deviousness and favoritism, with no legal machinery available to test the truth or falsity of the charges. The faculty meanwhile, as a fifth wheel, was placed in an uncomfortable and equivocal position in relation to students and trustees. Worst of all, no successors had been trained, and since there had been virtually no distribution of responsibility or delegation of authority, the vacuum created by the death of the leader hurt the college for many years to come.

But Nott's principal impact was on his students. He taught three generations of them: fathers, sons, and grandsons. His vehicle was the multifaceted moral philosophy course. Nott's method in this course was the conversational lecture in which he analyzed, confirmed, illustrated, and refuted the text, and when necessary engaged in long arguments with individual students. Though the personality and magnetism of the man are forever gone, a bit of the flavor of his sparkling performance may be conveyed by a mere recital of some of the topics touched on. The text was Lord Kames' *Elements of Criticism,* widely used at that time, especially in rhetoric courses. But the text was only the point of departure. Here is the introduction to the opening day's lecture, as one student got it in his notes:

"Young gentlemen: Your studies are intended to be such as are calculated immediately to improve the mind.—There are many, I have no doubt, in this class, as there are in all classes, who can't be persuaded to think. Them I could probably forward most by giving them longer lessons. But it has been my endeavour these twenty years, since I have had the care of youth, to make men rather than great scholars. I shall not give you long lessons, but shall lead you to exercise your own minds in much thought. Seniors should act for themselves, and from themselves. . . . It is easy to read, nothing is easier. The folly of most people is that they read too much. You should read but little, and turn that to the best account. You should analyze each book carefully so as not to loose [*sic*] any part of it. By this means you will understand it well and impress it upon your minds." [13]

There followed further hints on analyzing and note-taking, all humdrum enough. But then the course opened up in all directions. Here are a few highlights. Kames' statement that man is formed to be governed by reason was challenged: "Man seldom acts from reason. If you proceed to deal with men on this supposition you will surely fail. Individually men may be rational, but in society feeling rules all. In a small class a few students might be very rational. In the whole college there is very little reason. And if there were a thousand here there would be no reason at all." Other fragments may be paraphrased or abridged as follows: If a student gets into a scrape in town, the town's anger transfers to the whole student body. If you knew philosophy, you would stay home for a few days. The best time for courtship is when a young lady is in distress. Actors are worthless fellows, because they successively assume so many characters that they cannot build up their own. To illustrate Kames' statement that quick growth brings quick decay, Nott observed that the Irish are quick to anger and just as quickly mollified but Spaniards are the opposite. Little girls are brighter than little boys, but when they grow up, they become dull. Nott himself was considered a blockhead in his youth. A propos the current rage of phrenology and physical characteristics in general, Nott observed that he knew every student by his walk—a disturbing thought for potential evildoers. Training in eloquence and oratory are essential for honorable and decent public service, and will safeguard against backstairs behavior of crafty politicians. On animal magnetism: Nott knew a boy in Connecticut with mud turtle flappers for arms, the result of prenatal influence. One should not be too certain about the nonexistence of ghosts.

Clearly it was not a profound course, this strange mixture of shrewd common sense, naïve gullibility, and sheer sensationalism; yet it had a strong fascination for the seniors, and Union alumni by the hundreds remembered it, and the man who gave it, for the rest of their lives. Perhaps Francis Wayland, himself to become a famous college president, discovered the secret of its popularity. Sitting in Dr. Nott's class, he said, "We began to think ourselves men." [14]

Altogether different was the career of Charles Nisbet, first president of Dickinson. His was the oft-repeated story of the distinguished European scholar who comes to the New World with an idealized conception of the promise of American life, only to end up completely disillusioned by its actualities. The Pennsylvania Presbyterians who founded Dickinson believed, like those of Princeton, that some imported Scotch influence would lend strength and prestige to their enterprise and chose Nisbet, a Scottish theologian and scholar like Witherspoon, as their man. In addition to his scholarship, Nisbet's consistent and public opposition to the policies of the British government during the Revolution had commended him to the leaders of the new institution, which was founded in the first flush of a national patriotism so intense that the trustees had to take an oath that they had never aided the British after the fourth of July 1776.

At first everything was promising. Benjamin Rush, prominent Philadelphia physician and chief organizer of the college, had written Nisbet a glowing letter in which he pointed out the educational opportunities and excellent financial prospects, and furthermore assured the distinguished Scotsman that "Calvinism is the fashionable religion of our country." Nisbet came on, eager and full of high hopes. But soon the picture changed. Rush unaccountably turned cool toward his protégé (a habit he had), the climate of Carlisle did not perform as promised, and Nisbet came down with malaria. Homesick and disillusioned, he resigned and prepared to return to Scotland. But his funds had given out, and he was persuaded to change his mind and remain. He continued as principal (the title then used) of Dickinson College for twenty years, to 1804. The entire twenty years were a time of troubles. The difficulties were of a kind that confronted all American colleges in those days, but they were aggravated by Nisbet's stiff European attitude and his inability to adapt himself to American ways. To begin with, the college did not have the £10,000 which Rush's letter had promised, nor did it see that much money for the next fifty years. Expected legislative help was not forthcoming, and the "very liberal donation" that John Dickinson had given along with his name proved quite inadequate. Nisbet's contracted salary of $1,200 was reduced to $800 and was four years in arrears at the time of his death.

But the troubles went deeper, for this was a time of social upheaval as well as economic stringency. The turbulence of democracy in action, the bitter partisanship, the rioting over the Constitution and later over the whiskey tax were none of them reassuring. Worst of all, there was a prevailing attitude of contempt for scholars and scholarship that really got under Nisbet's skin. Even the trustees were not free of taint. Interested in show and numbers, "what they consider as the ultimate end of learning, is that the students may be able to speak readily in public." Whether they had anything to say was secondary. The trustees kept standards low by shortening the courses and pretending that just as much was being accomplished in less time; they made it virtually impossible for the faculty to drop even the stupidest student; and all this came about, Nisbet was sure, because they collected the fees for the diplomas. The trustees in turn might well have asked the president how he proposed to get the money to keep the college running and, incidentally, pay his own salary. But the whole system was wrong as Nisbet saw it. The autocratic and arbitrary power of the trustees and the subordinate hired-hand status of the president and the faculty—how different it all was from Scotland, where scholars were respected and where the rector and his colleagues controlled the university and directed its policies. As for American parents, they wanted their children educated, yes, but in a hurry; they did not know the difference between elementary school and college. Public opinion then was on the side of the trustees, and public opinion was all-powerful. In helpless exasperation, Nisbet exclaimed: "Americans seem much more desirous that their affairs be managed by themselves than that they should be well managed!" Andrew Jackson could not have put it better.

Nisbet cannot be called a failure. After all he lasted twenty years in his precarious post, which was better than par for college presidents. Throughout these years he kept his flags flying and continued to battle for higher standards. In his class lectures and public addresses, and in his Sunday sermons, which were always exactly one hour long, he preached the doctrine of excellence. "You have studied at a time," he told the student body in one of his last addresses, "when the most false and absurd opinions concerning learning have been current, prevalent, and even rampant. We mean these opinions which suppose that a liberal education may be attained in a very little time; that the study of the ancient languages is useless; that education may be completed in the course of a year." Short roads to learning were absurdity and folly. His students admired the scholarship of a man who had a library in six languages and was himself reputed master of twelve. The better ones tried to follow his lectures, overawing as they sometimes were, and they enjoyed his wit and winced under his sarcasm. In Carlisle and throughout Pennsylvania he gained many admirers and made some friends. Among the latter was Hugh Brackenridge, early American poet and novelist, who thought a great deal of Nisbet and worked him into his satirical novel, *Modern Chivalry*. No, Nisbet was not a failure; he was a voice crying in the wilderness.[15]

Not only in the original states of the Atlantic seaboard did students have the privilege of sitting at the feet of great men. Colleges west of the mountains had their outstanding teachers and leaders. Usually these were transplanted easterners. Idealistic young graduates of Yale and Princeton and Union and Harvard would move "Out West" to set up an educational utopia in some frontier community, hoping only that it would stand still long enough for their theories to work out. Two such knights-errant were Philip Lindsley, president for twenty-five years of the University of Nashville in Tennessee, and the brilliant Horace Holley, who had a brief and tragic career at Transylvania University in Kentucky.

Lindsley was a native of New Jersey and a graduate of Princeton. He studied theology and was licensed to preach, became tutor and then professor at his alma mater, and was called from there in 1825 to the presidency of Cumberland College, which styled itself in the next year the University of Nashville and was in turn the predecessor of Peabody College for Teachers. He found Tennessee a western state about to become southern. Its society, scarcely out of the blustering, unlettered frontier stage, was beginning to stratify. The cotton aristocracy was taking form, constantly recruited from the ranks of yeomen farmers and tradesmen, and was beginning, along with the professional classes, to lord it over poor whites and, of course, Negro slaves. In this environment Lindsley labored to build a rational system of education adapted to the needs of the community. His general aim was widespread schooling for all citizens from the elementary grades up, as a prerequisite for a smoothly functioning democracy. Here he encountered the conflicting interests of those who wished to use all the public education funds for the common schools and those who were willing to neglect the masses in favor of a well-financed state university to benefit the few. These interests clashed in other southern states too; in Missouri for example the former were winning out, in South Carolina the latter. Lindsley tried to reconcile the two, for he saw that they were interdependent, but his chief interest was in the university as the capstone of the system. His was the familiar ideal which had been reiterated from the foundation of the republic by Jefferson and others, and which was soon to be given new emphasis by Horace Mann. Lindsley tried to realize it in Tennessee. In a series of eloquent public addresses and papers he explained his program. "A free government, like ours, cannot be maintained except by an enlightened and virtuous people." This was no longer a new idea even as far back as 1825. Again: "The farmer, the mechanic, the manufacturer, the merchant, the sailor, the soldier . . . must be educated." This was the program of Francis Wayland of Brown a quarter-century later.

Lindsley's detailed plan called for six colleges, each with its separate land, building, refectory, and faculty. There were to be shops, gardens, and an experimental farm. Funds for all this were to come from state appropriations and individual gifts. A complete university would thus emerge, offering all liberal subjects and practical and professional training as well, and obviating the necessity of going east for a good education. The university was to have twenty professorships and teach, in addition to the standard classical subjects, international law, government, agriculture, commerce, statistics, manufacturing, riding, fencing, swimming, and gymnastics. Enlarged into twentieth century terms this would mean a college of agriculture, a school of business administration, and a full program of athletics and physical education. The classics would not be neglected but take their place as one of several options, and cease to hold the center of the stage. Lindsley hoped to have the program under way in five years but cheerfully admitted it might take five hundred.

Needless to say, the full university did not materialize, for all of its author's energy and eloquence. The obstacles confronting him were the same as have beset many an educational planner before and since his time. The people of Tennessee were unable or unwilling to supply the funds for so novel and ambitious a program. The rising southern aristocracy was not easily won over to support the schemes of a northerner, especially one who denounced its duels and its entire gentleman's code as sham and hypocrisy. Lindsley discovered that parents had to be educated first of all. Some of his commencement and baccalaureate addresses ascribed the difficulties of the university to parental objections to its purposes and parental interference with its discipline. When stupid or lazy boys failed of promotion, took to mischief, were punished and finally sent home, all in the interest of high standards and public order, the college authorities were immediately attacked by irate parents: "The son is a high-minded, honorable, brave, generous, good-hearted young gentleman; who scorns all subterfuge and meanness, and who would not lie for the universe! Not he. In this particular at least, he is above suspicion; and, like the Pope, infallible. While the Faculty are a parcel of paltry pedants, pedagogues, bigots, charlatans—without feeling, spirit, kindness, honesty, or common sense."

There was also opposition from organizations that hoped to share in the distribution of public money, like the church colleges. As head of the Nashville institution, Lindsley had repeatedly to complain of the mushroom growth of small denominational colleges contesting the prior claims of the university and supported by an obscurantist clergy. A licensed preacher himself, he aimed pointed shafts at the profession: "If people choose to have inspired men for their spiritual guides, the less of human science with which they may chance to be encumbered, the better—at least the more apparent and striking will be the evidences of their inspiration." The church colleges promised "to work cheap; to finish off and graduate in double-quick time, and in the most approved style, all who may come to them." The legal profession, too, seems to have crossed him. As for lawyers and their "intricate and almost unlearnable" science of common law, "they will abound and flourish just in proportion to the general ignorance and degradation of the mass of the people." Both preachers and lawyers could benefit from a thorough scientific education, the only safeguard against priestcraft and legal chicanery. Pounding away against such odds, Lindsley held his ideals and standards before the citizens of Tennessee for twenty-five years, winning the love and confidence of his students and the respect of the more thoughtful members of the community.[16]

The story of Horace Holley is a tragedy whose causes cannot be determined with finality, since the contemporary accounts of his career are so emotion-ridden. The people who knew him well seem to have been either enthusiastically for, or violently against, him. By setting off the one group against the other, one can gain a tolerably clear picture of the situation. Holley was a graduate of Yale and a favorite pupil of Timothy Dwight. He became pastor of Hollis Street Church in Boston, where his conservative theological views underwent a slow transformation into what was soon to be known as Unitarianism. He had acquired a considerable reputation as a preacher when he was called to the presidency of Transylvania University in Lexington, Kentucky. With an eighteenth century charter, Transylvania claimed to be the first institution of higher learning west of the Appalachians. Situated in "the Athens of the west," the college and its cause were taken up by a group of liberal and cultured Kentuckians who wanted to raise it into the state university and get all groups and factions to support it. But the college had been founded by earnest Presbyterians, and this denomination, though it included only a small percentage of the total population of Kentucky, was unwilling to relinquish its pre-eminence or let go its influence in the board of trustees. Holley was the choice of the liberal group, and was brought out at the staggering salary of $3,000. Lexington was perhaps the only community west of the mountains that could afford such munificence.

At first Holley lulled the suspicions of the orthodox group by his obvious integrity, eloquence, and personal charm. His own scholarly interest was not in the classics primarily, but in English literature. He thought himself forward-looking and regarded Latin and Greek valuable primarily as a help toward understanding English, the most important study of all. Holley was a pioneer, too, in suggesting the development and study of American literature. Among other, more tangible results of his presidency were a law school and a medical school, the latter probably as good as any in the country, even though the leading medical professor was a devotee of phrenology, which had quite a vogue among the highbrows of that time. Most of all Holley seems to have won his way by the force of his personality, which dazzled people. When his biographer and eulogist compares his eloquence with that of the Earl of Chatham and Bishop Bossuet, or describes his class lectures in philosophy as bordering on the transcendent, one feels that inflation has crept in and allowance must be made for the exaggerations of a friend; however, the statistics for his administration cannot be shrugged off. For its entire sixteen years preceding Holley, Transylvania had a total of twenty-two graduates; Holley's eight years produced five hundred and fifty-eight, the most famous of whom was Jefferson Davis. Unquestionably he raised an obscure school to the rank of one of the best institutions of higher learning in the country.

But the opposition was only biding its time. Holley's personal behavior and the tone he set for the life of the college, while quite acceptable to the *haut monde* of Lexington, was galling to the Presbyterian preachers. Rumors began to float about, and anonymous articles denouncing the president appeared in religious journals. His fashionable dress, his formal dinners sparkling with wine and witty conversation, his tolerance of card-playing, his occasional attendance at theaters and horse races, all counted against him. His use of the classroom to point up the futility of sectarian strife and his lofty assertions that he looked down on all theological hairsplitting "from a more pure and elastic atmosphere" did not endear him in orthodox circles. The attacks were now stepped up: He was a Socinian, a Pelagian, he did not believe in a personal devil, and, most reprehensible, he was disturbing the popular faith. Finally his opponents got to the legislature and had Transylvania's appropriation cut off, and that was the end. Holley resigned, the best students left, and Transylvania soon returned to its pristine mediocrity. When Holley, returning east via New Orleans, died of a tropical fever at the age of forty-seven, his victorious opponents in Kentucky felt themselves vindicated by the judgment of God.[17]

No recital of outstanding college presidents is complete without mention of Mark Hopkins. But this "grand old man" of Williams is so widely known that not much need be added here. As professor and president of the college in the Berkshires for forty-two years, he marks the end, at least in New England, of the reign of patriar-chal presidents who molded their students by their teaching, their direct discipline, and their personal counseling. Hopkins resigned the presidency in 1872, and when he died in 1887, full of years and honors, the old-time college was a thing of the past.[18]

Chapter Six

From Female Seminary
to Woman's College

American colleges, like European universities, were for men. Harvard had been in existence for two hundred years before any serious attempts were made to provide the same kind of higher education for women. The reasons for this lag lie deeply imbedded in the history of our culture. Through most of recorded time, women have been subordinated to men with the full approval of the latter, and have not been able to develop their talents or realize their ambitions as freely as the opposite sex. Matriarchies have been conspicuous by their rarity. In Hindu, as in Chinese civilization, women played a subordinate role, though the tightly knit family structure, especially of the latter, gave older women considerable authority if they lived long enough. Classical Athens, source of so much of our culture, was a man's world, where the most that an intelligent woman could aspire to was to become a hetaira. Phryne and Aspasia, among the few women in Athenian history who are known by name, enjoyed a brief and shaky pre-eminence in a small circle, and that was all. In the palmy days of the Roman empire the lot of women, by and large, was somewhat more tolerable; but when the empire passed its prime and started to decay, women's brief season in the sun also drew to a close and they returned to second-class citizenship.

Organized Christianity did little at first to improve their condition. Jesus, to be sure, had both men and women in His following and, as far as we can deduce from the record of the Gospels, showed equal understanding and respect for both. This is not surprising, since Jewish culture allotted a more dignified role to women than most contemporary pagan civilizations. Besides, Jesus dealt with human beings as individuals not as categories. But the church organized in his name took its cue from other leaders. It was St. Paul who had harsh things to say about women in his letters. Four centuries later St. Augustine gave tone and direction to medieval Christian theology. Augustine's *Confessions* emphasized the opposites of the mother and the temptress. The growing vogue of the monastic life as an escape from the insecurities of the Dark Ages gave currency among the Saints to the view of woman as a daughter of Eve and source of temptation. Even the veneration of the Virgin, romanticized in the arts from the twelfth century on, while it introduced the ideal of unattainable purity and so mitigated the coarseness of medieval life, failed on the whole to bring ease and freedom to woman. Meanwhile the manorial economy which overtook Western Europe pinned her down still further to a narrow domestic role of menial labor.

Neither troubadours nor humanists, for all their effusions in praise of women, succeeded in changing this situation. Their activities were largely a romantic façade, and their influence reached only limited circles. The female world of Tannhäuser was divided between the pious but colorless Elizabeth and the immoral revels of the *Venusberg;* he never seems to have met anybody like, say, Portia. The Reformation brought about little change in the relations of the sexes. Although Protestantism did restore marriage and the family to its pristine dignity for both clergy and laity, it did not do much, officially, to raise the position of woman in society. Catholic and Protestant clergy alike continued to inform women, vociferously and authoritatively, how God wanted them to behave.

What poetry and theology failed to accomplish, economic and social forces did. When Europe spilled over into the New World, men naturally took the lead, for pioneering required fighting and heavy physical labor. But that was only the first stage. To transplant a culture, women were needed; the processes of civilization could be carried on only by men and women together and by parents and children in family units. On the frontier, men were forever escaping the bonds of civilized life only to discover that it was not enough for them to subdue the wilderness; without women the wilderness would subdue them. Women were at a premium throughout the colonial period. Never equaling men in numbers until well into the nineteenth century, they attained a scarcity value and were cherished accordingly. European travelers in America began to notice that women—and children too, for that matter—were freer in the New World. Not that the laws had changed. British common law restrictions on women were still largely in force. But social relationships were changing, and the laws, geared to earlier and obsolescent conditions, were losing their meaning. Because of their greater contributions to the general welfare, women had to be granted wider freedom in practice. At the risk of oversimplifying a complex problem, one might maintain that the greater freedom and influence of American women, a phenomenon noted by European observers from the first settlements down to the present, was, at least in its initial stages, a function of the economic law of supply and demand.

It is in this framework that higher education for women in America must be understood. When the demand for it came, it was bound to get a sympathetic hearing, even though tradition and authority were against it. Patriotism was a powerful lever too. Just as the first men's colleges were supported as a means of securing an informed and trained citizenry, so it was pointed out that women needed to be educated to fulfill their growing role in the new republic; not in colleges just yet—that was too big a leap—but in elementary schools, academies, and seminaries, where they might receive systematic training in the subjects suitable to their sex. To state with any assurance when and where it all began is to invite trouble, for there are rival claimants for priority, all armed with impressive documents. What can be said is that in the early nineteenth century, ladies' academies and female seminaries appeared everywhere in the United States. A few dated back to the eighteenth. Famous among the early ones was the Moravian Academy in Bethlehem, Pennsylvania, which built up an enrollment of a hundred girls within two years, after its founding in 1786.[1]

As usual, the best-known ventures in women's education were in the northeastern states. In the Hudson Valley, in 1821, Emma Willard established her Troy Female Seminary, upon a plan of studies "as different from those appropriated to the other sex, as the female character and duties are from the male."[2] Conciliatory language such as this was necessary to forestall criticism and avert prejudice. After trying in vain to get legislative support, she became disenchanted, as she herself said, with the maneuvers of politicians and turned to private sources of maintenance. Here she succeeded. The seminary flourished and came to be widely known as an alert and progressive school.

It was a poor reform movement that did not have at least one Beecher among its supporters. Catherine was the member of this outgoing family most concerned about the education of women. She wrote copiously and sensibly about the problem, and tried her own hand at it too, in the Hartford Female Seminary begun in 1824. Here with one assistant and almost no equipment she taught girls of varying ages, and in short order had a hundred students. All were housed in one room where she and her assistant conducted recitation periods of fifteen minutes or less in ten to twelve subjects a day. It was rugged, but then it, too, was pioneering.[3]

Mary Lyon, another New Englander and a friend of both Miss Willard and Miss Beecher, launched an enterprise in 1836 that before long outdistanced the schools of both of her friends: Mount Holyoke Seminary. Miss Lyon was described by her contemporaries as warm and motherly and as lacking in natural dignity—this last from an Amherst professor; a student contrasted her cheerfulness with the solemn Atlas-like visages of some of her other teachers; another student never suspected from her looks that she was in the least intellectual. With these qualifications she turned out to be a huge success both as a teacher and principal of the seminary. For all her motherly warmth she was a driver and an autocrat, and confronted the two hundred and fifty girls who soon crowded the school, with a set of regulations for general conduct that ran to a hundred and six alphabetized items and were strictly enforced. Of course the laws of behavior in the men's colleges of those days were just as long and detailed, and more robust. While the boys were forbidden to bring guns into the rooms or to beat up instructors, their sisters were admonished to sit erect at tables and not to whisper in the corridors. To secure obedience to all these rules, Miss Lyon required every student to report her own infractions daily to the authorities in a sort of Puritan confessional. This self-reporting device was to cause much criticism and soul-searching in later years when Mount Holyoke grew up to be a college.[4]

For all its rules life in the seminary seems to have been pleasant enough. Intellectual activities alternated with domestic chores. There were breaks in the routine such as Mountain Day, when the entire school adjourned for a picnic on Mount Holyoke. This was doubly pleasant when, by coincidence, the Amherst boys happened to be out on a geology field trip on that self-same mountain. There were other ways for the girls to meet their fellow students from across the mountain. An Amherst student's diary in the 1840's records visits to South Hadley, a pleasant buggy-ride away, ringing the bell of the school "in great terror, for fear of Miss Lyon and assistant dragonesses," and spending a pleasant hour with a girl who shared his adoration for Longfellow.[5]

The course of study was the usual mélange of the ladies' seminary, but on a high level. There were the practical courses designed to make future home-making more efficient and agreeable; there was some English literature and a bit of French; the easier Latin classics, but no Greek; mathematics but with avoidance of its upper reaches; some history and geography; a little music and painting. Science at Mount Holyoke was kept at high quality by visiting lecturers, including such competent teachers as Edward Hitchcock, whose course in chemistry and mineralogy Mary Lyon herself had taken by special permission at Amherst, and who was one of the outstanding American geologists of his day.

Religion dominated the campus. Not polemical, denominational religion, but religion as a guide for personal conduct and an inspiration for social service. In the formal courses, Paley and Butler were read, just as in the colleges for men, but the chief concern of the school was to turn out missionaries and mission teachers and assistants. In time this meant missionaries' wives too. Thus graduates of Mount Holyoke spread over the face of the globe, wherever the evangelical missions led them. The combination of interest in missions and the strict rules of conduct built for the seminary a reputation for piety that proved embarrassing when the time came for expansion into a full college. As one critic, a sympathetic one at that, put it then, to secure a college charter, the institution would have to live down a reputation for "enforced pietism and religious terrorism." This it did, quite successfully.[6]

The female seminary, of which Mount Holyoke was a superior example, did not satisfy the demands of those who held that woman was man's intellectual equal in every respect and was therefore entitled to a higher education exactly like his. As a transitional institution, the seminary would do, but the movement must not stop there. To reach the college level, in terms of the educational philosophy dominant in the mid-nineteenth century, it would be necessary to slough off the many fashionable and vocational scraps of knowledge which cluttered the curriculum and concentrate on the solid subjects which sharpened the understanding and disciplined the mind. This meant the higher reaches of Latin, Greek, mathematics, mental and moral philosophy. Let a girl take four solid years of these subjects, and if she survived, she was entitled to the A.B. degree.

There were many who thought she would not survive. Alarm, indignation, derision, not all of them from men, greeted the proposals which now came with increasing frequency for full classical colleges for women. Such an experience, said one critic, "can only be hardening and deforming." And others chimed in: "This borders on the vulgar." "This is all very fine, but . . . how does it affect their chances?" Alarm verging on consternation is discernible in the comment of the Reverend John Todd, though, to be sure, his protest was directed against the imposition of a classical college on the already indigestible seminary course of study. "As for training young ladies through a long intellectual course, as we do young men, it can never be done," said Todd. "They will die in the process. . . . The poor thing has her brain crowded with history, grammar, arithmetic, geography, natural history, chemistry, physiology, botany, astronomy, rhetoric, natural and moral philosophy, metaphysics, French, often German, Latin, perhaps Greek, reading, spelling, committing poetry, writing compositions, drawing, painting, etc., etc., *ad infinitum*. Then, out of school hours, from three to six hours of severe toil at the piano. She must be on the strain all the school hours, study in the evening till her eyes ache, her brain whirls, her spine yields and gives way, and she comes through the process of education, enervated, feeble, without courage or vigor, elasticity or strength. Alas! must we crowd education upon our daughters, and, for the sake of having them 'intellectual,' make them puny, nervous, and their whole earthly existence a struggle between life and death?" [7]

. But no amount of alarming comment by preachers, editors, or any other spokesmen of the male sex could stop the movement. The girls insisted on going to college, though not in any great numbers at first. The earliest colleges for women were wispy and tentative. Notable among them were Georgia Female College at Macon, Mary Sharp College in Tennessee, conducted by an expatriate Vermonter, and Elmira College in New York. All three granted the bachelor's degree. Elmira came closest to the real thing. Its historian insists that priority in women's collegiate education belongs to Elmira, yet he admits that the curriculum for the first thirteen years after its opening in

1855 was a "compromise between the ideals of academic scholars on the one hand and popular opinion on the other." In his inaugural address the first president of Elmira, the Reverend Augustus W. Cowles, maintained, in terms of the then popular faculty psychology, that men surpassed women in pure intellection and profound abstract thinking, but that the retentive powers, the imagination, and the moral sensibilities of women were superior.[8] Such a concession was not acceptable to simon-pure exponents of equality. In the opinion of James M. Taylor, for many years president of Vassar, these early collegiate enterprises were conducted with much enthusiasm and earnestness and deserve the highest praise. But there was still too much of china painting and wax flowers about them; they were not real colleges, not like Vassar.[9]

Vassar *was* different, in a number of ways. When it opened in 1865 as the Vassar Female College, a well-thought-out prospectus was ready, offering a full collegiate program without seminary frills to three hundred and thirty students who came from as far as California for the exciting new venture. There was a faculty able and willing to turn the prospectus into reality, and the imposing college building was large enough to house and furnish classroom space for all the oncoming students. Best of all, there was a solid financial backlog of $800,000, the gift of Matthew Vassar, English-born businessman of Poughkeepsie who had made a fortune brewing ale. It was Vassar who put the case for the higher education of women simply and incontrovertibly. "It occurred to me," he said to his trustees, "that woman having received from her Creator the same intellectual constitution as man, has the same right as man to intellectual culture and development." Yet there was one difficulty: Scarcely any of the three hundred-odd incoming students had the proper training or background to take the courses that had been prepared for them. The college was ready for the girls, but the girls were not ready for college. They ranged in age from fifteen to twenty-four; enthusiastic, even gushing, they were "passionately fond" of this subject and "utterly detested" that, but they did not have the faintest notion what a higher education meant or involved. Neither did their parents. The faculty's first task was to explain to students and parents the meaning of a strict collegiate course. This took three years. By that time the institution had also shed the "Female" from its official title and could now, in 1868, square away a college in name as well as in fact.[10]

Others followed suit. The year 1875 saw the birth of Wellesley and Smith, 1885 of Bryn Mawr. Wellesley was the lengthened shadow of its founder and benefactor, Henry Durant. In the four years that its first college hall was in the building, Durant and his wife supervised every detail. Durant himself decided on the courses to be taught, picked the faculty—they were to be all women—and even selected the food for the dining commons. The Northampton institution, made possible by the bequest of Sophia Smith, had as its declared object from the start an education for young women equal to that afforded young men. It was not designed to fit a girl for a particular sphere or profession but to perfect her intellect and enable her to enjoy and do well her work in life, whatever that might be. Smith wanted the broadest and highest intellectual culture, together with completely developed womanhood. Vassar, by the way, had expressed the same ideals; in its literature one first encounters "the well-rounded woman." [11]

Not all wanted the general, rounded education. Bryn Mawr preferred its students sharpened to a point. Intellectual excellence and high scholarly achievement were the goals there, thanks largely to the influence of the first dean and long-time president, Martha Carey Thomas. Miss Thomas was one of the first women students at Cornell, took graduate work, under difficulties, at Johns Hopkins, then went to Germany to study philology, and became the first American woman to get a European Ph.D., from the University of Zurich, and *summa cum laude* at that. Before assuming her duties at Bryn Mawr, she was given a year's leave to acquaint herself with current educational problems and practices. She sought out President Gilman of Johns Hopkins, then visited Vassar, Smith, Harvard Annex (soon to be Radcliffe), and Wellesley. Vassar impressed her most favorably with its liberal spirit and the progressive ideas of its faculty, though in performance she found it still a glorified boarding school. Smith seemed more solemn, it lacked Vassar's freshness; perhaps, speculated Miss Thomas, because all its professors were men. The authorities at Smith in turn did not consider the new Bryn Mawr institution a college at all, because of its low entrance requirements. Carey Thomas saw to it that these were raised until they equaled Harvard's and were thus the stiffest in the country. In keeping with its high standards, Bryn Mawr had assembled an impressive group of professors. Of the first faculty of nine, eight had studied in Europe and four of these had achieved German Ph.D. degrees; the only one of the nine with no European graduate work to his credit was the young assistant professor of political science, Woodrow Wilson.[12]

With the opening of Bryn Mawr, the battle was won. Independent colleges for women had come to stay. They did not become numerous except in the New England states, but a number were founded elsewhere in the country before the turn of the century. Under the auspices of the Methodist church, Goucher, known until 1910 as Baltimore Woman's College, was chartered in the same year as Bryn Mawr. The same denomination sponsored Randolph-Macon in Virginia in 1891. This institution was to be fully equal to the best colleges for men, "without loss to woman's crowning glory, her gentleness and grace." Two small colleges in Wisconsin dating from the middle of the nineteenth century, one with the blessing of the redoubtable Catherine Beecher, merged in 1895 as Milwaukee Downer. Meanwhile a Presbyterian seminary in Rockford, Illinois, had gradually advanced its standards and began granting the A.B. degree in 1882. In Virginia a bequest by Mrs. Indiana Fletcher Williams of $500,000 and an eight-thousand-acre plantation for the higher education of "white girls and young women" was the beginning of Sweet Briar, which began to receive students in 1906. And a Mount Holyoke type of seminary on the Pacific coast, founded by a returned foreign missionary couple, the wife a graduate of Miss Lyon's school, became Mills College. As the Roman Catholic church grew in numbers and wealth, it, too, in keeping with its principle of separate higher education for the sexes, established numerous women's colleges, most of them in the twentieth century.[13]

Although separate colleges seemed the best answer to the educational needs of women in the older sections of the country, an altogether different pattern was emerging in the Middle West. This was coeducation. In the Mississippi Valley a younger and more fluid social structure together with a scarcity of financial capital made it seem natural and desirable, after some transitional maneuvering, to have women attend the same institutions and eventually sit in the same classrooms with men. In its early stages coeducation met with the same kind of opposition as women's colleges did in the East. Lyman Beecher knew it would not work. "This amalgamation of sexes won't do. If you live in a Powder House you blow up once in a while." Somewhat later the august authorities at Brown were to voice similar alarm at the suggestion of coeducation there. Such an innovation "in the inflammable years," they thought, would be most unwise.[14]

Oberlin began it. Believing that the education of youth of both sexes accorded with the spirit of the Gospel, the trustees in 1837 opened the college classes and the dining commons to women, with no discrimination. Almost none, that is. Women who took the required courses and passed all examinations were granted the A.B. but were not allowed to speak their piece at commencement. They had to write one, but a male classmate read it while they sat mute on the platform. Lucy Stone, a member of one of the early graduating classes, led a petition of protest, to no avail. Professor Fairchild laid down the law: "It is a thing positively disagreeable to both sexes to see a woman a public character." Not all the coeds were like Lucy Stone. President Mahan, who sincerely believed in coeducation, encouraged the girls in his rhetoric class to speak up, but they begged to be excused; they could not face the boys. Along with its college classes open to women Oberlin continued to maintain a parallel ladies' seminary which was more largely attended. By 1865 seventy-nine women had earned the A.B. degree, while two hundred and ninety had graduated from the scholastically inferior seminary course.[15]

Antioch in western Ohio, small but significant, was another pioneer college that admitted women from the start. The extent of their participation here can be deduced from a statistical summary of the postgraduate careers of the one hundred and thirty-three students who graduated from Antioch between 1853, the year it opened, and 1876. Eighty-seven of these were gentlemen, and forty-six were ladies. Of the former, nineteen were teaching in schools or colleges, twenty-two were lawyers, twelve ministers, five physicians, four editors, the rest presumably farmers or businessmen. The forty-six ladies included eighteen teachers, two physicians, one minister. Thirty were married, and twenty-three had children.[16]

The real surge of coeducation came with the opening of the great state universities of the Middle West. Here too there was opposition at first, but once the precedent had been established in one state, it was difficult for the others to resist. The state university of Iowa admitted women from the time it opened, in 1855. Michigan, the oldest, dating from 1837, resisted their intrusion for more than three decades. Not until 1870 were women received, and then grudgingly. The men resented their presence and shunned them until almost the end of the century. This becomes credible when one discovers that the first women students at Michigan were trainees for medical missionaries who show up on class pictures as a "most awesome collection of stony-faced females." [17] This was before the days of the sweetheart of Sigma Chi. The early Michigan coeds were clearly not the type. Wisconsin, theoretically open to women from 1866 on, began with a separate Female College of lower standards granting the degree of Ph.B. But over the years a number of things became apparent. The women were keeping up with their studies as well as the men; apprehensions of a decline of health and morals proved unfounded; it seemed a waste of time and money to run a separate female college; men students gradually ceased their objections. By 1874 the difficulties were overcome, and women were freely accepted at Wisconsin. At the commencement of that year all the honors were won by a woman graduate. Most opposition now disappeared, and coeducation became the normal condition, not only at Wisconsin but throughout the Middle and the Far West. It even spilled over a little into the East, where such institutions as Swarthmore, Bucknell, and, most important, Cornell took it up. Carey Thomas of Bryn Mawr, one of the first women graduates of Cornell, chose it in preference to Vassar because in her opinion it offered a more realistic education.[18]

In addition to the separate women's college and the coeducational college there was a third type which admitted women. This was the coordinate college, a term used to identify those separate organizations of women students, of full college caliber, that were established as adjuncts to and under the charter of already existing universities which hitherto had been catering only to men. Barnard was organized under the charter of Columbia in 1889, thanks to the untiring efforts of President Barnard and a number of prominent New Yorkers, male and female. Its beginnings were primitive enough. Virginia Gildersleeve, later dean and president of Barnard, has described the shabby old brownstone house in mid-Manhattan where the college had its being and where she climbed to the room on the fourth floor along with her twenty classmates, to the required class exercises of the freshman year. Two years later the college moved, with the rest of the university, to take its assigned share of the new campus on Morningside Heights. The same decade saw the emergence of Radcliffe from its embryonic stage of Harvard Annex. The Corporation of Brown, after fending off petitions for twenty years, admitted women to separate instruction in 1891. Seven entered that year, and five years later the number had risen to a hundred and fifty-seven. The following year the women were given a separate organization with their own dean and their own building: Pembroke Hall. That was the beginning of Pembroke College. Near the end of World War I the New Jersey State Federation of Women's Clubs, under the able leadership of Mabel Smith Douglass, secured legislative permission and support for an institution of higher learning for young women of the state, to be set up under the hospitable charter of Rutgers, and New Jersey College for Women, now Douglass College, came into being.[19]

Four of the oldest educational institutions in the nation, all with colonial roots, had thus admitted women to partnership. They had not all done it in precisely the same way, and the nature of the relationship varied from campus to campus. Radcliffe and Pembroke had no faculty of their own; their students were instructed by professors of the parent institution, though in separate classes. Barnard had its own faculty on an exchange basis, so that Barnard professors also taught at Columbia, and vice versa. Douglass evolved a separate liberal arts faculty with a good deal of autonomy within the general framework of Rutgers University.

To the question, Which of the three types of organization is the best? there can obviously be no categorical answer. The question rather suggests a second one: Best for what type of girl? All three have had their critics and their champions, the latter usually products or associates of the one they are defending.

Coeducation has been praised as the natural continuation of the family and social relationships in which both sexes have been reared and which they will resume after college. Presenting less of a break with normal conditions, it is therefore held the best preparation for adult life. Good-natured rivalry in class should be stimulating to both. It was also expected by some, as an early observer at Oberlin put it, that the young ladies would exert a civilizing influence. They might stop the young men from spitting in the classroom, which, according to another Oberlin observer, they incessantly did. Separate colleges for women, contend supporters of coeducation, present an artificial situation. Remote in their ivory towers, residents of such institutions are likely to grow one-sided and lose touch with real life.

By way of rejoinder, the champions of women's colleges could remind their critics that the ivory tower went out with the horse and buggy. There is a four-lane highway, and frequent railroad commuting service, between Bryn Mawr, Princeton, New Brunswick, and New York; a perfectly good road connects Lynchburg and Sweet Briar with Charlottesville; it is easy to get from Northampton to New Haven, taking in Amherst, South Hadley, Hartford, and Middletown on the way; and in the opposite direction even Dartmouth and Bennington are accessible. Newspapers are delivered on women's campuses, and television is not unknown. Besides, the vaunted equality of coeducational campuses is possibly illusory. In class it is the men who monopolize the discussion whether they have anything to say or not. Men are almost invariably elected to the top offices of the various campus organizations, while the best a coed can hope for is to be a decorative vice-president or queen of homecoming day or, more likely, a secretary toiling away in unglamorous drudgery while the men make the headlines. It is only in a college of their own that women can fully develop their talents. There the classroom is entirely their forum, and they can advance to the highest student office that they are capable of filling.

Students in coordinate colleges might well argue that they have the best of two worlds. To them the separate but equal status has more appeal than complete integration. With their own separately organized campus they can make full use of their talents, yet they are a part of the big, bustling university with its graduate and professional schools, its research library, and its manifold public contacts. And men are easily available!

There is obvious merit in each of the three forms, and, finances permitting, all three might well be continued. The greater the variety of forms and loyalties in education, in religion, in economics, the smaller the likelihood that our free and flexible society will degenerate into a monolithic totalitarianism.

In achieving the right to higher education women were moving in the same general direction as the larger feminist movement. Equal educational opportunity was one of the goals of the organized advocates of women's rights. It would be a mistake, however, to identify the two completely. The supporters of seminaries and colleges were not necessarily in favor of woman suffrage and general emancipation of the sex. In the twentieth century, yes, but not in the formative years of the nineteenth. At that time they could not afford to be so radical without forfeiting the support of the men and the money they needed for their schools. Their early educational ideals did not go much beyond those enunciated by Noah Webster, namely to make women "correct in their manners, respectable in their families, and agreeable in society. That education is always wrong which raises a woman above the duties of her station." This was substantially the goal of all the ladies' seminaries, including Mount Holyoke with its hundred and six rules of behavior. Mary Lyon was at opposite poles from Margaret Fuller, who demanded complete legal and political equality together with sexual freedom. Down to the time Mount Holyoke became a college, men gave its commencement addresses and told the students what their role in life was to be. No woman, professor or student, would offer public prayer at any campus meeting if a man was present. Holyoke students ridiculed the Seneca Falls convention for women's rights in 1848 and agreed with a male speaker that "woman descends from the pedestal of purity, dignity and true honor, when she calls her sisters into angry conventions, and wrangles and jangles about her rights and wrongs." [20]

This mood changed, and strong feminist sympathies were eventually generated on women's campuses. Even then the authorities held back. As late as the first decades of the twentieth century, professional suffragists were not in good repute at Vassar. Dean Gildersleeve of Barnard was taken to task by her feminist friends for not showing more enthusiasm in the cause.

Commenting on Calvin Coolidge's aspersion of women's colleges in the 1920's as hotbeds of radicalism, President McCracken of Vassar asserted categorically that on the contrary they were centers of conservatism. Since the high costs in most of them limited the enrollment pretty largely to the upper economic brackets, this is not surprising, even though college sophomores, male and female, are not averse to taking a political stand opposite that of their parents. In Presidential straw votes on the Mount Holyoke campus in the 1880's, the Republican candidate regularly came up with about an 8 to 1 lead; even the Prohibition candidate polled more votes than the Democratic incumbent of the White House, Grover Cleveland. Coeducation did not produce much radicalism either. Feminine emancipation was farthest from the minds of the Oberlin trustees when they opened the classes to women. On the contrary coeducation was held to be a device to keep women within their station. By continuing through the college years the same normal relationships that prevailed in their homes, women would remain content with their lot and not seek radical and unchristian innovations. It was when they went off to independent women's colleges in the East that they got delusions of grandeur. Coeds who wished to be acceptable to the men students were inclined to assume the cultural color of their environment and not to make themselves unpleasantly conspicuous by taking extreme positions.[21]

In an assessment of the role of women's colleges in the United States and their contributions to higher education in general, several things must be borne in mind. A dominant motive in the founding years was undoubtedly sex rivalry, even antagonism. Carey Thomas was unwittingly sounding this slogan when she wrote in her diary at the age of fourteen: "If I ever live and grow up my *one* aim and concentrated purpose *shall be* and *is* to show that women *can learn, can reason, can compete* with man . . . that a woman can be a woman and a true one without having all her time engrossed by dress and society." Her father's initial opposition to her career strengthened this determination. Many of her contemporaries shared Miss Thomas' sentiments. Their widely and energetically proclaimed desires were by no means entirely self-seeking but often had altruistic overtones. In her will which made possible the college in Northampton, Sophia Smith expressed the hope that "what are called the 'wrongs' of women will be redressed . . . their weight of influence in reforming the evils of society will be greatly increased."

To achieve this and prove their point, women had to work harder than men, and the requirements in their colleges had to be stiffer. Columbia professors teaching at Barnard in the early years of Dean Gildersleeve found the students there better than the men at Columbia College. This, said Miss Gildersleeve, was as it should be, for it was still necessary for women to do rather better work than men in order to get equal opportunities. Long before Barnard opened, Amherst boys comparing notes with Mount Holyoke girls when they met on the mountain, found the latter as good as themselves or better, even in Latin and mathematics. Frederick Jackson Turner's famous seminar of select seniors in American history at the University of Wisconsin, as far back as 1894, enrolled more women than men. Henry Noble McCracken, who taught English at Smith before becoming president of Vassar, was pleasantly surprised by the healthy give and take of his classes. In both places the students were ready to criticize the professor if he did not demand work of them. Men professors, they complained, were too easy, their assignments too low. "We took this course in good faith and we want to be taken seriously. We are not children." All this was in striking contrast to McCracken's earlier experience at Yale, where the students, particularly the "illiterate Sheffnecks," settled back on their haunches with a defiant "educate me if you can." [22]

Yet for all her extra effort and training and scholarship, a woman appointed to the faculty of a college established for her sex frequently found all the top positions occupied by men. It was a college run for women by men. Rarely did a woman get on the board of trustees. The president usually was a man. He had to be if the college was to win the confidence of the public and get access to funds controlled by men. He had to be efficient and he was often autocratic, but so were the presidents of men's colleges. There was Clark Seelye, first president of Smith. During his thirty-five-year term of office the college assets grew from $400,000 to $3,000,000, the faculty from six to one hundred and twenty-two, the student body from fourteen to 1,635, and the number of buildings from three to thirty-five. But Seelye was an autocrat, strong-willed and terrific in wrath, who read a psalm like an archangel and ran the college from his wife's rocking chair. One day a teacher disappeared and was never heard of again. After some time a more courageous colleague asked Dr. Seelye what had happened to her. "She scolded me," was his only answer.[23]

Some tried to meet situations such as this head-on; others bent before the blast and bided their time. There were colleges where the lower ranks of the faculty, mostly composed of women, made common cause against their increasingly conservative male department chairmen until they forced reforms on the latter. Then there were those who, as Mary Lyon had done, remained discreetly in the background while the trustees argued, but had plans ready for the favorable moment. Dean Gildersleeve similarly let male faculty committees view with alarm, bided her time, and then bored from within.[24] Mrs. Douglass, on the other hand, first dean of the college that bears her name, made frontal attacks and pulled out all stops in her dealings with women's clubs, trustees, faculty, and legislative appropriations committees. Differences of opinion between conciliators and direct actionists led to feuds which lasted for years, dividing entire faculties into academic Hatfields and McCoys. Professional jealousy between rival scholars sometimes added fuel to the flames. Such conditions, which are an occupational hazard of scholarship, were not of course unknown on men's campuses; college histories are full of instances. The more refined one's specialty and the more positive one's convictions, the more abysmal the stupidity and moral turpitude of colleagues who disagree!

With the passage of the Nineteenth Amendment to the Constitution tensions began to subside. By that time, too, women had more than adequately proved their ability both to take college work as students and to manage colleges as teachers and administrators. Militant feminism was slowly laid aside, and it now became possible to consider the educational problems of women in "that atmosphere of cool common sense" which, in the opinion of the historians of Barnard, had characterized that institution from the beginning. In a more relaxed atmosphere the very real advantages of intellectual cooperation between the sexes became apparent. Such cooperation had always existed alongside the antagonism. Without the moral and material support of men there would have been no women's colleges. Matthew Vassar, Henry Durant, Joseph Wright Taylor of Bryn Mawr, Henry Wells of Wells-Fargo fame, who wanted his college to be a real home for students, and many others, gave lavishly of their time and money that women might have the chance to which they were entitled. Prominent among those who labored toward this end was the Society of Friends. In their experience God spoke to women as to men, and the divine spark made no distinction of sex. Once a project, educational or otherwise, recommended itself as worth doing at all, it was to be carried out, vigorously and persistently, by and for women as well as men. Swarthmore, one of the few eastern coeducational institutions, was sponsored by the Friends; so, of course, was Bryn Mawr. Ezra Cornell was a Quaker. John G. Whittier and other Quaker members of the Corporation of Brown succeeded in breaking down resistance to women's education there.[25]

In women's colleges founded in the twentieth century, after the fight for women's rights had been largely won, the faculties could start with a clean slate, free of bitter memories. A "coeducational" teaching staff proved a distinct advantage, just as the patronizing male attitude of an earlier day proved unwarranted. Woodrow Wilson, who left Bryn Mawr because he had no use for intellectual women, was born thirty years too soon. It was no longer necessary, if it ever had been, for young men instructors to go slumming a few years in a woman's college while waiting for something better to turn up. Something better was turning up, right where they were. Women professors on the other hand could discard the pettiness and suspicion that at times had marred their achievements in earlier decades. In a healthier atmosphere men and women could now honestly cooperate, respecting one another's competence and integrity, to the benefit of themselves, the students, and the alumnae of the college they served.

Women's colleges have produced no revolutionary changes in higher education. It was not their intention to do so. They were founded to prove that women could also aspire to higher learning. Their courses of study were therefore patterned at first after those of men's colleges. They leaned over backward to be conventional and correct. Their leaders agreed on the whole with President John H. Raymond of Vassar that they "would have enough antagonism without adding a novel curriculum." Vassar's very first president, the Reverend Milo P. Jewett, had suggested, before he had a falling-out with Matthew Vassar, that the new college import and adapt the elective system of the University of Virginia; but he got nowhere with it. For a young college whose existence was still problematic to adopt a controversial curriculum from a rebel state in the midst of the Civil War was just not good sense.[26]

Yet the women's colleges were not tradition-bound. Once the languages, mathematics, and philosophy were firmly established at the heart of the curriculum, women's colleges felt free to experiment. And they did, in many directions. The catalogues and circulars of their early years make this perfectly plain. It was the time when the propriety of elective studies was being hotly debated, and the conservative leadership of the educational world was flatly opposed to them. Most women's colleges adopted them, not prodigally but judiciously. By and large they were abreast of progressive thought and practice in this field. They were also among the first—Bryn Mawr took the lead here—to initiate the system of group majors which was to become the almost universal pattern of American colleges. They were concerned from the beginning to have adequate libraries; they borrowed the practice of debating from the men's colleges and carried it to considerable lengths. They aimed to secure all-around development of their students by elaborate programs of hygiene, physical education, and planned physical exercise, which even included such imaginative fringe "activities" as grasshopper hunting and supervised rest.

Perhaps their main curricular contribution was in the fine arts. Painting and music, always a conspicuous part of the work of the old-fashioned ladies' seminary, were taken over, expanded, intensified, and made intellectually respectable. Appreciation courses, thin and watery at first, were gradually enriched and given scholarly content. Miss Thomas of Bryn Mawr dismissed appreciation courses as juvenile, but even she held out for Gothic buildings, encouraged the acquisition of sepia photographs of great paintings, and accepted twenty-six marble busts of Greek gods and heroes to decorate the corridors of the college. Women's colleges played a leading role in the transition that made English literature, rather than Greek and Latin, the chief bearer of the genteel tradition. Again it was Miss Thomas who gave what was probably the first required underclass survey of English literature. Dramatic art too received considerable attention and reached a high level of excellence. Closely related was an interest in pageantry, which, though not always artistic in the highest sense of the word, furnished an outlet both for imaginative fancy and physical energy and played a role comparable to organized athletics on men's campuses. Nearly every woman's college has some pageant or ritual, peculiar to itself and not duplicated anywhere else, as for example the Vassar daisy chain, which according to President McCracken has become almost as sacred as a wedding march, the academic pageantry of Bryn Mawr's lantern night, Barnard's Greek games, and the Christmas vesper ceremony at Douglass.[27]

The accent has always been on quality of teaching. This too may be a heritage of the pioneer days when women had to prove that they could learn and teach. Professors at women's colleges have generally considered it a prime function of their office to devise the most efficient means not only of communicating information but of encouraging student response and stirring student initiative. Underlying all this is the simple philosophy that a college exists for its students. In keeping with this rather obvious point of view, faculties and administrations have been hospitable to student self-government. At a time when the old paternal autocracy of president and faculty with its religious sanctions was breaking down on men's campuses, sometimes with demoralizing consequences, their sister colleges were experimenting with various forms and degrees of student-faculty cooperation. When Bryn Mawr first introduced a limited amount of student autonomy, President Eliot of Harvard told Miss Thomas: "If this continues, I will give you two years, and no more, in which to close Bryn Mawr College." [28] That was sixty years ago. In time such self-government was to extend on most women's campuses to the maintenance of honesty in classes and examinations, in many to dormitory and social regulations as well, and in some it even meant student participation in the construction of the curriculum. There was, in short, a disposition to hand over to students the maximum responsibility that they could bear and that the charter and the trustees would permit. Although there are still unresolved questions, such as the reconciliation of personal honor with collective responsibility, the varying systems of student self-government have been of inestimable worth in speeding the transformation of scatterbrained adolescents into responsible adults.

Another liberalizing influence was the absence of narrow sectarian control. Here again timing was important. Most of the influential women's colleges were founded at the time when denominational controls were weakening, though religious sanctions were still strong. Henry Durant stated unequivocally in the original statutes of Wellesley: "The college was founded for the glory of God and the service of the Lord Jesus Christ in and by the education of women"—and a course in Bible study was obligatory for all four years. Matthew Vassar expressed similar ideals for his college. The Quaker influence at Bryn Mawr was pervasive but not aggressive and was not allowed by President Thomas to interfere with the attainment of the highest intellectual standards. In the early years at Smith, students and teachers met daily in the social hall for worship. Somewhat more direct church control was exercised in denominational colleges like Rockford, Randolph-Macon, Hood, and Goucher. Yet even here the questioning mind was not discouraged. At Goucher, for instance, though all trustees had to be approved by the board of education of the Methodist church and the Bible was part of the required curriculum, this did not prevent the faculty from offering one of the earliest courses in sociology, in which Comte and Spencer were studied. And when a public lecture on evolution on the Goucher campus provoked a storm of criticism, the administration upheld the speaker's right to be heard and the students' right to hear him.[29]

When the domestic and international upheavals of the twentieth century shook American colleges and universities out of their complacency and caused a thorough reconsideration of aims and programs, the women's institutions were no exception. In the latter it took the form, specifically, of an examination of social problems, both from the theoretical and the practical side. President Mary Woolley of Mount Holyoke had sounded this new note when she took office in 1901, pointing out in her inaugural address that intellectual excellence, narrowly conceived, was not enough, and that the widening gulf between the rich and the poor called particularly for women's concern in social problems and social work. A quarter-century later Vassar introduced what it called its euthenics program, a formal study of the problems of home and family. Underlying this program was the assumption that both the biological and the social sciences had by this time amassed a sufficiently large body of tested and dependable data which could be brought to bear in rigorously scientific fashion on the problems of family and social life, with which women were primarily concerned. This was a far cry from the old rule-of-thumb domestic science courses of the ladies' seminary days.[30]

In the educational fermentation that followed World War I, when new ideals were being proclaimed and novel programs were proliferating, colleges for women again played a prominent part. For such experimentation, too, their more recent origin gave them certain advantages over men's colleges. They were more flexible and less weighted down by hoary traditions. Nor were they so likely to waste their substance on the specious ideals of intercollegiate athletics. Among the boldest of the innovators were two new institutions, Sarah Lawrence and Bennington, founded in 1925 and 1932, respectively. In these two colleges not only the traditional curriculum but all standard requirements, all uniformities, were discarded. Here young women were admitted, not because of satisfactory grades in entrance examinations, but on the basis of a complete personality inventory in which grades were only one item. On the strength of such analysis, and under the guidance of specialists in the faculty, an individual course of study was tailored for each student, designed to offer her the greatest challenge and to enable her to make the best use of her own peculiar talents. This was a more radical break with the conventions than most men's colleges of the time were willing to countenance, though many of these features have since then been widely adopted. The flexibility and originality of some of the women's colleges was reflected in their catalogue statements, which at times broke away from the clichés and conventions of college catalogues generally and stated their purposes in fresh and nontechnical terms. The "profile" of Mills College, in the introduction to its catalogue, is an example. One would have to read the Sarah Lawrence catalogue most carefully to discover that it is a women's college. A few fleeting feminine possessive pronouns and, in one place, the feminine form, alumnae, are the only clues.[31]

Significantly enough, heads of some of the older women's colleges were instrumental in helping their progressive sister institutions get on their feet. President McCracken of Vassar was called into consultation by the planners of Sarah Lawrence, and President Neilson of Smith gave valuable advice to the founders of Bennington. It does not follow that Vassar and Smith were in sympathy with all aspects of the new programs. There were, and are, differences of opinion as to educational aims and methods. The argument over vocational as opposed to purely humanistic and scientific subjects rages there as it does in colleges for men. The only difference lies in the nature of the vocations. There may still be bound up with it a bit of indignation harking back to the days when college women had to demonstrate their ability to do the kind of work that college men were doing, as well as their right to make free choices in a world of equals. That demonstration has been made, a hundred times over. Women have come out of the doll's house, and the rancors that made the issue such a burning one in Ibsen's day have largely subsided. Yet even today the advocates of women's colleges may well justify their position, not with anger but with calm assurance, in the words of Ibsen's heroine: "Before all else I am a reasonable human being, just as you are."

Chapter Seven

The Emergence of the University

We must now return to the story of the classical college for men, past its prime in the third quarter of the nineteenth century and on the eve of its absorption by the emerging university movement. The vigor of the old American college in its golden age derived from its clear purpose and simple philosophy, and the acceptance of both by its constituency. As long as everybody agreed that higher education meant character-building and that this was best achieved by adherence to a restricted intellectual program handed down from antiquity and applicable only to the fortunate few who had the stamina to take it and the means to pay for it, the classical college flourished and was all-sufficient. But its days were numbered, for soon after the middle of the nineteenth century, both the organization of American economic life and the intellectual presuppositions of the Western world were shaken to the foundations. Not all educational leaders were hospitable to the change or even aware that it was going on and that they were part of the most rapidly evolving society on the face of the earth. Under the collegiate elms tradition ruled. Many a venerable campus rumbled on as though nothing worth while had happened since Caesar found all Gaul divided into three parts. From their sheltered halls the sages of the academic world with few exceptions looked out self-satisfied on the turbulence of the market place and offered a centuries-old way of life and thought as the sovereign remedy for the ills of the age. "As stagnant as a Spanish convent," was the verdict of Andrew Dickson White on the older eastern colleges.[1] But in trying to hold back the tides of change they succeeded no better than King Canute. The flood that engulfed them in the last quarter of the century had three main sources: the new-styled western state university; German scholarship and higher criticism; and the theory of evolution. The first of these was a native product, the last two were foreign importations, for in culture as in economics America was still a debtor nation.

Under the steady pressure of these forces most institutions of higher learning gradually changed their character, and the age of the college gave way to the age of the university. At this point a definition of terms is in order. Unfortunately for the precisionists, such a definition is impossible, for our educational system, unlike that, say, of France, has never been nationally organized and no authority exists with power to define such institutions as *college* and *university* for the whole country. The best we can do is to describe prevailing practices and then generalize *ex post facto*. An American university as we know it today includes the historic college of liberal arts but is a much larger and more complex organization. From the original germ of the college it has grown horizontally and vertically. In addition to the college it now includes varying numbers of professional and vocational schools. Roughly, in order of their historic appearance, these are, first, the old medieval faculties of theology, law, and medicine; then schools of engineering and agriculture; in the twentieth century schools of pedagogy, journalism, business administration, and others. Meanwhile, in answer to specific community needs and by way of filling the gaps between the schools, a bewildering array of institutes, bureaus, offices, and authorities has sprung up as well, thus warranting the designation of the modern university as a public service station. Not every university has all of these schools; some even lack the medieval trinity of theology, law, and medicine. As the separate schools have multiplied, so have the subdivisions within each school, with a constant diversification of courses and of specialists teaching them.

Vertical expansion was achieved by the establishment of graduate work and the granting of advanced degrees. This change presupposed a new kind of professor. The classically and theologically trained pedagogue of the old-time college, who presided over so large an area of subject matter that he rarely found time to become an authority in any part of it, was superseded by the expert. This was a new type of teacher and research specialist who explored a limited segment of some science or art and passed on his findings in lectures to his students or in publications to the world at large. The result was an essential difference in structure and function between the new and the old institution. Instead of the organic whole of the college, the university tended to be an atomistic totality of scholars working, each in his own sector, to push back the frontiers of knowledge.

Not all colleges were thus metamorphosed. Some preferred to keep their simple historic structure, refusing both the title and functions of a university and trying to retain as many of the old values as possible. Occasionally even today a new institution is founded with the purpose of reviving what it fondly believes to have been the genuine classical and disciplinary college of an earlier day. But the trend has been the other way. Most colleges have changed, along with the universities that gradually enveloped them, into new forms in order to meet new conditions.

Of major importance in the transition to the new order were the state universities of the second half of the nineteenth century. These differed in a number of important particulars from the public institutions of the southern seaboard states. Of the latter, some were public in name only, getting their support largely from tuition fees, private and denominational contributions, since regular legislative subsidies were nonexistent or at best sporadic. This was true, for example, of the Universities of Georgia and North Carolina. South Carolina College did get regular and, on the whole, generous state support, but it was a narrow classical college like Amherst or Princeton, and in no sense a university. The University of Virginia, with its separate schools and other unconventional devices, was, more than any other, a pioneer moving in the direction of a true state university. But, as the pride of the plantation aristocracy, it was one of the most expensive schools in the land and did not reach the common man.

The state university west of the Appalachians was, by contrast, reared on the philosophy that public higher education was a responsibility of society and must be made available, in the interest of democratic equality and national unity, to everyone who qualified. All this had been said before by the proponents of the many church and community colleges which were already in existence. But they had not done the job. Competition had kept most of them small and inadequate, and unedifying denominational bickering had turned away many of their erstwhile supporters and weakened their claims to public subsidies. Increasingly, therefore, public opinion, especially in the Mississippi Valley, was moving in the direction of the state university as the better solution. An institution owned and supported by the whole state, free from local patriotism and sectarian strife, would be a more flexible instrument, it was hoped, for realizing a democratic society's educational goals. In such a school not only the classical student laying the foundations for the ministry or the law, but the farmer, the mechanic, the merchant—in short the *people*— could find the kind of training and information they needed. Here women as well as men would be welcome. Such an institution, furthermore, could serve as the capstone of the whole integrated educational system of the state, as Jefferson long before had visualized it. In sum, it offered something for everybody, not just for a social or intellectual elite. So said the supporters of state universities, from the Great Lakes to the Pacific Northwest.

They had been saying it in Michigan longer than anywhere else. Though Indiana preceded Michigan in time, with a state seminary which received students from 1820 on, the line of development of the state university idea is clearer in Michigan. After an abortive attempt to set up such an institution in territorial days, an effective charter was secured in 1837 and the first students came in 1841. There was much fumbling at first, and circumstances were not auspicious. "Well, we've got the buildings," said the governor of the state; "I don't think they're good for anything else, so we might as well declare the University open." And six students turned up that September in the raw, jail-like building rising out of a field of stumps that was the original college hall. By the time of the Civil War it had increased to six hundred students in all departments and was thus virtually as large as Virginia and Yale, the leading colleges of the country in size. In the course of the next decades Michigan drew ahead of all the eastern institutions and remained the largest university in the United States until about 1900. Much of this growth was accounted for by out-of-state students, who in some years made up almost half of the total. As the rapidly increasing body of alumni moved into positions of influence in the state, and the legislature came to be increasingly influenced by university men, the appropriations swelled correspondingly. An intelligent board of regents and excellent presidential leadership contributed to success. In the light of this unfolding record, educational leaders generally came to agree that the state university idea had passed the experimental stage. As one of them put it, state support was safe. Michigan had proved it.[2]

With variations the Michigan story repeated itself in state after state. Only a few of them will be singled out here to illustrate various facets. There was Wisconsin. Like Michigan, it had pre-Civil War beginnings and was launched with much popular enthusiasm. On the day of the inauguration of John Lathrop as first chancellor in 1850, all business in Madison ceased, the courts closed, and the legislature adjourned. The academic procession included the justices of the supreme court, members of the legislature, and almost all the male population of the town, who marched behind the Madison brass band into the assembly hall of the state capitol, while ladies in the balcony formed a decorative background. The chancellor's address was entitled "The Law of Progress." Progress or no, the first curriculum at the new university was narrowly classical and derivative. Over the years this situation yielded slowly to external pressure for a wider range of offerings and greater freedom of choice among them. Twenty years after its opening Wisconsin still had a rather heterogeneous student body consisting of four graduate students, eighty-three regular undergraduates, fifty-two unclassified university students, and a hundred and ninety-three preparatory school pupils. It was 1885 before the college undergraduate registration climbed permanently above five hundred. A mill tax coupled with land grants was considered adequate support to warrant free tuition. But though it achieved a kind of minimal security, this fixed tax made direct appropriations for rising current needs and for capital expenditures harder to get. The regents circumvented free tuition by setting a $10 incidental fee which was widely protested but stood up in the courts.[3]

The zeal for higher education was not long in reaching the Pacific coast. Five years after California had attained statehood in 1850, a College of California, the forerunner of the state university, was in existence. Following an older pattern, it began under church auspices, with the Presbytery of San Francisco and the Congregational association of California the chief sponsors. Most active among the founders was the Reverend Horace Bushnell of Connecticut, later to become known as a leader in adjusting Protestant Christianity to a scientific age. At the time, he was resting in California for his health. But rest is an elastic term which apparently did not mean the same to his fifth generation New England conscience as it does to most people. At any rate Bushnell spent his convalescence rushing about the state to find a suitable location and get subscriptions for the college. It was to be in a small town as far as possible from San Fran-

A Front VIEW of YALE-COLLEGE, and the COLLEGE CHAPEL, in NEW-HAVEN.

From *A compendious History of Yale-College, and a general Account of the Course of Studies pursued by the Students . . .* June 26, 1786. Printed by Daniel Bowen in New Haven.

Old East at the University of North Carolina was the first building to be erected on a state university campus in the United States. The drawing was made by John Pettigrew in 1797, three years after construction was finished.

The Apollo Room in the restored Raleigh Tavern in Williamsburg. Here, according to tradition, students of the College of William and Mary founded Phi Beta Kappa.

The Chapel and New College at the University of Georgia date back to the 1830's.

The Lawn at the University of Virginia in Jefferson's day. Böyë print.

Mount Holyoke Seminary, shortly after its founding in 1836. Lithograph by Nathaniel Currier from a drawing by Persis G. Thurston.

Maria Mitchell's astronomy class at Vassar College in 1878.

Office of Public Relations, Amherst College

College Row at Amherst. Flanking Johnson Chapel, left and right, are South College and North College, all erected in the 1820's. Noah Webster presided at the dedication of the original building, South College.

The Biology Laboratory at the University of Wisconsin in 1900.

At the turn of the century, when Oberlin's department of fine arts and Allen Art Museum were still in the future, the classes in painting and sketching sometimes made excursions to the shores of Lake Erie.

Radcliffe girls march in a suffrage parade in 1918.

A student's room at Harvard College in 1871.

Friends Historical Library of Swarthmore College

The tree-planting ceremony at **Swarthmore** College on November 10, 1869.
The small woman in Quaker bonnet, to the right of the tree, is Lucretia

Induction of new members of the Order of Gownsmen at the University of the South. The custom of the wearing of the gown has been preserved in recognition of the ties which bind Sewanee to Oxford and the English cultural tradition.

Cobb Hall, the University of Chicago's oldest building, was opened in 1892.

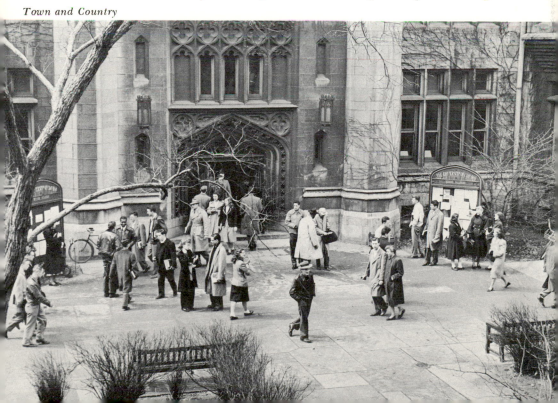

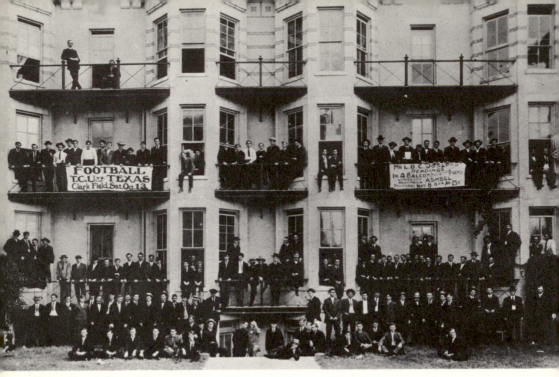

B Hall at the University of Texas about 1907.

The University of Kansas' first basketball team, 1898-99. Dr. James Naismith (*top right*), inventor of the game, was a member of the faculty for some forty years.

Dartmouth Snow Indian at a recent Winter Carnival.

Bob's

The Fine Arts Library at the University of Arkansas.

Joint concert of the Rutgers University Choir and the Philadelphia Orchestra.

F. J. Higgins

Memorial Church at Stanford University. The mosaic of "The Sermon on the Mount" was made in Venice after fifteenth century models.

Indiana University Memorial Union houses extensive lounge and dining facilities, as well as a ballroom and rooms for visiting artists and speakers.

Started in 1837 with forty acres of ground, the University of Michigan today has one of the largest enrollments in the country. Shown here are the main campus and the medical center.

Holder Court at Princeton University. To the left is a dining hall and to the right, student rooms.

The Commons Building and some of the student residences on Bennington's four-hundred-acre campus.

Commencement ceremonies at Columbia University.

cisco to safeguard the morals of the students. He found such a location in the country three miles northwest of Napa. Bushnell also believed, contrary to emerging trends elsewhere, that the job should be done by private enterprise. His published appeal for support was an eloquent call for civic responsibility in a new state, but by private effort and without benefit of politics. In his own words: ". . . the State University becomes of course a mere prize for placemen, subject to all the contests, agitations and changes of dynasty that belong to party politics. There is no place for that quiet which is the element of study, no genuinely classic atmosphere. The faculty come in at the same gate with the constables and marshals. . . . Meantime the students are rushing into the cabals of party to oust some obnoxious president or professor. . . . Elegant learning and science are draggling always in the mires of uneasiness and public intrigue. . . . No university can live in such an element. . . . You can never have a university worthy of your place as the central and first state of the Pacific, unless you call it into being by your own private munificence." [4] The college, representing eventually all Protestant denominations, lasted to 1868, when it transferred its assets and students to the newly chartered full-fledged state university. The latter opened in the following year and removed to the present Berkeley campus in 1873.

A glimpse of the campus in the middle seventies just before its first president, Daniel Coit Gilman, took off for Johns Hopkins, discloses a vigorous young institution. The *Register* for that year lists two hundred and thirty-one students, of whom thirty-eight were young ladies. Alongside the traditional classical curriculum were five parallel science "colleges." The physical plant included two main buildings and eight resident cottages; six of these were let out to students at $300 a year, the other two were occupied by faculty families, who paid $360 each. None of the cottages had baths or indoor toilets. An experimental orchard had been planted containing seventy-three varieties of grapes, as well as oranges, lemons, and limes. There were two chemistry laboratories, and philosophical cabinets and museums for the other sciences. Courses of instruction ranged widely. The president himself lectured on political economy and the origins of modern civilization. There was a course in Anglo-Saxon; it was even possible to get instruction in Hebrew and Chaldaic. Rules of conduct, which customarily filled many pages in the catalogues of the older church colleges of the East, were compressed into one short paragraph which merely stated in effect that students were expected to attend classes and behave as ladies and gentlemen. Prominently displayed, in capitals, was this statement: "Tuition in all departments of the University except the Medical College, is ABSOLUTELY FREE." Such were the beginnings of what has become, with all its branches, the largest state university in the country.

Ohio, first state of the old Northwest Territory, was among the last to get a state university. The reason was simple. Ohio was saturated with independent and church-controlled colleges, some of which maintained high standards and were of good repute. Collectively, they formed an effective pressure group to delay the coming of the state university. After the passage of the Morrill Land Grant Act it took five successive boards of trustees ten years to decide whether the beneficiary of the law was to be one of the existing colleges or an entirely new institution. They finally voted for the latter and set up the Ohio Agricultural and Mechanical College in Columbus in 1875. This became Ohio State University. The pattern of Ohio, by the way, was pretty much that of Illinois, which was even more dilatory. In these more recent midwestern state universities things were different and new winds were blowing. Here farmers and mechanics had things their way, and the old classical influence was hardly noticeable at all. Of the first faculty of six at Ohio State, for example, none were ministers, two had no college degrees at all, and two came up from teaching positions in the public schools. According to its first president, the Columbus institution had a serenity almost utopian. "The order of the University is excellent," he proclaimed. "We have been happily free during our short history from the relics of that barbarism that still survives in so many colleges in the shape of hazing and the reckless destruction of property. Hazing and class insubordination are unknown in our experience—not a single class exercise having yet been interrupted by college tricks." [5]

Sometimes the beginnings were really primitive, especially in those vast sparsely settled quadrilaterals that were the Great Plains states. Kansas ambitiously organized a state university in 1866, but when the faculty of four looked over the first year's crop of students, they found none capable of college work and had to start as a preparatory school of twenty-two boys and eighteen girls. The first A.B. degree was granted in 1873. At one time in the early years the entire junior class consisted of one girl—and when her professor married her, there were none! State support was chronically scanty, and even that little was shaved almost below the subsistence level in the grass-hopper plague year of 1875. On a visit of inspection to the campus that year the governor of Kansas noticed a fine hardwood handrail pieced out with a length of unpainted pine. "That," explained the chancellor, "is where the appropriation ran out." By the end of the century, however, the University of Kansas had made great strides in buildings and equipment and had assembled a competent and, and in some areas, distinguished faculty.[6]

Even more elementary conditions prevailed in Arizona and Oklahoma, where the universities antedated statehood. The territorial university at Tucson, though organized in 1890, had only thirty-nine college students and a hundred and fifty-five in the preparatory department as late as 1906, and ran on a total budget of $30,568. In Oklahoma the beginning was in 1892, three years after the first white settlers had begun to carve up Indian Territory. The charter was modeled after that of the University of Nebraska, and two of its first three presidents were former superintendents of schools, one in Kansas and the other in Boston. One member of the first faculty of three got the job primarily because he was a Democrat, inasmuch as his two colleagues were Republicans. The regents insisted on this. With virtually no high school graduates available in Oklahoma, the admission requirements were scaled down the point where anyone who could handle "arithmetic through percentage, English etymology, read ordinary newspaper English, parse a sentence, spell correctly and write legibly" could get in. Even these conditions were waived for the sake of getting students, and the president stated categorically: "The doors of the University are open to any young man or woman . . . who will work." Not a bad criterion, incidentally, as far as it goes; and one may fairly ask how many of the hundreds of thousands of freshmen who throng our universities today can parse a sentence, spell correctly, and know English etymology. Oklahoma, like Kansas, soon outgrew its primitive beginnings. By 1909, two years after statehood, it had a complete college of arts and sciences together with the usual professional schools, and doctors of philosophy from eastern universities were drifting into the chairs of instruction.[7]

In Texas the story was slightly different. Here the university movement began when Texas was still an independent nation. In 1839 the Republic of Texas set aside public lands for the support of higher education. A state university was chartered in 1858, but the Civil War and Reconstruction prevented its establishment. Authorized anew by the new Constitution of 1876, the university was incorporated in 1881 and located at Austin by popular vote. Two years later it opened its doors to men and women, and tuition was free. When oil was discovered on university land, the income from leases and royalties, added to the regular legislative appropriation, laid a solid financial foundation for what was to become one of the noteworthy state universities.

While the central and western states were thus struggling to establish adequate institutions of higher education for all their citizens, major support for the undertaking came from the Congress of the United States. This support took the form of a series of laws granting financial subsidies of various kinds. The first of these laws, based on the congressional power to tax for the general welfare, was the famous Morrill Act of 1862, which granted to each state thirty thousand acres of land from the public domain, or its equivalent in scrip, for each Senator and Representative to which the state was entitled. The money realized from the sale of the land was to be used to maintain at least one college whose leading purpose was, without neglecting other scientific and classical studies, to teach "agriculture and the mechanic arts." A later amendment to the law provided for direct federal contributions to states from the sale of public lands. The program was further enlarged by the Hatch Act of 1887, which set up agricultural experiment stations in all the states, and the Smith-Lever Act of 1914, which established a network of agricultural extension and home economics programs.[8]

The Morrill Act gave every state an incentive to establish a public college of some kind or to strengthen one already existing. Through its emphasis on the agricultural and mechanical arts, America's rapidly growing technical knowledge and efficiency in these fields was to be made available for public use. Some states bypassed the state university in favor of separate colleges of agriculture and engineering, schools that came to be popularly known as "Aggies," or just "State." Michigan State, Purdue, and Kansas State are examples. Most southern states established separate, parallel schools for Negroes and whites.

It was by means of the Morrill Act that the state university invaded the East. Here the impressive array of independent colleges of great age and prestige made a frontal attack inadvisable, but through the land grant the state university did establish itself. In some instances the Morrill funds were diverted to already existing private institutions. Sheffield Scientific School of Yale was the recipient for Connecticut until 1881, when Storrs Agricultural College was erected, the present University of Connecticut. New Hampshire granted its allotment to Dartmouth until it established its own state university in 1903. The meteoric rise of Cornell is accounted for in part by its designation as the land grant beneficiary of New York state, and then the highly efficient and profitable management of the Morrill funds by Ezra Cornell himself.

In New York and New Jersey, incidentally, the state university system remained incomplete longer than anywhere else, and its development continued beyond the middle of the twentieth century. New York never did get around to setting up a state university in the conventional sense. It has had instead, from the late eighteenth century on, an administrative agency known as the University of the State of New York, which maintains standards through a board of regents. In 1948 the state created an additional agency, the State University, which was authorized to establish a number of brand-new colleges and to extend the state's jurisdiction over the professional schools of various already existing universities, Cornell among them. Meanwhile the City of New York had established its own tuition-free municipal colleges. These city colleges must, in turn, be distinguished from the large, influential, and privately controlled New York University, which dates back to the 1830's. If a foreign scholar, studying the organization of higher education in the United States, were unfortunate enough to begin with New York, he might work himself into a delirium trying to untangle the identities of, and relationships between, Cornell the land grant college, New York University, the College of the City of New York, the State University of New York, and the University of the State of New York. British institutions are often accused of having no logic but the logic of history. When it comes to higher education, the state of New York is their match.

In New Jersey, Rutgers has become the state university. Originating as one of the nine colonial colleges, under auspices not unlike those of Yale or Princeton, it was designated the land grant college of the state in 1864. Ninety-two years later, after a succession of partial steps, the Rutgers trustees adopted, and the state legislature approved, a charter amendment giving the state effective control. New Jersey thus acquired a state university by a historic process that might be called the Dartmouth College case in reverse.

For all their belated efforts, eastern state universities, whatever their form, have not achieved the prestige of those to the west. In the Mississippi Valley the state university has become a focus of loyalty and devotion to a degree that no private institution in that area can command. This was natural enough as the alumni found their way into positions of prominence in the state and as the cost differentials became more apparent. Thus the president of Michigan, speaking for state universities in general, could exult in his report of 1887 over the difference in tuition costs between West and East: At Michigan tuition was $55 the first year, $30 a year thereafter; at Wisconsin, $18; Ohio State, $15; Iowa, $10; California and Nebraska charged state residents no tuition at all. By contrast the cost at Cornell was $75; at Brown, $100; at Yale, $125; and at Harvard, $150. That, thought President Angell, should keep the Michigan boys where they belonged.

With all its advantages, the state university suffered from certain drawbacks. As a tax-supported institution operated by agents responsible to a popularly elected government, it was subject to the shifting whims of public opinion. It could become a pawn of designing politicians, in whose hands the management of the land grants, for example, was often wasteful and sometimes dishonest. It could be whipsawed between the conflicting interests of rival pressure groups, and could become the innocent victim of such democratic devices as the initiative and referendum.[9] Its program of teaching and research was likely to be a compromise between the educational philosophy of the president and faculty and the varying demands of the most influential or most vocal segments of the population. Amid such hazards the university had to tread warily.

One of the tenderest areas was its relation to organized religion. Historically and ethically rooted in a religious philosophy but subject more and more to diversified secular interests, the new state institutions had to learn to walk the razor's edge between denominational commitment and religious indifference. In the early formative years of the state university movement, the churches had played a prominent part. Ante-bellum South Carolina College was under Presbyterian domination; in the Civil War decade the Methodists virtually took over the University of Michigan. Clergymen presidents were still the rule. Even the University of Illinois, one of the later and more secular foundations, chose a Baptist minister for its first president. The initial faculty of four at the University of Kansas was carefully selected by the regents to include an Episcopalian rector as chancellor, a Methodist, a Baptist, and a Congregationalist. But experience and common sense dictated freedom from denominational involvement as much the better course, together with a benevolent neutrality toward religion as such. That came to be the position of most presidents and boards of control. The regents of the University of Wisconsin prided themselves on the nonsectarian atmosphere of their campus. They had abolished compulsory chapel in 1869, and had all major Protestant groups and Roman Catholics represented on the faculty. Yet a Catholic priest complained in 1872 that the commencement exercises that year had an unpleasantly Protestant character. If, on the other hand, the university proved its religious neutrality too well, it was likely to run afoul of the opposite charge that it was a godless institution. The weakening of the old Puritan controls and the growing campus prestige of science, which was ethically and theologically neutral, lent some color to this charge. It has of course been heard many times since. Religious and moral denunciations were sometimes blurred with economic criticism and all pet aversions put into one category, as in Kansas, where a prospective student was warned, apparently in ascending order of menace, against anarchists, atheistic evolutionists, and free traders on the faculty.[10]

Liaison between the state university and its public was, as in the case of the older private colleges, the external board of trustees. But it was a different kind of board. It was known more often as the board of regents, and its size was usually under ten, as opposed to the older type of board with from twenty to forty members. Besides, its membership was rotating or staggered, which made it a changing not a permanent body. It was variously chosen: by the governor, the legislature, or popular vote, and always for a limited term of years.[11] These were the men and, in more recent years women, who interpreted the state university to its constituents. Any generalizations as to the success or failure of the institutions which they served and managed would require such huge documentation as to be impossible in a work of this compass, and would entail so many qualifications as to crumble off into meaninglessness. Still, the general attitude toward these new instruments of higher education in their early years was probably that expressed in an article in the *Atlantic*

Monthly. Writing at a time when fraternity politics was still in its infancy and football scholarships were unheard of, an eastern critic commended the new state institution for its intellectual and moral vigor. Its campus life, he felt, was sound. "Hazing and vandalism are seldom seen in the west. There is little dissipation. The student . . . strives to put away childish things and does not forget that his chief business is to prepare himself for the performance of social duty." That was in 1891.[12]

The state university and the land grant college challenged the supremacy of the traditional classical college. Admitting the validity of the demands of the farmer, the merchant, and the mechanic for technical training and vocationally useful information, the new institutions proceeded to meet these demands by setting up new courses, departments, and schools to take their place alongside the older, privileged liberal arts. The result was an expansion of educational opportunities for great numbers of young people who otherwise could not have gone to college at all. Along with this broadening of opportunity came another form of expansion which called attention in a different way to the limitations of the old-time college.

The generating force behind this expansion was intellectual, and it came from Europe. The surge of philosophical speculation and scientific research that characterized nineteenth century Europe was, by the middle of the century, beginning to affect America and to demand recognition and appraisal. The channels of communication were various. There had of course always been some contact with English scholarship, if only because of the common language. But the principal impact this time came not from England but Germany. For a variety of reasons, of which a cultural patriotism was not the least, the universities in the several German states had enjoyed an intellectual renaissance and by the end of the Napoleonic age were coming to be recognized as the best in Europe. It was to the German universities therefore that American scholarship turned for answers when the old, inherited theological answers no longer satisfied. It all began in 1815, when two young Harvard graduates, George Ticknor and Edward Everett. set out for two years of travel and study abroad, most of the latter at Göttingen. There a new intellectual world opened up before them; they were astonished and delighted with the freedom and the opportunities of the German university, so different from the cramped schoolboyish performance of American colleges, even Harvard.

Ticknor and Everett, with George Bancroft who joined them later, did not precipitate a mass exodus to Germany among American students. They were ahead of their times. Another generation of theological conservatism was to intervene before American educational and philosophical thought was attuned to the liberal and critical scholarship of Germany. The trek to the German universities really gained momentum after the unification of the German states by Bismarck in 1871, and reached its height in the last two decades of the century. All told, in the hundred years from 1815 to 1915, over nine thousand Americans studied in Germany. Once there, they drank in the ideas and pondered the judgments of some of the keenest minds of Europe and soaked up new knowledge so fast that, as one of them put it, the entries in his diary on Sundays often contradicted what he had recorded the Sunday before.[13] Hundreds came back with the coveted Ph.D. degree, which had become the open sesame for virtually any university chair in the United States.

At the German universities Americans studied philology and comparative literature, history and philosophy, chemistry and medicine, economics, and the new science of psychology. What impressed them most was the freedom of choice and of expression allowed both students and professors, the insistence on rigorous scientific method for the establishment of all facts, and the utter devotion to truth, rationally determined. In the words of one American student, the objective of the German universities was the "ardent, methodical, independent, search after truth in any and all its forms, but wholly irrespective of utilitarian applications." [14] The historian in retrospect can point out that they did not always attain it, and the modern psychologist may insist that such complete objectivity is impossible to begin with. Yet it was a noble effort and its achievements were impressive. There was no prescribed curriculum: German students could move from one university to the other, enroll for any course that attracted them, attend classes or not, as they pleased. Those who wanted a degree had to pass the final examinations, and they were formidable. Teaching methods, too, were different. The professor lectured on his specialty without demanding day-by-day textbook recitations or giving daily marks. All that was put behind when the German student finished the *Gymnasium*. Students of science were not content with lecture-demonstrations but worked in laboratories, a pedagogical device of the chemist Liebig and his associates, where by observation and rigorously controlled experimentation they could test the facts for themselves. Counterpart of the laboratory in the philosophical faculties was the seminar. In the historical seminars of Leopold von Ranke and his colleagues, for example, students would examine the primary sources individually and jointly, report on their findings, receive the criticism of the master and their fellow students, and, in the end, write their own history.

The lecture, the laboratory, and the seminar were the new educational methods that the returning scholars brought with them from Germany and the means by which they hoped to bring American higher education to maturity. In a large measure they succeeded, though the American university which emerged from their efforts was by no means an exact replica of the German. In America the new type of scientific research had to be carried on by the existing college of liberal arts or by some kind of extension of that college. In the new state universities it had to find a place, somehow, among or above the various vocational departments and schools. The German universities were not burdened with such encumbrances and could devote their entire resources to pure research, lecturing, and publication.

The American answer was the graduate school, grafted on to the undergraduate college. Henry Tappan had tried this, unsuccessfully, in Michigan in the 1850's. But now the time was ripe. In the last quarter of the century graduate schools appeared in most of the leading institutions. Where fully developed, and not stunted by the undergraduate college and the vocational departments, they were the equivalent of the faculty of philosophy in a German university. A few tried to duplicate the European example completely by organizing solely as a graduate university. Johns Hopkins was the first and most famous of them. Others were Clark University in Massachusetts and the Catholic University in Washington. The latter existed as a theological school from 1889 on and added graduate schools of philology and the social sciences five years later.[15] But experience soon showed that such an exclusively graduate institution was still too exotic a plant for American conditions. Sooner or later an undergraduate college had to be added, both for financial reasons and as a feeder producing qualified students for the higher school. But with or without the undergirding of a college, the graduate school became the vehicle for the transmission of scientific research and productive scholarship from Europe to America.

While the state university was broadening the scope of higher education and scientific method was giving it precision, a new philosophy was in the making that was to change its fundamental character. This was the theory of evolution. Cautiously advanced in a limited field by Charles Darwin, expanded into a universal philosophy by Herbert Spencer, and carried directly to the lecture-loving and magazine-reading American public by popularizers, its influence was soon all-pervasive, inescapable. Scholars going to Germany absorbed it in the lectures of Haeckel and his disciples. It was the evolutionary approach, the idea that the world and everything in it is the result of a process that began eons ago and is still going on, which gave the final impetus to scientific study and eventually raised the scientists to the position of pre-eminence in the intellectual hierarchy once held by the classicists. It offered a fresh point of view in other fields as well and called for a reappraisal of accepted values throughout the curriculum. It made possible the organic approach to history and literature and revolutionized teaching in those subjects, and it speeded the emergence of the social sciences as a separate division of teaching and research.

All this was not accomplished without a struggle. Unlike the state university and the German research technique, evolution had to fight its way into the fold. The orthodox both in church and school offered dogged resistance. The length of the battle and its details varied from campus to campus, but its outcome was nearly everywhere the same: The champions of the old order lost the day. Some went down fighting, and some retired to the ivory tower. Many compromised, perhaps on the principle that if you can't lick 'em, join 'em. The colleges did not reorient themselves overnight, though it looked that way in retrospect to some of the enthusiasts of evolution. Charles Francis Adams, speaking for historians, said in 1900: "We of the new school [of history] regard as the dividing line between us and the historians of the old school the first day of October 1859,—the date of the publication of Darwin's 'Origin of Species.'" In reality the acceptance of the organic or evolutionary thesis was itself something of an evolutionary process, since the new views replaced the older orthodoxies not so much by direct frontal assault as by gradual infiltration. After all, the idea itself was not entirely strange. The science of geology had been flourishing for a generation, and new vistas of the earth's age, accepted by Agassiz of Harvard, Dana of Yale, Hitchcock of Amherst, and others, had already blurred the focus of

Biblical literalism. The naturalistic speculations of Thomas Cooper of South Carolina College antedated all of these.[16]

The Darwinian hypothesis did not therefore come as a major shock to college scientists. In one way or another they managed to absorb it or to reshape it in harmony with their religious beliefs and philosophical positions. A case in point is Asa Gray of the Lawrence Scientific School of Harvard, whose urbane and well-informed review articles on the *Origin of Species* in the *Atlantic Monthly* went far toward making Darwinism palatable to his colleagues. Gray's general conclusion was that Darwin had proposed a tenable hypothesis, "not harmful to religion, unless injudicious assailants temporarily make it so." As long as the argument for design was left intact—and Gray thought it was—it seemed rather silly to "hold the original distinctness of turnips and cabbages as an article of faith." This remained his position, and he expressed it many times. An unwavering theist, Gray saw in the evolutionary struggle the assurance of ultimate higher and nobler forms. A similar position was taken by Joseph Le Conte, eminent biologist of the University of California, who lectured on evolution with the admitted purpose of reconciling science and religion, saw an immanent divinity in the Darwinian data and the ideal Christian man at the summit of the evolutionary trail.[17]

It was arguments such as these that created a sympathetic atmosphere for the new theories and gradually undermined the opposition. Chief among the popularizers, because he reached a wider audience than either Gray or Le Conte, was the historian John Fiske. A brilliant undergraduate at Harvard, Fiske had been suspect to the authorities there ever since he was caught reading the positivist philosopher Comte in chapel, and he never secured a permanent appointment at his alma mater. He did, however, with President Eliot's consent, give the first series of lectures on evolution on the Harvard campus. His fluent style and captivating platform manner facilitated the acceptance of the Spencerian philosophy which he introduced, somewhat prettied up, to the American public. Not a scientist himself, Fiske insisted, on philosophical grounds and in opposition to the German scholar Haeckel, on the need of a personal God in the process; he equated evolution with progress, and he made it a basis for racial theories that flattered his hearers.

Although the *Atlantic Monthly* and the *North American Review* carried much of this controversial literature, the principal outlet for the exponents of the gospel of progress through evolution was the

Popular Science Monthly, begun in 1872 by Edward Youmans, an enthusiastic disciple of Spencer and Huxley. Two years after its founding this magazine reported a circulation of twelve thousand—excellent for such a journal for that time. Support of a different kind came from Chauncey Wright, mathematician, philosopher, and occasional lecturer at Harvard. Wright was not concerned to reconcile the new hypothesis with traditional religion but to demonstrate its scientific validity. A regular correspondent of Darwin and a student and critic of Spencer, Wright was a "scientists' scientist," with little popular appeal. "The strategy of science," he insisted, "is not the same as that of rhetorical disputation, and aims at cornering facts, not antagonists." [18]

Meantime the opposition was not inactive. It was largely theological in origin, even though the Puritan version of Protestantism, under whose auspices most of the colleges had had their beginnings, was by no means hostile to science, and many a clergyman-professor, when mathematics and natural philosophy was assigned to him, took this subject matter seriously and acquired considerable competence. The Darwinian implications, however, were too much for him. He dismissed the entire evolutionary hypothesis as not proved, then usually went on to denounce it as immoral. A theory that tended to promote unbelief and to subvert Christian morality must be opposed, no matter what the evidence showed. Among the theological leaders of the time, Charles Hodge and Horace Bushnell feared for the foundations of faith and morality and were not ready to follow Henry Ward Beecher in his sentimental espousal of the progress version of the theory. For a while the clerical conservatives thought they had found a champion among the scientists in Louis Agassiz, eminent Swiss biologist and Harvard colleague of Asa Gray. Agassiz was not, however, quite the shining champion of orthodoxy that his admirers made him out. He had accepted the idea of development as such, geologic eons were no impediment to his faith, and he merely entered a *caveat* against the uncritical acceptance of all phases of the Darwinian thesis. The emergence, by natural selection, of varieties within a species he could admit; but the species themselves, he insisted, were successive creations emanating from the mind of God. Thus he salvaged the teleological principle while remaining scrupulously attentive to evidence. For a time the controversy between Agassiz and Gray made Lawrence Scientific School a lively place, but after the death of Agassiz it faded out; and as the growing fossil collections and expanding "philosophical cabinets" on a hundred campuses piled up the evidence, the few recalcitrant scientists capitulated and the new theory took over.[19]

It was not so much the professors, however, as the college presidents who had to make the momentous decision and then explain the change of course to their constituents. Interpreters of the college to the community, they thought it their duty to reassure a bewildered public that whatever novelties might be dispensed in the classroom and laboratory, the seats of learning were safe against moral sabotage. By and large the presidents were men of integrity and superior ability, concerned to advance and disseminate the truth. Their truth was of course the truth as it had been committed to them by their classical, metaphysical, and theological training. Should they now throw their lifetime convictions overboard in favor of a novel theory, the scientific evidence for which few of them had actually examined? Then there were the trustees and the alumni to consider, among whom the clergy were influential if no longer very numerous. Above all, in the highly competitive business of higher education, no college could afford too much unfavorable publicity, and that in itself made it difficult to decide the highly explosive issue of evolution on its merits alone. This equivocal situation explains the half-challenging, half-reassuring note which echoes through the voluminous baccalaureate sermons, inaugural addresses, and presidential reports of those years. We must keep abreast of the times, they all agreed, we must move forward, for this is an age of science and progress. On the other hand, science must not presume to dictate but must approach sacred things with reverence; eternal verities cannot be challenged, and ethical foundations must stand secure.[20]

So they backed and filled. When an influential religious journal asked nine college presidents in 1880 whether they permitted the teaching that man in his physical structure was evolved from irrational beasts, the answer, with some qualifications, was no. Yet when one of the nine, Noah Porter of Yale, tried about at this time to dissuade William Graham Sumner from teaching his famous sociology course in a naturalistic framework and with Herbert Spencer's *Study of Sociology* as text, he found the popular professor too strongly entrenched and had to give up the attempt.[21] Porter, by the way, was a sound scholar and no bigoted obscurantist. But every campus had its own peculiar situation. At Michigan, urgent requests for the enlargement of facilities for the sciences were balanced in President Angell's annual reports with reassurances that the university was not forsaking the old paths. Christianity, he pointed out, was honored at Michigan even though there was no compulsory chapel or religious instruction. Of the teaching and administrating staff of eighty, three fourths were communicants of local churches, and every Sunday school in Ann Arbor but one had a professor as superintendent.[22] Barnard of Columbia, one-time president of the American Association for the Advancement of Science, never quite overcame his misgivings. His inaugural address at Columbia in 1864 was so happily phrased that both the scientists and the preachers claimed him for their own, but his first report to the trustees a year later made much of the fact that in his lectures to the senior class he had defended religion against "the recent very plausible and insidious theory of Darwin." In a still more conservative vein, he remarked in 1873: "If the final outcome of all the boastful discoveries of modern science is to disclose to men that they are more evanescent than the shadow of the swallow's wing upon the lake . . . give me then, I pray, no more science. I will live on in my simple ignorance as my fathers did before me." [23] Barnard's lingering nostalgia did not keep Columbia in the paths of the old orthodoxy.

Among the many who had to make both a personal and a public adjustment Chancellor Francis H. Snow of the University of Kansas may be singled out. A New Englander, graduate of Williams and student under Mark Hopkins, he came to Kansas in its first year with a license to preach and a cheerful but unexamined religious conservatism. Assigned the scientific branches, he was soon forced to come to grips with the evolutionary hypothesis and was gradually convinced by the cumulative evidence. By the time he became chancellor in 1891 he had not only worked it into his courses but was giving public lectures on the subject in Kansas City, thus trying to get both students and constituents to accept it as a demonstration of divine foresight and the assurance of progress.[24] Most successful in absorbing and adapting the evolutionary thesis without denying his religious convictions was President James McCosh of Princeton. A Scottish theologian, McCosh was brought to New Jersey in 1868, as John Witherspoon had been a century before, to invigorate Princeton. Though widely acquainted with university conditions and leaders in Europe, he remained in many ways the paternal college head of an earlier day and the personal disciplinarian of individual boys. As such, he soon sensed that an unequivocal stand against evolution at this time might undermine his and the faculty's influence with the students and prove disastrous for the cause of religion. Unlike many of the clergy, McCosh tried sincerely to understand Darwin and to reconcile natural selection with a sound theism. His adjustment was the familiar one: "I have been defending Evolution but, in doing so, have given the proper account of it as the method of God's procedure." And again: "We are not to be precluded from seeking and discovering a final cause, because we have found an efficient cause." And harking back in his farewell address to the things that had given him the greatest satisfaction during his twenty years in office, he made special mention of the conversion of tough students like the "open-mouthed infidel, perpetually quoting Huxley and Spencer," who ended up lecturing for the Y.M.C.A.[25]

More commonly the new views prevailed by default. President Julius Seelye of Amherst, one of the nine who had answered "no" in 1880, was a religious conservative but a tolerant man. He permitted his science professors to teach geology in a thoroughly naturalistic manner, and the latter gratefully acknowledged: "The old fellow lets us alone." What happened at Amherst happened elsewhere. Evolution-slanted texts like those of Gray, Dana, and Le Conte were more and more widely used, while the philosophy of the college remained theistic and the general public was assured that the professors were in Sunday school. But inside their laboratories the scientists held sway. If they were competent and produced results, "the old fellow let them alone." By the turn of the century even so devout an institution as Illinois College (not the University of Illinois) had accepted the new theories and was no longer frightened by evolution. When Billy Sunday came on a revival tour to Jacksonville in 1908, where he denounced the college, proclaiming that "Darwin is sizzling in hell," and that "all scientists can go plumb to hell so far as I care," students and faculty remained cool and unimpressed.[26]

When we turn to examine the general effects of the triple impact of the new forces on the traditional college, several things stand out. The college was shaken to its foundations. These foundations had been the intellectual authority of the classical curriculum and the moral authority of a theologically oriented faculty. Knowledge of Hebrew, Greek, and Latin, and the belief in the inerrancy of the Scriptures buttressed each other. In the turbulent history of English and American Puritanism from which the college movement stemmed, familiarity with these languages had been of inestimable worth for defining and defending the church's official position, and in the process they had achieved an aura of sanctity second only to the Bible itself. This had of course also been true of the original Protestantism of Martin Luther. Now the credentials of both the classics and the Bible were being challenged. Knowledge of the world was increasing so fast that no one category of studies could any longer encompass it. Science, confident and arrogant, was crowding the classics to the wall, and English literature, history, and economics were clamoring for admission to the college curriculum on the same basis as the hitherto privileged ancient languages. In the light of the new situation there seemed no longer any good reason for requiring students to take Latin and Greek rather than any other subject. President Eliot of Harvard, as we shall see, was soon to raise this idea to the level of a full-fledged educational philosophy.

If the classics were no longer sacred, what chance had the Mosaic cosmogony? Darwin and Spencer had made a myth of the Garden of Eden, and the entire Christian epic of redemption seemed threatened by the doctrines of natural selection and survival of the fittest. What was worse, the students in their search for answers would no longer come to their theologically trained professors but would go to the scientists in their laboratories. Any light that the sophisticated disciples of Darwin, Spencer, and Huxley could shed on the origins and meaning of human society was eagerly sought after. While their religious and philosophical unities were thus slowly disintegrating before their eyes, the displaced oracles of the old order could only cry over and over, like the character in the Saroyan play, "No foundation! No foundation!"

Chapter Eight

Prophets of New Ideals

~~~~~~

New foundations were being prepared, and the men who laid them were among the greatest names in American higher education. Pre-eminent among them were Charles William Eliot, president of Harvard from 1869 to 1909; Daniel Coit Gilman, first president of Johns Hopkins, from 1875 to 1901; Andrew Dickson White, first president of Cornell, from 1867 to 1885; James Burrill Angell, president of Michigan from 1871 to 1909; David Starr Jordan, first president of Stanford, from 1891 to 1913; and William Rainey Harper, first president of the University of Chicago, from 1892 to 1905. These men, together with a few others almost equally brilliant or effective, reassembled the pieces of the old order, added new ingredients which the changing social structure had produced, infused the whole with a touch of their own genius, and brought forth the modern American university.

They had certain common characteristics. For one thing they welcomed and did not deplore the new scientific thinking. In contrast to the conventional clergyman-educator, they had adventurous minds and accepted the challenge of the age. Critical of their own narrow undergraduate training, they were aware of European university methods and developments. Significantly, they were not theologians but secular by profession and predilection. Harper carried a theological degree, perhaps for protective coloring, but his real interest was philology. These men personified the onset of lay instead of clerical control in higher education. Up to this time an occasional college had experimented with a lay president—Columbia as early as 1787— only to return to theological leadership. From now on, at least in the larger universities, the tide would run the other way.

Yet this group of new-style university leaders could hardly be called radical in any general sense of the term. Certainly they were not, in their religious and philosophical thinking, complete positivists. Hospitable though they were to innovation in matters academic, they maintained liaison with the absolutes of their inheritance. Eliot could ram the appointment of John Fiske the evolutionist down the Overseers' throats without giving up his personal faith in a transcendent intelligence which gives the universe meaning; and he loved to sing the old hymns. In the early days of Cornell, White had to battle the heresy-hunters, whom he described as mostly older theologians who had learned nothing and forgotten nothing and professors who did not want to rewrite their lectures. But he indignantly denied that his university was a hotbed of infidelity and atheism, and more than once expressed his personal belief in "a Power in the universe, not ourselves, which makes for righteousness." In retrospect he seems almost a religious conservative. Jordan came closest, perhaps, to the positivist stand: William James would have classified him as tough-minded. An ichthyologist of note, Jordan knew that biological natural selection did not prove the inevitability of human progress. "As science advances in any field, philosophy is driven out of it." Yet even Jordan, at the end of his lectures on evolution, postulated an Infinite Being as a logical necessity.[1]

The hospitality to innovation of this group did not extend to the economic and political fields either. Here they accepted, by and large, the prevailing *laissez faire* views of the business community, that social Darwinism which could be so neatly tailored to fit the interests of the captains of industry. Gilman could hardly help accepting the economic *status quo* when all the assets of his university were invested in common stock of the Baltimore and Ohio railroad. White was a businessman himself, and had served in the New York state legislature. He admitted that he tried to learn from such "foremost business men" as Cornelius Vanderbilt and Daniel Drew, and he was converted from the theoretical free-trade views of his Michigan teaching days into a pragmatic protectionist later in life. Harper of Chicago saw "incalculable injury" to democracy in what seemed to him a trend toward socialism at the end of the century. Jordan at Stanford was an economic individualist who believed that poverty was inefficiency. Yet they all prided themselves on permitting and encouraging free discussion of controversial political and economic issues on their respective campuses.[2]

It is their educational views, however, that interest us primarily, and here each of the men made a distinctive contribution. Most far-reaching was that of Eliot. Member of a family that had been identified with Harvard almost from the beginning, he graduated there in 1853, became a tutor of mathematics at his alma mater, then assistant professor. He left Harvard for two years abroad, where he studied educational methods and philosophies of European countries. Then he returned to be professor of chemistry at the new Massachusetts Institute of Technology. As a teacher, both at Harvard and M.I.T., he distinguished himself by his organizing ability, constant attention to methods, and by the introduction of such novelties as laboratory work and written examinations. In his classes he was considered eminently fair but cold as an icicle. He was not a popular teacher. Yet he made such an impression by his all-around competence that in 1869 the Overseers of Harvard, after much soul-searching and in the face of considerable faculty opposition, elected him president of the university.[3]

At the time of Eliot's accession the older American colleges were stagnant. Even Harvard had not entirely escaped the blight, though it had by far the largest library, an imposing array of professional schools, and men like Agassiz, Gray, Lowell, Holmes, Sparks, and Peirce to give prestige to its faculty. Yet in the opinion of its chronicler "Harvard College was hidebound, the Harvard Law School senescent, the Medical School ineffective, and the Lawrence Scientific School 'the resort of shirkers and stragglers' . . . something must be done, and that quickly, or Harvard would degenerate into a mere cultural backwater: desire under the elms, and not much desire at that." [4] For twenty years the announcements of courses in the Law School had not been altered by a single letter. Its classes were not graded, and no examinations were given. The entire program was covered in a two-year sequence of lectures. A student might start in at any time of the school year, remain until the merry-go-round of lectures returned to his point of entry and then, with a "here's where I came in" walk off with his diploma. The three professors who made up the law faculty considered this arrangement eminently satisfactory. A decade earlier Henry Adams had dismissed his whole Harvard education, with the exception of his work under Agassiz, as a failure: "The entire work of the four years could have been easily put into the work of any four months in after life." [5] Although Henry Adams could hardly be called an average student, it does seem that the Cambridge undergraduates of those decades were far from working at maximum efficiency. Harvard, like the rest, was wallowing in the doldrums.

All this was changed when Eliot got to work. In his inaugural address he announced a philosophy of education and a plan of procedure that he was to follow consistently for the next forty years, until he had made Harvard the foremost and richest American university. The theme was stated in the first sentence: "The endless controversies whether language, philosophy, mathematics or science supplies the best mental training . . . have no practical lessons for us today. This University recognizes no real antagonism between literature and science, and consents to no such narrow alternatives as mathematics or classics, science or metaphysics. We would have them all, and at their best." Not only the classics, not just the genteel tradition, but every subject that interests the mind of man was to be taught at Harvard and at the highest possible level. To each subject professors and students must bring "an open mind, trained to careful thinking." Routine recitation of remembered facts and dogmatic lecturing had no place in his ideal university. "To learn by rote a list of dates is not to study history." And again: "Philosophical subjects should never be taught with authority. . . . Exposition, not imposition, of opinions, is the professor's part. . . . Two kinds of men make good teachers: young men and men who never grow old." And as for the president of the university, he must consult and execute majority decisions. "A university is the last place in the world for a dictator. Learning is always republican." [6]

By way of translating this program into action, Eliot proceeded at once to urge the enlargement of Harvard's curricular offerings, both as to quantity and quality, looked around for suitable new instructors, agitated to secure the necessary funds, and kept up this pressure for forty years. His emphasis at first was on teaching rather than research. Eliot himself was a first-rate teacher and a great administrator, but not primarily a research scholar. He did provide for graduate instruction, but in the interest of better teaching rather than for the purpose of extending the frontiers of knowledge. As a matter of fact his immediate predecessor in office, Thomas Hill, seems to have had at least as much interest in research as Eliot. President Hill's last annual report, after pointing out that the buildings were in poor repair, that campus landscaping was nonexistent, and that any burglar could get through the college fence, went on to say, among other things: "If our University desires to maintain her position as one of the first institutions in the country she must not be content with hearing *memoriter* recitations from a text-book in the undergraduate course, but must devise stimulants to original investigation, research, and experiment, creating a class of students whose ambition it shall be to advance science rather than to receive knowledge and diffuse it." [7] From there he went on to outline a program of graduate fellowships.

One consequence of Eliot's proposed curricular reforms stood out clearly, and he faced it fearlessly. If every intellectual activity is important when properly organized and pursued at its highest level, it follows that no subject or group of subjects, neither the classics nor any other, can claim priority as one that every student should be required to take. This was exactly what he meant. He had said on one occasion: "The vulgar argument that the study of the classics is necessary to make a gentleman is beneath contempt." [8] Since no student could possibly take all the courses offered, there must be some freedom of choice; in Eliot's opinion there should be complete freedom. And he set about to secure it. It took fifteen years, for neither the Corporation nor the faculty were ready for such a radical departure all at once, and much persuasion was necessary. But piecemeal, class by class and year by year, subject by subject, the requirements were whittled down and the range of choice was widened, until in 1884 Eliot could announce that the development was practically completed. Two years later a Harvard undergraduate could earn the A.B. degree by passing any eighteen courses, no two of which need be related.[9] Thus there was introduced into the world of higher education what has ever since been known as the elective system.

The idea was not entirely new. The University of Virginia, from its opening in 1826, had permitted its students to choose any one of a number of parallel programs but had then required completion of all the work in the program selected. William and Mary, Brown, Union, and others, had at one time or another experimented with limited electives, but without much success. Now the oldest university in the land was getting behind the idea and taking it all the way. The impact on the college world was tremendous. For the next thirty years the greatest controversial issue on nearly all campuses, even more exciting than evolution, was that of electives as opposed to the old required curriculum. Should Harvard be imitated or opposed? Or could one find middle ground? Harvard's tercentenary historian flatly accuses Eliot of "the greatest educational crime of the century against American youth—depriving him of his classical heritage." [10] Yet he admits that the educational sideshows into which the free-wheeling undergraduates of Eliot's day sometimes strayed could produce astonishingly satisfying cultural experiences. In general the newer institutions welcomed the Harvard innovations and adapted them to their own needs, while the older centers of tradition viewed the whole development with alarm.

Leaders among the conservative forces were once again Princeton and Yale. President McCosh of Princeton believed fervently in maintaining the old disciplines, and in a public debate with Eliot in 1885 on the merits of the elective system he ridiculed the "mental monstrosities" currently turned out at Harvard who, unable to take solid intellectual food, dabbled in music, art, and French plays.[11] Yale was even more determined to salvage the ancient values. Under President Noah Porter, a scholar and gentleman of the old school, it took a determined stand against the alarming heresies of Eliot, just as it had in 1828 against the errors of that generation. A student of Porter's day remembered the spirit of Yale in his memoir: "In those classical days, none questioned the right and few the ability of the college faculty to prescribe the subjects best suited to training the mind. Mental training rather than intellectual interest was then the watchword and our professors held fast to the procedures which had been hallowed by immemorial service. Harvard had, to be sure, recently gone modern and optional. Her vagaries we viewed with alarm and saw in them all the more reason why we should hold high the firm torch of learning. Sheff [Sheffield Scientific School] had long since had well-established and successful elective group courses manned by distinguished scholars, but Sheff did not count, at least not in the affirmative. Under a former Sheff professor, Johns Hopkins had become a pathfinder. Cornell and Michigan and others were extending their courses into new fields of science and technology, but we knew better." [12] So the good old curriculum was good enough for Yale. There were some defections. Frederick A. P. Barnard, a Yale graduate and one-time champion of the earlier "Yale Report on the Classics," had changed his mind. By the time he became president of Columbia, in 1864, he had come to regard the Greek and Latin requirement more as a sedative than a stimulus, a fetish whose utility ended when the new-made bachelor of arts had laboriously construed the Latin on his diploma. From than on Barnard labored steadily to introduce electives at Columbia.[13]

By the turn of the century Eliot's views had apparently prevailed. The large universities had nearly all fallen into line. Even Yale and Princeton were moving cautiously in that direction. The smaller colleges followed suit as far as their finances permitted, for the elective system was costly. Then came two world wars with a depression sandwiched between, and educational leaders, jolted out of their complacent assumptions of the inevitable triumph of reason and progress, decided to take a second look at free electives. Perhaps something precious, after all, had been lost. But that is the story of a later chapter.

While Eliot was launching his program at Harvard, another educational experiment of far-reaching consequences was taking shape in Baltimore. There in the 1870's an educational bequest of the unprecedented amount of $3,500,000 from the Quaker merchant Johns Hopkins was being translated into a university of a new type by its first president, Daniel Coit Gilman. A graduate of Yale, Gilman had studied two years in Europe, then returned to New Haven for educational posts of various kinds. Passed over for the presidency of Yale in favor of the more conservative Noah Porter, he was soon after elected president of the new University of California. Pressure groups and politics made his stay in California uncomfortable, and when the offer came to take charge of the new enterprise in Baltimore, he gladly consented. His first step, after being given carte blanche as to the kind of institution to be fashioned out of the Hopkins money, was to ask the advice of his friends Eliot of Harvard, White of Cornell, and Angell of Michigan; but having consulted them, he presented a plan that was essentially his own. He proposed a real university in the European sense of the term, to be the first of its kind in America. Instead of starting with the usual college nucleus which would gradually add professional divisions and a graduate school to become a university, he wanted to begin with a carefully selected faculty of scholars who would establish a center of research and would also direct the studies of a body of qualified graduate students by means of lectures, laboratories, and seminars. A library must be provided first of all, professional schools would be erected as time and money were available, and an undergraduate college added only as a minor appendage, if at all.[14]

In his inaugural address Gilman further developed his ideas. The new university, he suggested, was being launched under exceptionally favorable auspices, free from control by either church or state. His experiences at Yale and California had led him to the conclusion that the privately endowed university, built on the profits of capitalistic enterprise, had in the long run greater opportunity for the disinterested pursuit of truth than either of the other two American types, for it would be unhampered by denominational or political bias. As for the program itself, it must be both broad and deep, with all subjects entitled to equal recognition, and it would be conducted by teachers who also did research and researchers who also taught, for the one endeavor re-enforced the other. The faculty would not be asked what was their college, their social status, or their church. Rather, "what do they know, what can they do, and what do they want to find out." [15] And they should not be allowed to bog down in details of administrative routine.

Hopkins opened in 1876, organized pretty much along the lines of Gilman's specifications. A faculty of scholars had been assembled from both sides of the Atlantic. It included an Irishman from the University of London who had been an assistant to Huxley, a famous British mathematician, a New Yorker who had studied chemistry and medicine in Germany—that was Ira Remsen—and a Confederate veteran. The last choice was good politics for a Yankee operating in Baltimore, and it also secured a first-rate classical scholar in Basil Gildersleeve. An undergraduate college had to be established after all, both as an obligation to the city and the state, and to build a reservoir of qualified graduate students. The growth of the university was steady not phenomenal. At the opening in 1876 it had twenty-three undergraduates to fifty-four graduate students; twenty years later the numbers were one hundred and forty-nine and four hundred and six, respectively. Seven distinct major programs were offered with complete freedom of choice between them, but unlike the Harvard system, the component parts of the program selected had to be rationally put together under the guidance of the faculty. Throughout, the lines between undergraduate and graduate work were kept flexible, and remain so to this day; every student was encouraged to move at his own pace to the highest degree of which he was capable. Johns Hopkins thus became the first adequate American source of doctors of philosophy, and from Hopkins the rapidly growing colleges and universities of the country obtained some of their ablest teachers and most productive scholars.[16]

The two friends whom Gilman had consulted about plans for Johns Hopkins were themselves conducting creative educational experiments. Andrew Dickson White's specific problem at Cornell was to weld together a land grant institution of many vocational schools and a German university of research scholars and graduate students, and thus to promote both horizontal and vertical expansion at one and the same time. Even though he was unencumbered by tradition or powerful vested interests, this took some doing. White began by insisting that all subjects of instruction be held equally valid and thus anticipated Eliot by a year in the dethronement of the classics. In actual practice the five hundred students who entered Cornell in 1868 each chose a certain field of study, and these fields gradually identified themselves as the classics or modern literature or science or vocational studies like agriculture. The student then built a program around the field of his choice, somewhat in the manner of Virginia or Hopkins. Later, under White's successors, this freedom was somewhat curtailed for a time, but eventually Cornell went over completely to the Eliot plan.

White tried by various devices to keep standards high and to avoid falling into the boarding school regime which he remembered from his own college days. Distinguished scholars were brought in as visiting professors for varying terms as a stimulus. The energetic president had no use for pedants on the faculty, describing them as "gerund-grinders" who mistook the husks for the kernel, substituted dates for history, syntax for literature, and formulas for science. He himself continued to give his course of lectures on European history as he had done at Michigan, teaching the subject, as he put it, in that "most stimulating atmosphere coming from the great thought of Darwin and Herbert Spencer,—an atmosphere in which history became less and less a matter of annals, and more and more a record of the unfolding of humanity." Whether his enthusiasm for the new was matched by his scholarship is open to question. In the opinion of one of Cornell's great historians of a later generation, Carl Becker, White was not a profound scholar but essentially a crusader. His crusading spirit extended to every aspect of life on campus. By way of insuring maturity of conduct, rules of behavior were reduced to a minimum, and students were encouraged to manage their own affairs. The daily marking system was also abolished. Students were "expected to attend" chapel, but nobody checked up on them. Thus under the impact of White's personality and a new combination of social forces Cornell emerged as an institution that was different.[17]

James Burrill Angell's long career at Michigan, almost identical in time with Eliot's at Harvard, was marked by the emergence of that institution as the foremost of the state universities. A major contribution of Angell's was his insistence on state responsibility for higher education. Civil society, he maintained, had not only the negative duty of repressing crime but also the higher positive responsibility of promoting the intellectual and moral growth of its citizens. It must therefore place the means of obtaining the highest culture within reach of the poorest and humblest citizen of the state. (Here was the welfare state, suggested sixty years before the New Deal.) Corollaries of the educational premises of this transplanted son of Rhode Island and new-modeled Puritan included a wide and diversified range of studies with considerable freedom of choice, as well as graduate work of the highest rank. All this was substantially what Eliot, Gilman, and White were saying, with minor changes in emphasis. Scholarships and all forms of self-help would also be necessary (since Michigan did not have free tuition), if the university was to function successfully as the apex of the public school system.[18]

The final decade of the nineteenth century saw the establishment of two more universities that were to have considerable influence on the course of higher education in the twentieth. They were Stanford and Chicago, both dating from 1892, the former under the leadership of David Starr Jordan and the latter the embodiment of the ideas of William Rainey Harper. Jordan was one of the early science students at Cornell and would be remembered as an outstanding research biologist even if he had never headed a great university. After teaching in various schools he became president of Indiana University, where Mr. and Mrs. Leland Stanford found him. They took him out to Palo Alto, promised him a salary of $10,000, an endowment of $30,000,000—more than Harvard had at that time—and told him to build a university. When he got to the coast, Jordan found things not quite as rosy as they had been portrayed. There was, for one thing, the competition of the state university, whose supporters did not look with kindly eyes on the rival upstart. His freedom of action was circumscribed. Though empowered to introduce almost any educational innovation, he did not control the budget; in fact there was no budget. Mr. Stanford and, after his death, his widow handed out "what was needed." She gave liberally, to be sure, and her rubber-stamp board of trustees always consented, but it was decidedly a lady bountiful situation. When the estate was tied up in a federal suit and suffered further shrinkage in the depression of the nineties, the young university went through lean years. But Jordan had a youthful and enthusiastic faculty, with a zest for teaching and research, and he began with an initial enrollment of five hundred students, many from poor homes since tuition was free.[19]

The dominant note at Stanford was freedom of choice and specialization. As at Hopkins and Cornell, a student chose a field of major interest and built his program around it. Jordan, like Eliot, dismissed the argument for the classics as pedantry. They were good for "Greek-minded men." A strong advocate of early specialization, he was skeptical of cultural values that were supposed to come like the gentle rain from heaven as a reward of all liberal arts study. "The average first-class engineer is better educated than the college student who goes in for culture, with no definite purpose of action in connection with it." [20] Chemistry and mathematics are good for the medical student, not as general culture; they will have no broadening effect unless taken with a vocational purpose. Jordan thought of a university as primarily a place where scholars and specialists associate for original research. Though living on the largess of private millions, perhaps because of their uncertainties, he favored public control of higher education as more compatible with democracy.[21]

The first phase of the expansion movement came to a climax in the University of Chicago as it sprang full-panoplied from the brain of Harper and the purse of Rockefeller. The story of Chicago was not that of an old classical college suffering from growing pains and reluctantly, unsymmetrically, adding a school here and an activity there, like Harvard or Yale or Princeton. Chicago was launched as a university, more nearly complete than any other at its outset. There was a junior college and a senior college with an assortment of courses that few institutions could equal and a faculty to teach every one. The professional schools were all assembled too: law, medicine, divinity, fine arts and music, together with a graduate school of science and one of the arts. A library, a museum, a division of university extension, and a university press completed the picture, and there were buildings and endowment to support it all.[22]

William Rainey Harper, who presided over this marvel, was a dynamo of energy and ideas. Graduating from a small Ohio college at the age of fourteen, he had earned a Ph.D. at Yale four years later. He was thirty-five when picked to head Mr. Rockefeller's fabulous university. There he burned himself out in fifteen years of tireless activity. He was likely to open an important conference with a professor, for which he had managed to allow fifteen minutes, with the greeting: "I have forty points to be discussed this morning." He died at fifty.[23]

His educational theories were realized in the university that he created. The marks of a true university to Harper were self-government and freedom from external control, especially church control; freedom of expression; and advancement of learning on all fronts. It was not an ivory tower but a public institution by virtue of its charter, even though its support might be private. It was the prophet, spokesman, interpreter, and critic of democracy. Among Harper's specific contributions, one of the most important was the idea of the junior college. No friend of complete freedom of choice, he believed that there was a common cultural heritage to be transmitted, but that this could be completed in the two lower college years. From his third, or junior, year on, the student would then be ready to begin advanced work on the university level, with his general education behind him. The length of time required to complete the work for the bachelor's degree or, for that matter, for any advanced degree, might vary; at any rate there was no reason to maintain the four-year block of time as a fetish. The general courses in the lower years, furthermore, were to be taught as such and not as introductions to a specialty which the student would continue until graduation. Here the difference between Harper and Jordan is marked. In Harper's opinion the scientists were making the same mistake that had ruined the classicists, namely assuming that everyone enrolled in their introductory courses was going to be a professional scientist and thus making the subject distasteful to those students who were taking it only for general cultural purposes. To a surprising degree Harper's ideas anticipated those of Chancellor Hutchins of the same university thirty years later.[24]

The creative leaders whose work has been described here were not singled out with any intention of disparaging the achievements of others almost equally important. It was the philosophical breadth and administrative skill of Frederick Barnard, for example, that began the transformation of Columbia from a stagnant little college into the complex metropolitan university it is today. What Barnard had begun Nicholas Murray Butler carried to fruition in the twentieth century on the new campus on Morningside Heights.[25] In the same year in which Butler began his reign at Columbia, 1902, Woodrow Wilson was elected president of Princeton by the unanimous vote of the trustees and without consideration of any other candidate. Wilson converted Princeton from a complacent college slowly turning into a country club and made of it a modern university where intellectual interests were paramount. Given complete freedom by the trustees to "create such vacancies in the teaching force as he may deem for the best interests of the university," Wilson imported fifty young scholars, the best he could find, to pump "oxygen into the blood of an anaemic institution, long inbred." The preceptorial system of small discussion groups inaugurated by these fifty scholars became a chief means of promoting respect for scholarship and stimulating interest in things of the mind among the undergraduates. Wilson, as is well known, did not succeed in all his ventures at Princeton and finally resigned over the question of control of the graduate school. Apart from this specific issue, some of the alumni deeply suspected the new president's attempts to make over a comfortable old college into an institution of learning. Increasing opposition among faculty and trustees, brought about in part by his too precipitate pace of reform, defeated some of his later plans. Yet he convinced his constituents before he left for broader fields that "the chief glory of a university is always intellectual glory." [26]

Yale was loosened from its conservative moorings during the administration of Arthur T. Hadley, a contemporary of Butler and Wilson. It had of course always boasted nationally prominent scholars, had in fact been the first American college to grant earned Ph.D. degrees. The faculty at Yale wielded more power than in most places and had tried earlier to nudge conservative presidents into a faster tempo of change. By means of the educational reforms of the Hadley regime Yale maintained its place among the leaders.[27]

Many other leaders of the era of transition might be mentioned, among them G. Stanley Hall, guiding spirit of Clark University, William Pepper of the University of Pennsylvania, and James H. Kirkland of Vanderbilt. Their story would be a repetition of the central theme with minor variations. But no matter how much one narrows or widens the circle it was this group of leaders who, between about 1870 and 1910, hammered out the modern American university system. In their actions and their writings can be found nearly every issue that has agitated the world of higher education to this day.

Chapter Nine

Transformation and Rival Loyalties

By the opening of the twentieth century the old independent college had yielded precedence to the university. Colleges
continued to function, they even increased in numbers, but henceforth they carried on their activities as units of, or in competition
with, the larger many-sided universities. A new set of problems now
faced the colleges, and they had to adjust to a new frame of reference. Even the language of higher education was new. No self-
respecting college in the nineteenth century felt under any obligation to "adjust" to any "frame of reference."

Clearly, in an age of multiplying intellectual complexities and discordant philosophies the single-minded college of an earlier day with
its simple formula for turning out scholars and gentlemen was not
fit for survival. Mastery, or even a survey, of all knowledge was an
eighteenth century ideal which, by the end of the nineteenth, had
become palpably absurd. A few years earlier it had still been possible
for John Bascom, who afterwards became president of the University
of Wisconsin, to write four textbooks within a decade, dealing respectively with political economy, esthetics, rhetoric, and psychology.
And Harvard's great geologist, Nathaniel Shaler, disturbed by Darwin's declaration that his absorption in scientific research had dulled
his interest in poetry and drama, set out to show that this was not
at all necessary by writing an eight-hundred-page dramatic romance
called *Elizabeth of England.* But Bascom and Shaler were a vanishing
type. Few scholars and fewer college presidents would henceforth
have the temerity, even if they had the time, to cover so much
ground. Nor was it likely any longer even in the smaller colleges that
an instructor would be asked, as was David Starr Jordan in his first

position at Lombard University, to teach science, political economy, evidences of Christianity, German, and Spanish, and to pitch for the baseball team besides.[1]

Among the characteristics of the new age was an increasing emphasis on externals and quantitative values, which created a variety of new interests in place of the old inner unity. Symptomatic of this trend were expansion in size, standardization of practices, diversification of functions, and multiplication of extracurricular activities. Compulsory chapel lost its purpose, and rapidly growing fraternities and intercollegiate athletics set up rival loyalties. Evolution and the elective curriculum, meanwhile, continued to rearrange the philosophical foundations. Under the combined impact of all these forces, some of which have persisted unabated to this day, the old-time college was transformed into a different kind of institution.

The sheer growth in numbers was phenomenal. Between 1870 and 1910 the enrollment of students in institutions of higher learning increased, in complete reversal of earlier trends, four times as fast as the population of the United States. The broader variety of subjects of study combined with the rapidly increasing wealth of the nation to bring this about.[2]

Standardization made itself felt in various ways. First of all, the age and method of admission to college, which had been fluctuating and haphazard up to now, were regularized. The age of college students had fluctuated considerably over the centuries. In the late eighteenth and early nineteenth the average age of entrance to college was fourteen or fifteen, but the range was wide. By 1880 it had risen to about nineteen, at least in older institutions like Harvard, as a result of rising quality of work and stiffer entrance examinations.[3] Meanwhile, however, the public high school had, in the last quarter of the century, become a standard feature of the educational picture, and its four-year course, on top of the eight-year elementary school, tended to equalize and standardize the age at which young people were ready for admission to college, scaling it down to eighteen and presently to about seventeen-and-a-half. Several factors now contributed to a smoother articulation between school and college. State universities were put under pressure to admit without examination all certificated graduates of public high schools whose program was approved by the state board of education. Meanwhile, the older universities and colleges of the Atlantic seaboard, each of which had been setting its own standards and conducting its own entrance examinations, also came to agree on a common basis of admission. At the instigation of Nicholas Murray Butler and Charles W. Eliot the College Entrance Examination Board was organized in 1900 to frame and conduct examinations for graduates of private preparatory and also public high schools, the results to be accepted by member institutions in lieu of entrance examinations of their own.[4] The "College Boards" grew in range and authority, steadily improved or at any rate modified their examinations in form and content, and came to enjoy the confidence of most of the leading universities of the country.

All this was probably necessary to keep the competitive, almost anarchic, system of higher education in America from going completely to pieces. A further aid to standardization came about at this same time with the invention of that boon to administrators and academic bookkeepers, the credit point system. Academic credits were an answer to the need for assessing the value, in comparable terms, of the multitude of new subjects and courses which appeared on campus after campus as the elective system slowly displaced the solid core of linguistic and mathematical studies of earlier days. Credit points were also a logical extension of the growing practice of the high schools, which, in answer to demands from the universities, began to describe their work in terms of measurable units of time. This was achieved largely through the work of the Committee of Ten that was created in 1892 under the chairmanship of President Eliot and made its final report in 1899. The high school principal could now say: Our boys and girls have successfully completed the following sixteen units, each unit representing five forty-minute class periods a week for thirty-eight or forty weeks—three in English, three in mathematics, two in a foreign language, two in science, one in history, and the other five in miscellaneous subjects. The subjects and proportions might vary a bit from state to state, but, once again, a standard practice had been evolved.

If the high school thus explained itself to the university, why should not the university explain its requirements to the high school in the same quantitative terms? Appropriately enough it was at Michigan, the state university which from the beginning had thought of itself as the apex of the public school system, that the practice began. The Michigan catalogue of 1892 for the first time added those little Arabic numerals in parentheses to the course descriptions, soon to be used in nearly all college and university catalogues.[5] One credit hour was to be awarded for the satisfactory completion of the work of one period a week, usually fifty minutes in length, for one semester. After four years of this and with a hundred and twenty credits—more or less—the senior was duly recommended by the faculty for the bachelor's degree. Then it occurred to someone that the week, excluding Sundays, divided itself into two equal dovetailing parts, so that half the courses could be run on Mondays, Wednesdays, and Fridays and the other half on Tuesdays, Thursdays, and Saturdays, each for three points credit. Here was a uniform measuring device for all the mushrooming courses and departments and schools that were swamping the academic world and threatening it with chaos. Small wonder that college after college adopted the Michigan system or a related one, to achieve orderly housekeeping and statistical symmetry.[6]

The growth in numbers and multiplication of functions called for building programs of hitherto undreamed-of magnitude. More classrooms and laboratories were needed, more library shelves and dormitory space, bigger and better gymnasiums and stadiums, offices for administration and faculty, space to house the expanding clerical staffs and store the accumulating records. When Dean Van Amringe of Columbia College retired in 1910, he handed over all the records of his office to his successor in one large brown envelope. Down to 1892 Franklin B. Dexter of Yale was secretary to the Corporation, assistant librarian, professor of American history, and registrar of the college. In his spare time he wrote important works on the early history of Yale. "Had he returned in 1950 he would have found his functions requiring the services of five professors of American history, a whole registrar's office, two associate librarians and a dozen department heads—to say nothing of the staffs for reference, circulation, and cataloguing—and finally the University Secretary with his office staff, the Clerical Bureau, News Bureau, Alumni Records Office, and assorted stenographic services."[7]

What happened at Yale was happening in varying degrees on all campuses. As a result there now began a tremendous expansion of the physical plant, made possible by the munificence of captains of industry in steel, oil, soap, automobiles, and tobacco, or by appropriations of state legislatures or federal grants. The advance was not at all even. Illustrating once again that to him that hath shall be given, Harvard, Columbia, Chicago, and a few others, were adding building to building with apparently little strain, so that Harper of Chicago, for example, could loftily protest: "I don't ask for money. I offer opportunities." [8] At a respectful distance behind the leaders followed hundreds of smaller institutions. In many of these, modest college yards grew into far-flung university campuses where a bewildering agglomeration of Romanesque arches, Tudor mullions, and Georgian façades completely overshadowed the chaste simplicity of the original college hall together with the simple philosophy that had flourished there. University authorities received these blessings with mingled gratitude and apprehension, for the donor of a building acquired a leverage that might become powerful enough to dictate policy. It was just such a policy dispute over a $2,000,000 bequest that catapulted Woodrow Wilson out of the presidency of Princeton and onto the national scene. There are those who maintain that somewhere in the process of expansion American higher education lost its soul.[9] If it did, it was in the attempt, so characteristically American, to build more stately mansions.

If it has not already been done, a sociological study ought to be made of the history of American architecture, using university campuses as laboratories. There the fat and the lean years are as distinctly recorded as in the annual rings of the giant redwoods, by the style of architecture that predominates. They are all on view, from the colonial Georgian of the oldest building, through Greek revival, on to the red-brown arches and slit windows of Henry Hobson Richardson, to other Victorian adaptations, to the Tudor Gothic of Ralph Adams Cram, the second round of pink-and-white Georgian, and finally the severe "functional" glass-and-concrete structures of the present; to make no mention of those monstrosities that have been variously described as railroad depot and firehouse style, French-and-Indian renaissance, and Custer's last stand. Unlike business and industry, where profits are the chief determinant, universities cannot so readily tear down the old just because the new is more efficient. Sentiment plays a part too, and alumni may be heard from if ruthless hands are laid on sacred halls. As for functionalism, virtually every new style was recommended in its day as both functionally and esthetically superior to the one immediately preceding it.[10] We can expect this to happen again. The next generation will shake its head over the stark austerity and lack of beauty and ornamentation in mid-twentieth century structures, and will regard our glass-and-aluminum slabs with the same sophisticated condescension that we now bestow on the Tudor and Georgian frills of the generation before ours.

Insofar as the university is an agency of research and investigation, it will from time to time need new kinds of structures in which to carry on its work most efficiently. The cyclotron cannot be housed in the same quarters as the old philosophical cabinet. Libraries must provide for microfilm, and classrooms for television screens. A library erected merely as a monument to its donor or to fill in one side of a quadrangle is likely to prove a disappointment. Light, air, and warmth are conducive to scholarship. More than one student who failed an examination might have crawled over the passing mark if the ventilation had been better. Just because medieval scholars were uncomfortable in their authentic medieval lecture halls, we have no call to neglect the findings of modern engineering science when building ours. On the other hand the university, or at any rate the liberal arts college from which it springs, is also the bearer of the cultural tradition of the race. As such, it is concerned with enduring human values. Would it not be proper therefore for a liberal arts college to select an enduring historic style, any style, that has been associated with higher learning through the ages and is regionally appropriate, provide it with the necessary modern conveniences, and stick to it? Is variety quaint or discordant, and is symmetry pleasing or monotonous?

While the multiplication of buildings went on at an impressive rate, an even greater expansion occurred in the curriculum. Mute testimony to the proliferation of courses and subjects is offered in the annual catalogues.[11] The Yale catalogue for 1829 managed to include the entire four-year course of study in one page; in 1955 it took two hundred pages to list the undergraduate courses of study. First among the subjects of instruction to benefit from the post-Darwin and post-Eliot expansion were the sciences. Course offerings were multiplying and nomenclature was changing, too, as the continuous accumulation of data and growing specialization everywhere led to the establishment of new chairs of teaching and research, while the academic "settee" of pre-Darwinian days, whose occupant taught all the science there was, went on its way to the pedagogical junk pile. The omnibus designations of natural philosophy, natural history, mental and moral philosophy, had about disappeared from the catalogues by 1890, to be replaced by the now familiar departmental categories: chemistry, physics, geology, zoology, psychology, each of these again subdividing according to the size and complexity of the institution. When Francis Snow went out to Kansas to join the faculty of the new state university in 1866, he was assigned the conventional teaching field of mathematics and natural philosophy, which comprised about one fourth of the whole curriculum. Thirty years later, as an experienced teacher and renowned specialist, he was responsible for only a small segment of this field, being now "professor of entomology and organic evolution." [12]

Parallel expansion and subdivision were taking place in English literature, the modern languages, history, and political economy. English literature, which had customarily included about everything from Shakespeare to Tennyson in one course, was broken down into period courses dealing with such limited topics as Chaucer, the Elizabethans, the Restoration, and the Romantic age. French and German literature were similarly split up. History was subdivided, separate courses appearing in the catalogue offerings on Greece and Rome, the Middle Ages, the Renaissance and Reformation; or else it was organized along national lines, such as England and the British Empire, and of course various periods and aspects of American history.

Thus higher education was in its own development illustrating Herbert Spencer's famous definition of evolution as a whole: Its curriculum was passing "from an indefinite, incoherent homogeneity to a definite, coherent heterogeneity," and was doing so amid a considerable "dissipation of motion." [13]

With the multiplication of departments and course offerings came an increase in the number of electives, ranging from the complete freedom of choice of Harvard and Cornell or the group elections of Hopkins and Stanford to the few alternative choices reluctantly conceded by the remaining classical strongholds. A transitional structure maintained by most colleges and leading ultimately to the now familiar major-minor system was that of three separate schools or divisions: the classical, the scientific, and the literary, with the three corresponding degrees of A.B., B.S., and Ph.B. or Litt.B. The first of these was the old college, the other two were frills or concessions to philistinism. But Greek and Latin were moribund, and the future lay with the philistines. Grudgingly, incredulously, the votaries of the classics saw their claims to mental discipline and precision of thought appropriated by the cocky scientists, while the mantle of the genteel tradition was coming to rest on the shoulders of the burgeoning departments of English literature.

For a time the English departments wore their new honors with diffidence. To raise *Beowulf* to the stature of the *Iliad* and to supplant Sophocles with Shakespeare or Aristophanes with Restoration drama took some doing. But no such false humility plagued the scientists. Darwin had furnished them with a rationale, and in their new laboratories they were working out dependable techniques. These laboratories were now forthcoming, for a large part of the wealth that alumni and business philanthropists were beginning to lavish on the universities was, if not needed for a football stadium, being channeled into the science departments. From Harvard to Stanford and from Michigan to Tulane the sciences were now being supported in a style to which they had not been accustomed. The dingy philosophical cabinets and the routine lecture-demonstrations by the professor of natural history had vanished into the paleozoic past, while now in modern surroundings the undergraduates "got glimpses of the passion and confidence of science in a day when it seemed that all wisdom as well as all knowledge was to be its province." [14]

Here again the larger institutions were more fortunate than the more modest ones remote from the centers of wealth and publicity. As far back as 1865, Allegheny College in western Pennsylvania had boasted some electrical equipment, a stock of chemicals, "the greater part of which has been imported from Paris and Berlin," and an eleven-thousand-specimen fossil collection which was about to be added; twenty-seven years later the college catalogue mentioned the same items plus two new ones: a phonograph and a double stereopticon. But the twentieth century saw vigorous expansion and modernization at Allegheny too. President Hyde of Bowdoin complained in 1892 that the chemistry laboratory, once a source of pride as one of the oldest and best in the country, was sadly out of date; that it was high time to begin to teach physics by the laboratory method, and that if something drastic was not done soon the Brunswick high school would have better equipment than Bowdoin College. He got a new science building the next year. Stirrings in the war-impoverished South are reflected in a report of President Crowell of Trinity (now Duke University) in 1888. In it Crowell urged that even a Christian classical college must make room for the new sciences that were making the road to graduation quite different from that of fifty or even thirty years earlier. He would establish new subject matter departments; beyond that he appealed to the faculty to serve the larger public by lectures, writing, and research, to give intellectual guidance to the community and to take the lead in movements of social reform. Unfortunately the professors who were to initiate the new program had been sharing an annual deficit and, though entitled to salaries of $1,000, had actually been living during the past decade on incomes that ranged from $231 to $550 a year.[15] The munificence of Benjamin F. Duke eventually helped the college over this difficulty.

But the ferment spread beyond the physical and biological branches. Nowhere was the proliferation of subject matter and the trend toward specialization more in evidence than in the social sciences. Though the term social sciences, which in itself marks the beginning of a return to integration, did not gain currency until later in the twentieth century, the area of teaching and research that it was to include had been staked out and its subdivisions defined before the end of the nineteenth. History, no longer a matter of chronology or an aspect of literature, was receiving a new, twofold orientation from the *Quellenstudium* of the German scholar and the organic evolutionary approach of Herbert Spencer. All this did not change immediately and completely. Many an institution continued to boast of men like Arthur Wheeler, dramatic professor of European history at Yale, who drew overflow audiences to his annual hero-worshiping lecture on the battle of Waterloo until 1911. Some students went to hear it every year they were in college. But Wheeler and his kind were about to give way to a new breed of historians who were being trained in a series of lively seminars conducted after the manner of the German universities by various scholars named Adams. As the products of these seminars began to find their way into college positions the country over, the emphasis in the teaching and writing of history shifted from the mere narrative of events to the verification of sources, the search for causes, and the organic development of institutions. Henceforth the soaring passages of the dramatic lecturer would be anchored down by footnotes.[16]

Government, long a by-product of history, was establishing itself in its own right, and political economy, itself an offshoot of the old moral philosophy course, was tightening its structure, sharpening its focus, and, in the hands of such men as Ely of Hopkins (later Wisconsin), Taussig of Harvard, and Patten of Pennsylvania, was becoming economics. Last of the group to gain academic respectability was sociology, still a little starry-eyed and inclined to claim the world as its oyster. When Lester Ward, founder of the discipline in America, was appointed to the newly created chair of sociology at Brown in 1906, he offered as his principal course "A Survey of All Knowledge." William Graham Sumner, Yale's pioneer sociologist, had little reverence for tradition. When on one occasion the Yale faculty was about to rehabilitate the disorganized philosophy department, Sumner's advice was to abolish the department entirely as an anachronism on a par with astrology. "We might as well have professors of alchemy or fortune telling." But then, sociology was charting new courses and had little ballast of its own. Edward A. Ross, for example, pioneer sociologist with service at Stanford, Nebraska, and Wisconsin, never had an hour's instruction in sociology as either an undergraduate or a graduate student. He took his Ph.D. in economics at Johns Hopkins under Ely. Neither Ross nor Ward, by the way, subscribed to Sumner's Spencerian dog-eat-dog philosophy of extreme *laissez faire,* but showed deep concern for problems of social welfare.[17]

Not satisfied with breaking new ground, the students of society tried to emulate the physical and biological scientists by creating a new vocabulary to fit new concepts. An extremist in this respect, Lester Ward tried to acclimatize such synthetic terms as karyokinesis, tocogenesis, and ampheclexis, which meant romantic love. Most of these mercifully died in infancy. But other men produced more lasting additions. In his epoch-making study of the psychology of adolescence G. Stanley Hall, president of Clark University, is said to have introduced four hundred new words into the language. As long as the supply of new facts and concepts kept pace with the output of new terms, there was sense in this expansion of the vocabulary, but each new enthusiastic coiner of words increased the danger of runaway inflation.[18] Unlike the natural scientists, who were forced by a host of new discoveries to create a new and precise vocabulary, the social scientists dealt with human society, which can more readily be discussed in everyday language, and whose changing issues and values do not lend themselves to definitions and labels as precise as H_2SO_4 is to a chemist or, for that matter, a grand-slam home run to a baseball fan. To some extent the specialists in literature were also concocting a special vocabulary of their own though perfectly good words of general usage were already available. The result of all this was gobbledegook. And professors were not the only offenders. Gobbledegook is known in business and government. One is reminded of the placards displayed in New York City shops and offices during the second world war, which read something like this: Illumination is required to be extinguished when these premises are vacated at the conclusion of business. What they meant to say was: Turn out the lights when you shut up shop.

Symptomatic of the substitution of new values for old was the disappearance of compulsory chapel. On campus after campus this venerable rite of an all-college religious service conducted by the president now went into the discard. A multipurpose institution, it had always been more than a service of worship. Chapel was an information center, an instrument of discipline, and a rallying point for morale. First to give it up were the newer state universities where the student body was religiously heterogeneous. The decentralized nature of university life had much to do with its disappearance. With engineers going off to class in one direction, agricultural students in another, and the classical contingent in a third, and with students living in rooming houses all over town, it became difficult if not physically impossible to find a time or a place for daily or even weekly chapel meetings which all could be required to attend.

Wisconsin began it, abolishing the compulsory feature in 1869, and within the next quarter-century other state universities followed suit.[19] Cornell eliminated the requirement as a matter of educational policy. The Johns Hopkins catalogue announced chapel for every morning at 8:45 and added: "No notice will be taken of the presence or absence of anybody." [20] Of the older universities with religious antecedents, Harvard was the first to make the break. In 1886, after having presented the Lord with a captive student audience for two hundred and fifty years, the oldest American university gave up the practice. At Yale, where graduating seniors regularly voted in favor of retaining it, the compulsory feature continued for another fifty years, to 1926, and at Princeton it lasted still longer. At Columbia compulsory chapel ended in 1891, through the action of President Seth Low.[21]

The vacuum was filled, in most cases, by a voluntary religious service conducted by various members of the faculty and administration, or featuring a sermon by prominent preachers and public figures from the outside world. Though valiant and intelligent efforts were made by university chaplains and professors of religion to make these services attractive with the aid of excellent music and well-trained student choirs, often in impressive auditoriums or memorial chapels, the results were disappointing. Attendance diminished, sometimes to the vanishing point. This was the almost universal experience, for the religious unity of the old college was gone. Chapel preachers faced a dilemma. If they preached positive sermons of strong convictions, they risked the charge of narrow dogmatism and unsuitable partisanship; if on the other hand they strove to find a common denominator of all faiths, the result was likely to be a thin ethical broth of washed-out platitudes. Of course, they could always talk on current social problems. There have been distinguished exceptions, especially in those institutions that have remained under direct church control and where the old rite still lives and flourishes, but generally speaking college chapel in the old sense is defunct.

In other ways, too, secularism was in the ascendant, and accelerated the transition from old to new. With the increase of vocational and "practical" studies, the cash value of a college education was more apparent than ever before, and the A.B. degree became the magic key to open all doors to material success. A college degree had always been a badge of status and carried certain prestige. Now specific economic values were added. It was material success rather than scholarship or character that now began to attract the multitudes. The older eastern institutions set the pace, as usual. Princeton students, vigorous and lusty, were not very studious but eager for advancement and success. Woodrow Wilson, introducing the preceptorial system there, tried to create respect for scholarship among the undergraduates.[22]

Yale, still the guide and mentor for scores of inland colleges, was also caught up in the new drift. Strenuous, loyal, and conformist, Yale men expected the richest material rewards that the booming country had to offer, and college was the means to this end. About their studies they were somewhat less than enthusiastic. Let Harvard go in for that sort of thing. There was a complacent belief that Harvard intellectuals after graduation found themselves working for Yale men. The Yale campus was energy itself, with no lassitude anywhere except in the classroom. There, as Henry Seidel Canby of the class of '99 saw it, "we could sit and sit while ideas about evolution or Shakespeare dropped upon us like the gentle rain from heaven, which seeped in or evaporated according to our mental temperatures." Brilliant professors like Lounsbury and Sumner were completely frustrated by undergraduate indifference. An all-time low in scholarship was reached at Yale in the first decade of the twentieth century, then intellectual interests again came out of hiding, oddly enough at about the same time that Yale's football primacy was coming to an end.[23]

Elsewhere in the country the anti-intellectual phase sometimes expressed itself in widespread rowdyism. Not that student pranks or riots were anything new, for all the older colleges had had their share. But now they were appearing in the new universities, which had prided themselves on their seriousness of purpose and freedom from adolescent horseplay. At Michigan, which among other things set itself up now as the fashion arbiter for college clothes, town and gown riots repeatedly got out of hand. Stanford, for all its interest in research and scholarship, suffered from seasons of drunkenness and rioting which led, in 1908, to the expulsion of forty-one students. A nightshirt parade of male undergraduates at Wisconsin in 1899 broke into a women's dormitory and stole coeds' clothes, in what may well have been the first "panty raid" in the history of American higher education. The girls, perhaps taking their cue from Aristophanes, retaliated by refusing all social invitations until the offenders were punished and the losses made good.[24]

It would be unfair to draw sweeping conclusions as to the low character of student life from these admittedly sporadic occurrences. Then, as at all times, there were serious, dependable students in all institutions. In fact these complained, at Wisconsin, Princeton, and elsewhere, that facts were being distorted and rowdyism exaggerated by sensation-hungry newspapers. Yet, when all due allowance has been made, the evidence is overwhelming that intellectual interests on American campuses at the turn of the century were far from satisfactory.

There was also widespread evidence that cheating, that perennial campus evil, was flourishing once again. All the familiar dodges were in use: bootlegged translations of the classics, direct copying from texts or notes during examinations, burglaring of examination questions in advance, and files of past examinations and term papers in dormitories and fraternity houses. Faculties, some of them, wrestled manfully with the problem but without much success. The supposed moral influence of religion does not seem to have been very effective, for some of the most lurid forms of cheating were prevalent in church colleges. The evil could be curbed and kept under varying degrees of control, but apparently it could not be eradicated. Many campuses talked about the honor system, that device of the University of Virginia whereby a student's pledge as a gentleman of honest performance rendered proctoring and penalties unnecessary, but few adopted it. Among the few were Oberlin, Ohio Wesleyan, which tried it for twenty years and then gave it up, and Princeton, where the faculty adopted it in 1893 upon recommendation of the student newspaper and where it has been successfully practiced ever since.[25] Women's colleges have been unusually successful in maintaining bona fide honor systems. They are relatively new and not burdened with sinful traditions. There were, then, encouraging exceptions. By and large, however, faculties and administrations took a fatalistic attitude. Cheating, they felt, was endemic, a disease which should be checked but which would always be there.

With the breakdown of the old controls came "activities." As intellectual and spiritual unity vanished and guidance weakened, students devised their own pastimes and gradually evolved that mélange of entertainment, self-improvement, community service, and busy work which came to be dignified as extracurricular activities—the sideshows of which Woodrow Wilson complained. As long as students sat in the same classes together, met daily in chapel for instruction and reproof, shared common study hours in a common dormitory, and grumblingly observed—or surreptitiously violated—the same code of behavior, there was not much room for anything extracurricular. But when all this was replaced by the heterogeneous university, the new activities came into their own. From then on, incoming students on most campuses were encouraged not only by upperclassmen but by their deans and faculty advisers to find an activity beyond their studies through which they might become socially adjusted and develop a sense of mature personal responsibility. Let them "heel" or "buck" for the student newspaper or literary magazine; let them try to make an athletic team or the glee club, let them become campus politicians and go in for a career in student government; or let them undertake some profit-making service to pay their college bills. Whatever the area selected, there the student should try to become as much of a BMOC—Big Man on Campus—as it was in him to be.

The function and value of these sideshows in the general process of higher education continued to be one of the liveliest subjects of debate among educational leaders. A few would have liked to abolish them lock, stock, and barrel; many found them useful but only if kept subordinated to the main show; others gloomily predicted that the sideshows would soon swallow up the circus; and some complacently proclaimed that they should. Unquestionably they have produced a new kind of student in a new kind of college. Of the many types of extracurricular life that American campuses have spawned, only two will be examined here: secret fraternities and organized athletics. The first was regarded with apprehension by faculties and administrations, the second usually with pleasure and gratification.

College fraternities are of long standing, but their purpose and character have changed. For completeness the story should begin with the founding of Phi Beta Kappa at William and Mary in 1776. This of course was an honor society, not a social fraternity in the conventional sense. Though provided with grip and password and a stately ritual, Phi Beta Kappa was and is for the intellectual elite, and its membership is carefully limited to students of demonstrated and certified scholarly excellence. Nothing else is required, and there is no other way to get in. The national social fraternities date back to the second decade of the nineteenth century. In 1825 Kappa Alpha was founded at Union College, and Sigma Phi and Delta Phi followed two years later, on the same campus. These three were known as the Union triad. From there the practice spread. In the competitive scramble which followed, certain fraternities emerged as the stronger and managed to establish chapters in many institutions. But the founding of new societies continued into the twentieth century.[26]

The extraordinary success and universal vogue of fraternities and sororities in American college and university life are due to a complex of social and economic causes which require more analysis than is possible here. A few obvious explanations suggest themselves. The exclusiveness, the shared secrecy, and the thrill of solemn vows appealed to adolescents. They did not appeal to deans and professors, responsible for the good of the whole. The fraternity movement, furthermore, was the campus version of the general American passion for joining something that promised exclusiveness, drama, and ritual, as well as occasions for exhibitionism in outlandish costume, all by way of compensation for the drabness of democracy. The fraternities did not have all smooth sailing at first. There was opposition, even among students. This grew so strong in the days of the political anti-Masonic movement as to produce some antisecret societies. One of these, founded at Williams in 1834, was acclimated and regularized eventually as Delta Upsilon, the one nonsecret national fraternity.

Some institutions managed to stave off or at any rate to reduce the influence of the national organizations. Harvard and Yale developed their own rather intricate and uniquely different system of honor societies and social clubs, and the national fraternities have never had chapters there. At Princeton a determined president and faculty suppressed them in 1875. Meanwhile innocent little eating clubs had appeared with faculty consent. These in time became such an incubus that President Wilson set as one of his first tasks the conversion of the eating clubs into more democratic organizations for group living in whose advantages all could share. But for all his prestige and enthusiasm, Wilson was unable to reform or remove these vested interests. The whole weight of alumni displeasure came down on his head, and he met his first defeat.[27] In recent years much progress toward democratization has come through student action.

The secret societies found the midwestern and southern state universities made to order. They existed at Michigan as early as the 1840's, and the first legitimate fraternity house was built on the Michigan campus in 1880. The first sorority there dates from 1879. College sororities in general go back to the fifties. At Ohio State, Oklahoma, and elsewhere, they got in on the ground floor, appearing soon after the first classes opened. They might not have grown so powerful had the trustees of the most rapidly growing universities built dormitories to keep pace with the rising tide of enrollments. But dormitories were expensive, and some university administrators doubted their value. In university towns like Ann Arbor owners of student rooming houses organized lobbies to fight against legislative appropriations for dormitories, successfully staving them off until World War II. The segmentation of student life resulting from such neglect widened the gap between rich and poor, playboy and grind, and was made to order for fraternities, sororities, and special-interest groups of every description.[28]

Fraternities had a blighting effect on the old literary and debating societies which had offered such a wide field for intellectual interests and student initiative. This was not a coincidence; there were causal connections. Bowdoin felt the blight, and Amherst and Princeton, and state universities, too. Princeton tried to stay the decline of its famous societies, Clio and Whig, by rebuilding their two Ionic temples in grander style. But even though they now dwelt in marble halls, the debating clubs did not recover their former vigor or prestige. Social fragmentation and the quest for material success were too strong. Wisconsin managed to keep the interest alive a little longer than most schools. There the winner of the intercollegiate speaking contest was still in the 1880's hailed as a campus hero, like the captain of the football team a few decades later. But then not every university could produce debaters of the quality of Wisconsin's champion, Robert M. LaFollette. Partly through LaFollette's continuing interest in the university, partly because of a group of unusually able social scientists on the faculty, student debating continued and maintained a high standard into the third decade of the twentieth century.[29]

With the exception of athletics, no issue of modern campus life has stirred up more controversy than fraternities. Defenders of the system still point out the advantages that derive from the association of small groups of like-minded young people, the social polish they acquire, the sense of group responsibility that is engendered, and the loyalties that continue long after college. Such educational values, they say, are worth cultivating and maintaining. To which the critics reply: If these values are so great, why confine them to the privileged few who already have more than their share of the good things of life and are the only ones who can afford to join fraternities? Why not extend these benefits to everybody? Furthermore, say the critics, the fraternity system widens economic and social barriers and creates false values. When a potentially good student goes home in despair because he has failed to be pledged by the society on which he, or his father, had set his heart, something is radically wrong. The social stigma attached to such failure works even more havoc among coeds. The power of the alumni, who usually hold financial control, is unsound. Conservative to the point of reaction, alumni governors of national fraternities and sororities have curtailed the freedom of action of the current undergraduate membership, who are likely to be more socially aware than their elders and willing to take constructive action to reform the evils. Such behavior by the older generation is altogether inconsistent with the philosophy of a nation that prides itself on its democracy and wants to be the leader of the free world. And so the argument goes on.[30] One may reasonably suppose that the national leadership of the secret societies, aware of the widespread criticism, will move to abolish the evils, if the critics are proved right, and to convert the fraternities and sororities into a force for individual and social good, as they were intended to be.

Best known to the layman of all the activities of educational institutions are their athletic programs. Colleges and universities are likely to be rated and classified in the popular mind according to the prowess of their football teams. When track and field contests, and all the other modern competitive team sports and games which are now included in the term athletics, began to filter in to the campuses soon after the middle of the nineteenth century, they were welcomed by administrations and faculties as a useful aid in the solution of the problem of discipline. Along with gymnastics, which was also becoming popular—Amherst was the first, in 1860, to arrange formal work in physical education under a member of the faculty—they promised a harmless outlet for adolescent animal energy, which had hitherto been largely dissipated in hazing, class fights, and the cruder forms of horseplay. Thus President Crowell of Trinity College in Durham sanctioned the introduction of football there as a "bulwark against social and individual vices incident to collegiate student life." His concern was so great that he coached the first team himself and led it to victory over "the Chapel Hill Eleven." [31] Though the president might occasionally take a hand at helping the cause along, the management of athletics was, on the whole, left to the boys. They found a suitable location, sometimes with the aid of trustees who provided a convenient pasture, secured the necessary equipment, set up conditions and methods of play, formulated and changed the rules with great freedom in the light of experience.

The most popular sports in order of appearance between about 1855 and 1895 were rowing, baseball, football, and basketball. The first had British antecedents. It was at a Boston City Regatta that the Harvard crew, to identify their shell among the many entries, tied bright crimson silk handkerchiefs around their heads and thus initiated the practice of distinctive college colors. The other three sports bore little resemblance to the polished and highly organized activities they have become today. Baseball regularly ran up astronomic scores of 63 to 48 and the like. There were no gloves, and the pitcher had not yet learned the overhand throw or experimented with speed and curves. The first intercollegiate football games, like the one between Princeton and Rutgers in 1869, were mob scenes with twenty players, more or less, on each side. There was no throwing or running with the ball. It was really soccer with pugilistic trimmings. The ball was of black rubber and round. Play often lasted from noon to dark. Meanwhile Harvard and Yale were putting their heads together to standardize the game, coming up eventually with a hybrid that was a cross between soccer and English rugby, out of which the present American football evolved. The team of eleven men, according to Harvard's historian, was an accident. McGill University of Canada was coming down to Cambridge to play Harvard in 1874. At the last moment four of its team of fifteen were unable to leave Montreal. Such things as substitutes, second-stringers, and a bench were then unheard of. So Harvard obligingly dropped four of its own players, the two teams played with eleven on a side and that became the rule.[32]

It was of course the competitive element in athletics that gave it status and prestige. Higher education was itself competitive, just like the economic system, and it was the most natural thing in the world for American colleges to try to excel among their peers. One might suppose that the real yardstick for comparative excellence would be intellectual; and often it was. But this kind of competition left something to be desired, for it was not conclusive. The evidence for intellectual or, for that matter, ethical and esthetic superiority could not always be interpreted with precision. But when you could pit the best nine or eleven men against your rival's best, under conditions agreed upon in advance and subject to the judgment of an impartial arbiter, superiority was clearly established. You can't argue with the final score. A tie game? Wait till next year. And so competitive sports became an oversimplified symbol and fetish for excellence. All the self-effacing loyalties of campus life, the pride of achievement, the nostalgia of alumni, were channeled into this one direction and in a flood of sentiment swept other values before it. At the annual homecoming game old grads stood awkwardly at attention while the strains of the alma mater song floated over the autumn hills, and even flippant sophomores felt the benison of something bigger than themselves. The words might be trite, the tune borrowed, but it bathed the world in a golden glow and stirred the old half-forgotten loyalties to new life.

Faculty and administration could not check the flood. Few tried and many rode along in full approval. Even the great university leaders at first welcomed the new trend. There were exceptions. Andrew Dickson White was not amused. When Michigan sent a challenge to Cornell for a football game to be played on neutral ground in Cleveland, in 1873, President White refused, saying: "I will not permit thirty men to travel four hundred miles merely to agitate a bag of wind." Eliot of Harvard, on the other hand, considered games and sports "of great advantage to the University" because they generated qualities in the students that had lasting values, were body- and character-building. President McCosh on his trips about the country to get students for Princeton mentioned athletic victories over Harvard and Yale as an inducement. Only when Princeton lost did he complain of overemphasis on athletics. In fact he allowed sports to rise to such a level of prestige that his successor, President Patton, felt it necessary to come out to watch football practice occasionally in order to scotch the "appalling rumor" that he was hostile to athletics. And Princeton's political science professor, Woodrow Wilson, helped coach the team, just as he had done when at Wesleyan.

Professors elsewhere lent a hand too. Vernon L. Parrington, later known as author of *Main Currents of American Thought,* coached the first football team of the University of Oklahoma. President Harper of Chicago, in being all things to all men, even resorted to the between-the-halves pep talk when his boys were at the short end of the score in a critical game with Wisconsin: "Boys, Mr. Rockefeller has just announced a gift of three million dollars to the University. He believes the University to be great. The way you played in the first half leads me to wonder whether we really have the spirit of greatness in ambition. I wish you would make up your minds to win this game and show that we do have it." David Starr Jordan was sports-minded himself and played on the faculty baseball team at Stanford until he was fifty-eight. He approved of Stanford's athletic program at first. In later years, dismayed by the growing commercialism and the coddling of athletes, he changed his opinion. But by that time matters had gone too far.[33]

Chief protagonist of intercollegiate football was Yale, where close-knit campus loyalties offered scope for the enthusiasm and organizing genius of Walter Camp. And President Hadley saw eye to eye with Camp. Just as Yale graduates had been sought out to be presidents and professors by colleges of the interior a generation earlier, so Yale football men were now top-heavy favorites to become coaches of the football teams in these same institutions and many newer ones besides. With this development football became a technique and coaching a profession, and the era of carefree sports, when students coached and managed the teams, perhaps with an obliging professor of English or political science lending a hand, came to an end. When Amos Alonzo Stagg, Yale '88, went out to the University of Chicago in 1893 as director of physical culture and athletics with professorial tenure, college sports entered the age of big business.[34] In the decade of the 1890's forty-five graduates of Yale, thirty-five of Princeton, and twenty-four of Harvard were teaching football in colleges the country over.

A final step in this transformation was the discovery that college games and especially football were interesting to watch, not only by students but by the general public. Football was becoming a spectator sport, for which thousands were willing to pay top prices. Harassed physical directors and university bursars saw undreamed-of sources of income which might render the whole physical education program self-sufficient, might in fact even pay for the upkeep of the new stadium, which would otherwise prove a white elephant and an endless drain on the precious university resources. In 1881 a Columbia-Harvard game at Cambridge before what was then considered a large crowd grossed all of $342.[35] Now the day was dawning when a "big-time" game between major teams would yield an income in six figures. The show must therefore go on, come blizzard or hurricane, especially when television contracts had been let. The original ideal of physical exercise for every student as an aid to his intellectual development was largely lost sight of. *Mens sana in corpore sano* was a remote echo.

Coaches now became more important than players. They gained faculty standing, their influence on the students exceeded that of most professors, and their salaries were often higher. The football coach was likely to be a good teacher, for he knew his subject and could impart it. Sometimes real educational values emerged. A fatherly coach might understand his boys better and show more human concern for their welfare than many of their classroom instructors. But the pressure to turn out winning teams made such relations difficult to maintain; here too the cynic might exclaim, with a recent manager of the New York Giants, that nice guys finish last. The urge to win made serious inroads on the vaunted spirit of fair play that college sports were supposed to engender. Meanwhile, as Stagg passed his magic on to Rockne and Rockne to a host of his disciples, and as Warner at Pittsburgh, Yost at Michigan, and Haughton at Harvard all developed systems of their own, football became an institution with traditions, legends, and a literature of its own. On some campuses the athletic board's decision to switch to the T formation was likely to cause wider comment than the trustees' choice of a new president or a faculty resolution launching an undergraduate honors program. A university president might be a world-renowned nuclear physicist, but that did not excuse him from the chore of crowning the queen of the ball after the annual homecoming game.[36]

As a form of big business, football developed its by-products and "fringe benefits." It provided endless copy for sports writers on metropolitan newspapers. It produced new activities and techniques, as for example that of the cheerleader, and new uses for existing ones, such as the intricate maneuvers of the university marching band between halves of a game. Hours of rehearsal were necessary to make the cheering section and the band letter-perfect in their antics, so indispensable to college spirit—and so incomprehensible to foreigners. To the French literary critic Charles Bourget, who was spending a year in the United States gathering data for the usual book of "impressions," the performance of the cheerleaders at a Harvard-Pennsylvania game in 1893, in the antediluvian days of bootball, was completely unintelligible. Football to his uninitiated eyes was a "fearful" game, the players "beasts of prey" scrimmaging in "murderous knots." Weirdest of all, however, were the "propagators of enthusiasm" roaring the war cry of the university, and all in the name of higher education.[37]

By the early twentieth century faculties and university authorities in general were showing concern over the Frankenstein they had so unwittingly created. Earlier complacency now gave way to real alarm. In the 1890's the president of Northwestern University could still report that competitive athletics, though becoming controversial, were on the whole a good thing and that at Northwestern they could be kept under control, for "in the West, college athletics have never been carried to the excess that has characterized the Eastern institutions."[38] President Jordan's growing alarm at Stanford was soon shared by many others, and from that day to this university faculties have attempted to find ways and means of bringing athletics under control and restoring their original purpose. Some abuses were corrected. Through faculty action on individual campuses, coupled with the efforts of self-policing regional associations like the Big Ten, eligibility rules were established. In the good old days "students" played on the varsity for six and seven years, and university teams were riddled with professionals.[39] To end this abuse the freshman rule was adopted, and minimum standards of grades were set up. But the problem continued unabated. Athletes learned the short cuts. Somehow, eligibility rules were constantly having to be tightened, or loosened, as the case might be. Real reform was made difficult by sports writers and by alumni, who, in the words of Chancellor Hutchins of the University of Chicago, played "a weird and often-times terrifying role" in university affairs.[40] The alumni, to be sure, might retort to the faculty: Why did you let us get these false values in the four years you had us under your influence?

Those who would remedy this state of affairs must begin by facing a fundamental question: Is the university an educational institution or is it in the entertainment business? Once this question is properly answered, a number of things will follow. Athletic scholarships of all kinds, including every form of under-the-counter subsidy, will be abolished, and the university agents and alumni scouts who now beat the bushes and the mining towns of Pennsylvania for healthy flesh will have to find something else to do. Parents who now boast openly of the number of athletic subsidies their high school senior son has been offered will need to have the real meaning of a college education explained to them. The specious argument that the abolition of athletic scholarships means discrimination against athletes will be shown up for the nonsense it is; for scholarships, *if* universities are educational institutions, can in fairness be based only on such criteria as comparative scholastic achievement, superior intelligence, and promise of social usefulness, mental independence, and creative productivity—all this combined, of course, with evidence of financial need. How many touchdowns the lad scored in high school is irrelevant. If students who have been properly selected choose, in their spare time in college, to play football or basketball, fine! Interest in competitive sports is normal for healthy young men. But they will no longer be commercially exploited or publicly exhibited for such purposes.

A few institutions have managed to resist the pressure of big-time athletics and to keep the game in the hands of the students, thus saving themselves much trouble and keeping their purposes clear and their energies intact for the main business of education. These are usually small institutions where a slim purse has re-enforced a virtuous purpose. But some of the larger universities of considerable prestige have avoided involvement. Johns Hopkins is a notable example. More difficult and requiring greater courage is the decision to withdraw from such competition after having played a leading role. Prominent among those who have done so is the University of Chicago, which thought matters through and dropped out of the Big Ten. In the East, Fordham University in New York, with an "enviable" record in football, made a similar decision. Others found the solution in a policy like that of Washington University in St. Louis, which abolished all forms of athletic subsidies and preferences in 1946 and went completely amateur. In spite of its self-denying policy, Washington has for the past ten years carried on a lively and diversified athletic program, and has attracted some of the finest coaches in the country.[41]

Still another suggestion is sometimes made, half facetiously but with a serious undertone, for the guidance of institutions that would like to be simon-pure scholastically, and yet find themselves so financially involved that they need to continue to draw revenue from their costly stadium and retain the good will of their public: If a university wants to be both an educational institution and in the entertainment business, let it openly hire athletes as cities in organized baseball hire ballplayers, make them the varsity team and continue playing the usual schedule to the usual admission. But these men would not be required to attend any classes and would not be given a degree. They would not be students or officers of the university but employees, rendering service for pay like janitors and stenographers. The same enthusiasm could be generated for the team, and without hypocrisy; for one can become attached to a team of hired players as well as to one's own tuition-paying fellow students. The pageantry and suspense and drama of a great spectacle would all be retained. Over the years such teams as the Brooklyn Dodgers and the St. Louis Cardinals have called forth intense and unshakeable loyalties. Except for the fact that the field of professional sports has been pretty well preempted, this proposal might have some merit.[42]

There are phenomena that appear at an early and relatively primitive stage of a culture, reach their zenith, and then, as the culture grows more mature and sophisticated, slowly slough off and disappear. College athletics may be following this pattern. At any rate there is some indication that they have passed their prime in the very institutions where they first appeared. The seeds of disintegration may have been sown back in the 1920's, when Henry L. Mencken of the *American Mercury,* bible of all college radicals in those days, reviewed Percy Haughton's book, *Football and How to Watch It,* in one sentence: "But why watch it?" Today the Ivy League is beginning to "de-emphasize" football. It has raised its scholastic requirements for membership on varsity teams, has abolished spring football training and generally tightened controls. Perhaps these Atlantic seaboard universities of colonial origins have discovered that other paths to greatness are more rewarding. A good many years have elapsed since Yale could claim the mythical national championship, but in these years it has become a university of international repute and no longer needs football to bolster its ego. The same can be said in varying degrees of the other Ivy schools. The football scepter meantime has moved west and south where newer schools are going through the kind of athletic phase that Yale and Princeton suffered half a century ago. A decade or two hence we may expect the student bodies of these present-day football powers to emphasize other values besides blocking and forward passing.

In spite of the time and effort diverted to fraternity initiations, junior proms, and bowl games and other Hollywoodish frills many institutions recorded solid educational achievement in these transitional years. The large universities were in a better position to absorb or ignore the sideshows and to offer intellectual adventure to those of their students who, in the gilded age, could discern the real gold. Professors were beginning to come off their perch and to discover that their students were people; students meanwhile were making the same discovery in reverse. A Charles Townsend Copeland of Harvard and a William Lyon Phelps of Yale had their counterparts on many campuses. The first dawn of a literary renaissance at Yale coincided with the decline of its football fortunes.[43] The age of Haughton, the big-time coach, and Brickley, the drop-kick artist, was also, however, a time of high intellectual achievement at Harvard, which had assembled a brilliant body of scholars and lecturers. Harvard also had the most heterogeneous student body in the country, and this combination made for an exciting time. " 'My roommate,' said Rollo Walter Brown, a student at that time, 'was a German Catholic from Ohio; another close friend was a Quaker from Pennsylvania; another was a Mormon from Utah; one was a Presbyterian from Indiana; two were pure pioneers from the Dakotas; another was from Iowa; another from Virginia; another from Japan; another from France; another from Bulgaria. . . .' "[44] Such were the students. The professors were men like James and Santayana in philosophy, Copeland and Kittredge in English, Channing and Turner in history, Taussig in economics, and Shaler in geology. Harvard was by no means unique. In these same decades, Lounsbury and Sumner at Yale, Giddings and Robinson at Columbia, Wilson at Princeton, McMaster at Pennsylvania, Dewey at Chicago, Ross and Ely at Wisconsin, Fling at Nebraska, Parrington and Smith at Washington, and many, many others were offering a variety of opportunity and stimulus. The university was beginning to be all things to all men.

To make sweeping generalizations about it was, as it is today, a hazardous undertaking. But sweeping generalizations were being made, nonetheless, and some of them were highly critical. In the light of such criticism and of radical changes in the structure of society in the twentieth century, the colleges and universities entered a period of self-examination which resulted in widespread reorganization in curriculum and method.

Chapter Ten

Dewey vs. Hutchins

~~~~~~

If the colleges and universities, as they entered the twentieth century, had some of the aspects of a variety show, they were merely reflecting American life as a whole. With the utmost confidence in the future Americans were still advancing in many directions and taking up any occupation or activity that suited their fancy. Individually or in organized groups, they were exploiting the resources of the continent and converting them into ever greater comforts and luxuries for themselves. This was known as progress. Similarly, in the institutions of higher education, choices and opportunities were multiplying, but the sense of direction was weak. The student could, if he came with a serious purpose, find much to challenge him to solid achievement; but he could also lose himself in busy work or, attracted by the glitter and the tinsel, come out with a tawdry counterfeit of a real education. Such a state of affairs could last as long as America's happy-go-lucky age, and no longer. That age, once reportedly characterized by a European statesman as one in which God takes care of fools, drunks, and the United States, was now drawing to a close. An unthinkable world war shattered national complacency; and at its close the country plunged into a decade of escapism and make-believe. There followed an economic and social upheaval, the like of which Americans had not seen before, to bring it back to reality. This was topped off by a second world war which in turn released powerful, disciplined philosophies committed to the destruction of everything that America stood for. Sobered and alarmed by the succession of blows, Americans were forced to reassess their values and re-examine their first principles. Precisely the same thing happened in American higher education. There too the first half of the twentieth century was marked by a broad and deep self-examination, which led to great changes.

In the course of this soul-searching, which began even before World War I, a central focus of criticism came to be the elective system, that device which in its most liberal form gave the student almost complete freedom of choice of courses and subjects and permitted him to graduate upon completion of a definite *number* of courses, or *quantity* of work, taken in any sequence or combination he desired. Reaching its ultimate form at Harvard in the last decade of the nineteenth century, the elective principle had spread over the land to enrich and enliven—or contaminate, according to the point of view—the curriculum of virtually every institution of higher learning in the United States. Few adopted the Harvard plan in its entirety, but all campuses felt the pressure and found themselves compelled to make some concessions to the new viewpoints. By 1910 there were few institutions that had not capitulated at least in part.[1]

Free electives did not fulfill their promise. As experience with them mounted, so did criticism. For the able student who came to college already equipped with cultivated interests and a disciplined mind, they were a liberating influence, as Eliot had intended; the unfit and inadequate who would make a hash of their elective opportunities did not much concern him.[2] But it was the latter kind that was crowding the admissions offices in the early decades of the twentieth century when college enrollments were increasing four to five times as fast as the population. The average high school graduate who thought of the A.B. degree merely as a means of achieving material success, and whom the state university nevertheless had to admit, did not in most cases have the background or judgment to make an intelligent choice among the bewildering profusion of elective courses that confronted him in the college catalogue. Was it not therefore the duty of the university authorities, who, after all, should know what higher education is about, to make some of these choices for him, or at any rate to offer him direction and guidance and so prevent him from making a complete mess of things? Critical questions such as these began to multiply.

They gained further momentum when Harvard itself abandoned the system that it had foisted on the academic community. In his inaugural address in 1909 Abbott Lawrence Lowell, Eliot's successor, announced a philosophy of higher education that took issue with the free electives of his predecessor, for, having seen them in operation, he had become increasingly skeptical. As Lowell saw it, the ideal college "ought to produce, not defective specialists, but men intellectually well rounded, of wide sympathies and unfettered judgment. At the same time they ought to be trained to hard and accurate thought, and this will not come merely by surveying the elementary principles of many subjects. It requires mastery of something, acquired by continuous application." And again: "The best type of liberal education in our complex modern world aims at producing men who know a little of everything and something well." [3] Suiting the action to the word, Lowell, through a faculty committee, secured basic changes in Harvard's elective system. These changes operated in two directions. In the freshman and sophomore years students were required to choose courses from groups of subjects, each group representing a wide range of related knowledge. In this way they would be forced to sample all important areas of knowledge and yet retain considerable freedom of choice within each. For the upper two years each student had to pick a narrower field of major concentration, usually one of the organized departments of instruction such as chemistry or economics or English, thus achieving that "mastery of something" which Lowell demanded. Outside the area of concentration there would be room for considerable unfettered choice.

Here was a compromise solution which recommended itself to program planners and educational theorists everywhere. Without giving up the elective principle, it eliminated its irresponsibilities. It reintroduced plan and direction into the chaotic and competitive jumble of unrelated courses which college curricula had come to be. What Lowell was saying at Harvard, other university leaders were saying elsewhere. Some, like those of Yale and Princeton, had never really stopped saying it. Following their lead, college after college now revised its courses of study in the direction of distribution and concentration, either adopting the Harvard plan or moving ahead on lines of its own.

In its most common form, as evolved between about 1910 and 1930, this curriculum consisted of the following elements. All courses in the catalogue were grouped under three or four large categories, each composed of a number of departments of instruction that were presumably interrelated as to subject or method, or that contained some other common denominator. The first of these groups consisted of the physical and biological sciences, with mathematics usually included. The second was that of the social sciences: economics, political science, sociology, usually history and philosophy, sometimes psychology. These were the disciplines that dealt with the structure of society and were held necessary for intelligent performance of one's duties as a citizen. In the third group were the humanities. Largest and vaguest, it included literature in all languages, drama, music and painting, the fine arts in general. It was in this area that individual human beings expressed their response to the universe in the form of creative productions in words, music, or color. History, insofar as it was a record of such individual achievements, was sometimes included in the humanities, and so was philosophy, as an attempt to interpret the whole of this experience.

In his first two years in college the underclassman took a prescribed amount of work in each of these three large fields or groups. He might be asked to take a year of physics or chemistry and one of botany or biology. Or a year of mathematics might be substituted for the physics or chemistry. Two of the social sciences were usually required also, say a year of history and one of economics, or government, or sociology. There was finally a required course or two in the third field, that of the humanities, usually including a broad survey of English or American literature. In addition to all this the freshmen had to have a course in composition or theme writing, to insure their ability to express themselves intelligibly in other college subjects. To top it off students were often asked to take two years of a foreign language, any foreign language, ancient or modern. This was what the Greek and Latin of the old-time college had simmered down to.

By the end of his sophomore year the student had chosen a field of major concentration to be pursued for the remainder of his stay in college. If he was headed for a professional career like medicine or engineering or law, this choice had to be made earlier and a larger proportion of his freshman and sophomore studies was devoted to his professional preparation. But if he remained in the liberal arts college, the major was one of the subjects or departments that he had sampled in the first two years. Half or a little less than half of his time in the last two years was given to advanced work in the major field, the rest to related or nonrelated subjects freely chosen.

This was the new curriculum that emerged to replace the free electives of Harvard; the earlier group electives of Virginia, Johns Hopkins, and the first years of Stanford; and the four-year classical, or literary, or scientific course of those colleges that had not entirely succumbed to the Eliot plan. With minor variations it became the prevailing pattern. Probably three out of four college men and women who graduated after 1920 and before 1950 will recognize this as their own college experience.

Distribution and concentration was a first step on the road back to unity. In the eyes of its proponents the process of disintegration growing out of complete freedom of election had been checked and a semblance of purpose and meaning restored. But for many this was not enough. Critics continued to point out that even with these changes the college experience was still largely specialized training, a job that should be left to the technical institutes and the professional schools of the universities. The common cultural experience and the unified general education which the old classical college had at least tried to provide were still lacking. The departments of instruction were still competing like so many salesmen, recommending their wares to the bewildered freshmen. The introductory courses in the three broad fields of learning were taught by the professors of the major departments, not as contributions to general culture, but as first courses in the major subject. Thus the required introductory course in physics assumed that every freshman in it was planning to be a physicist, and the introductory course in government became a direct feeder for the advanced courses in that subject, as though every student had in mind a career as a professional political scientist.

Researches in psychology meanwhile were weakening the old argument of mental discipline. The typical nineteenth century pedagogue had held that a disciplined mind was the main purpose and desired outcome of all higher education, and his twentieth century counterpart believed that this could be achieved not only by Greek and Latin and mathematics but by any subject of instruction properly taught, that it could become an intellectual habit which would hold in any other subject or situation. As Abraham Flexner summed it up in 1930, in his penetrating analysis of higher education, the principal aim of the university was intelligence, capable of being applied in any field whatsoever.[4] But a new generation of psychologists was demonstrating by now that this thing called mental discipline was not a general attitude but a pretty specific thing. Though learned and rigorously applied in one field, it was not therefore equally effective in all others. A man might be completely logical and rational in his own specialty and yet quite illogically emotional when he moved to unfamiliar ground. To confound matters still further, Sigmund

Freud and his disciples were pointing out that underlying man's vaunted reason and logic was a dark substratum of irrationality, most difficult to get at, which affected behavior in profound and unexpected ways. Scientific knowledge and method in one field by no means insured a scientific approach to all others, because irrational forces of unknown power might blur the picture. The chemist who insists on factual accuracy and unemotional precision of thought in his own subject may behave quite differently in questions of international relations. The sociologist proceeding from positivist premises may be altogether blind to the rational claims of philosophy or the mystical insights of religion. When the *Maine* was sunk in Havana harbor in 1898, President Harper of the University of Chicago called a student mass meeting at which he asked two professors to speak, a historian and a physicist. The historian counseled objectivity and suspended judgment until all the facts were in, but the physicist, a Nobel prize winner "who had made a creed of precision and suspended judgment, with blazing eyes and choked voice, emotionally demanded that the United States declare war immediately." [5]

In another field, too, there was a new need for agreement on principles by the college-bred leaders of the future. This was in the matter of American ideals. For some years now, ever since the Civil War, the American people had coasted along on easy assumptions of democracy, equality, and progress, polishing up the phrases on the Fourth of July and the rest of the time taking them for granted, much as mutual affection is taken for granted in a normal, healthy family. But normal health was fading fast in the twentieth century world. Two million of our young men had to be sent overseas to "make the world safe for democracy," and soon after that an economic depression rocked the nation and threatened those very foundations on which our philosophy of freedom had grown strong and careless. It was high time to re-examine this philosophy. If there was a body of ideals that had made us free and strong, then surely it was the duty of the schools to formulate and teach them to all pupils, and of the colleges and universities to analyze and evaluate them for the benefit of all their students. And so the social and civic purpose, inherent in American public education from the beginning, was given a new impetus and swelled the demand that the disjointed college curriculum be further unified and really integrated. And with that the magic word "integration" became imbedded in the jargon of educational philosophy.

But just how would one go about integrating the college program, and what would such an integrated program include? Here opinions differed. Before long these differences expanded into two conflicting schools of thought, and a major war of ideas got under way. We cannot follow all the ramifications of this conflict or do justice to all shades of opinion; however, the two principal opposing views will be delineated. For the sake of clarity but at the risk, as always, of oversimplification, we can apply to them the conventional labels of progressive and conservative. We can also identify their leaders. Creator of the progressive viewpoint was John Dewey, with his disciples; the conservative position, somewhat more complex, was most clearly and unequivocally stated by Robert M. Hutchins, when chancellor of the University of Chicago.

John Dewey has become "the Philosopher" of the American public school, enjoying almost as much authority among professional educators as Thomas Aquinas did in the medieval church or Karl Marx among Communist theoreticians. For more than half a century, from 1888 on, Dewey taught, lectured, and wrote from his successive chairs of philosophy, first at Michigan, then at the University of Chicago, and then finally at Columbia; he continued writing and lecturing for another twenty years, until his death in 1952. Though his dominance is most complete over the elementary and secondary schools, he has had considerable influence on the course of higher education as well.

Dewey's educational philosophy [6] is based on the major assumption that human beings, like all living things, are part of the natural world and grow and decay along with everything else. Man is superior to, but not different in kind from, all other living creatures. What we call our mind is not something separate, or different in essence or quality from our body, but is a part or aspect of our whole person. It is that instrumentality or part of us through which we direct our growth by adjusting to new situations. Life constantly confronts us with such new situations, for it is in continuous process of change. Everything is everlastingly waxing, waning, expanding, contracting, becoming something else. To live successfully we must recognize this fact of change and learn to deal with the endless succession of new problems it presents. We do this by applying to every problem our experience, our memory, and the skills and habits that we have formed: in other words, our intelligence. We learn things by doing them; thinking is solving problems. This process of problem-solving, which we call education, goes on all through life, in school and out. It does not begin with kindergarten or end with graduation. Its chief tool is science, which by constantly enlarging the field of verified knowledge about the world and about ourselves as part of the world, enables us to meet new situations more and more successfully, to recognize our problems and define them more precisely, and to solve them with a smaller margin of error. Our constantly maturing intelligence meanwhile organizes the data that science presents and formulates rational concepts and abstractions, which are the further tools necessary to solve problems on the highest level.

To expedite all these processes is the principal purpose of the educational system, from nursery school through the university. If it does its work well, it will enable us to adjust more smoothly to the changing world, meet new problems with greater efficiency, and, as the crowning achievement, combine with our fellow men to change the whole social order and mold it nearer to our hearts' desire. To succeed in all this, the educational system must meet the needs of all people by offering to every individual the kind of educational experience that will enable him to meet his particular problems with the kind of tools that he is best fitted to use. Only by thus diversifying its methods to meet the needs of all citizens, can education be called democratic. This principle holds for higher education as well as for the lower schools. A college curriculum designed to satisfy Dewey would have to be a flexible affair. It would include every subject and every method, no matter how novel, that help to solve those problems which the college, or the society that supports the college, considers of prime importance; and it would eliminate every subject and technique, no matter how venerable or respected, that does not contribute to this end. In fact such a curriculum would probably not be divided into subjects and departments in the conventional sense at all; rather its formulators would select and regroup material from all departments into an ever-new, ever-changing pattern of problem-solving activities.

And right there Dewey's principles ran head-on into the determined opposition of the conservatives. To the educational as to the religious conservative there are some things that do not change. Surface conditions may change, appearances are always ephemeral, but behind these loom the unchanging values and eternal verities which alone make human life worth living. To conserve these values and transmit them intact to future generations is the chief purpose of a liberal college education. These enduring truths and insights were recorded by sages and seers of the past whose names are known to everyone and whose writings should be familiar to every educated man and woman. Accumulating over the centuries, this body of literary, philosophical, religious, and scientific writing has come down to us as the Great Tradition of our culture. It concerns itself with the hopes and fears, the problems and aspirations, of mankind, which are, after all, because of our common, unchanging human condition, the same in all ages. The answers and observations offered in these great books of the past are so profound and so permanently satisfying that to this day they serve better than anything else as a lamp unto our feet, a light upon our path.

These sentiments are not new. To anyone in the habit of attending college commencements or other inspirational campus occasions they will have a familiar ring. They represent the philosophy of many prominent leaders in higher education in all ages including ours, and they have been embroidered and elaborated many times over. In recent years Irving Babbitt, Paul Elmer More, Abraham Flexner, to mention but a few, have expressed this general point of view with varying emphases. But the man who has given it the most precise and vigorous contemporary expression is former Chancellor Hutchins of Chicago, currently president of the Ford Foundation's Fund for the Republic.[7] In independence of thought, though not perhaps in profundity, he is Dewey's equal; in vigor of expression, his superior. Hutchins flatly rejects the idea of the university as a public service institution, overly sensitive to public opinion, and busily setting up courses with short-run objectives in any subject that looms up at the moment as a problem to be solved. Problem-solving courses in simulated "life situations" are to Hutchins a waste of time, for the problems the student "solves" will not be the ones he will have to deal with when he is old enough to play a responsible part in community affairs. It is similarly not the university's business to teach practical professional and vocational courses, for again practice changes too rapidly. What the student learns in such "practical" courses, even if his professor is up to date, will be out of date when he gets around to using it. "All that can be learned in a university is the general principles, the fundamental propositions, the theory of any discipline."[8] The essence of university education is intellectual, not social or moral or vocational. These other values are of course not denied, but their inculcation is the business of the home, the church, and the job, *not* the university. And the essence of intellect is the power of thinking in abstractions, not of solving problems. If the college goes in for social adjustment primarily and the professional schools for vocational training, the university of which these schools are a part is anti-intellectual. A profession must have intellectual content; it must teach why one does a thing, not how. Schools of journalism and of education, as Hutchins sees it, have no such intellectual content. "All there is to journalism can be learned through a good education and newspaper work. All there is to teaching can be learned through a good education and being a teacher." [9]

But what is a good education? Here Hutchins becomes specific. It is not any sequence of sixteen or eighteen courses, chosen at random or from prearranged groups; it is not a major and a minor. Nor is its end-product that threadbare cliché, the well-rounded man. The good college education has the following constituent parts: "It is, first and foremost, the study of those books which have through the centuries attained to the dimensions of classics." [10] And he defines a classic as a book that is contemporary in every age. Here then we have again the thesis of the Great Tradition. An educated person is one who knows and understands our cultural heritage. To develop the critical powers necessary for a full understanding, proficiency must be attained in grammar, rhetoric, logic, and mathematics (almost the medieval *trivium* and *quadrivium*). The information and ideas to be extracted from the great books arrange themselves around three centers. The first is metaphysics, that is a set of general principles along which all knowledge is organized. The mere accumulation of knowledge without such metaphysical direction and unity is meaningless. Then there are the social sciences, which establish the principles of the relation of man to man: ethics, politics, economics, each with appropriate historical background. There is finally the study of the natural sciences, or the relation of man to nature. These three concentrations, pursued with philosophical breadth and intellectual vigor, are the sum and substance of a real education. And the program must be the same for all. Doctor, lawyer, merchant, chief, all will take it undiluted and with no sordid vocational aim. The objection that some students may not like this monolithic course is "irrelevant." They will learn to like it or get out. In teaching it, one starts, not where the student is, from the known to the unknown, as Dewey's disciples would do it, but "from first principles to whatever recent observations were significant in understanding them." The perfectly legitimate desire of students to prepare for a career or a vocation can be met by technical institutes and trade schools, whose teachers should not be members of a university faculty. The latter should include only those who do teaching and research in first principles, for the essence of the university is the quest for truth in the light of a rational principle. Hutchins held to his belief in an intellectual elite to the end of his career as Chicago's president, telling the students in his farewell address in 1951 that the general public has no idea what a university is or what it is for, and that this is due in part to the "fantastic misconduct" of some of the universities themselves.

By the second quarter of the twentieth century the controversy tended to revolve around the two centers of Hutchins and Dewey, and educational leaders found themselves caught up in the orbit of the one or the other. The two philosophies, labeled conservative and progressive, might also be described, with some distortion, as the aristocratic and the democratic positions. In the former, higher education is for the intellectual elite. Only a minority have the mental powers and discipline to achieve full understanding of the ideas of the original thinkers and the great systematizers of the past, and genuine appreciation of their timeless worth. Having done so, these same superior individuals must pass on to the rest of the people, whose mental powers are only average, as much of this treasury of wisdom as they need to know or are able to take in. Hutchins and his school did not consider this undemocratic. On the contrary it was for them the only way to discover and train leaders possessing that discipline and vision without which democracy founders. In Dewey's scheme, on the other hand, all were to have their chance. A democratic society owed all its citizens the opportunity to develop their talents, of whatever nature, to the highest possible degree, so that their collective competence, be it in words and ideas, or techniques and manual skills, could be brought to bear on the problems of that self-same society and ensure its continued progress.

In actual practice, university leaders did not of course immediately choose sides and commit themselves irrevocably to the Dewey or the Hutchins camp. Each had his ardent supporters who sometimes— and this was particularly true of the Deweyites—went beyond their master. But many others saw values in each position and tried to salvage the best of both worlds. In the philosophical spectrum most professors and presidents could be found somewhere between the

infra-red of Dewey and the ultra-violet of Hutchins. The more independent their own thinking, the less likely they were to be complete
devotees of either school.

George Santayana challenged the traditionalists. In *The Genteel
Tradition at Bay* (1931) he denied that every worthwhile experience
or every possible human problem had come up in the past. A classical scholar himself, he maintained that the Greeks had not faced
every situation or originated every great achievement of thought and
culture. The past was useful for comparisons, but our choices must
grow from present experiences.

A member of Hutchins' faculty, Harry D. Gideonse, later to become president of Brooklyn College, took immediate issue with his
chancellor. In his book *The Higher Learning in a Democracy* (1937),
written in response to the Hutchins credo, *The Higher Learning in
America,* Gideonse began by agreeing with most of Hutchins' stric-
tures of current educational practices. But he disagreed with the
solution, particularly the comprehension of all learning in a particular metaphysical system. Though Hutchins does not say it, the
system he favors seems to be the Aristotelian world view rendered
palatable for a Christian society of the thirteenth century by St.
Thomas Aquinas. Although a gigantic intellectual achievement in
its day, the Thomistic philosophy, maintained Gideonse, is a cramp-
ing strait jacket for the dynamic American society of the twentieth
century. Logic and philosophy have passed far beyond the medieval
synthesis, and modern scientific thought and discovery have shattered
the Aristotelian categories of thought with which Aquinas operated.
For that matter—and here Gideonse cited Whitehead—the enthrone-
ment of any particular system of rational thought as the final authoritative one is itself the ultimate anti-intellectualism. Education must
be forever testing all systems, and science and philosophy must work
out new syntheses. Besides, the college must deal with the whole
person and is concerned with the understanding and enrichment of
twentieth century life in all its phases. The Great Tradition is not
finished. It continues to grow and therefore to change, and the twentieth century has its contributions to make as well as the thirteenth.
And he might have added that the time will come when John Dewey
will be a part of it.[11]

Presidents of some of the leading universities, including Lowell
of Harvard and Angell of Yale, ranged themselves on the side of the
cultural as opposed to the pragmatic approach. Angell even com-

mended the aims of the famous Yale report of 1828.[12] A dramatically phrased contrast between the two viewpoints seasoned with a bit of nostalgia is found in a passage of a recent Phi Beta Kappa address: "Fifty years ago we taught liberal subjects and strict disciplines in courses that were expected to provide information, knowledge, training, culture, and the elements of wisdom. Out of these basic ingredients it was presumed that valuable end-products would naturally come, and through them the student was expected to move on toward becoming an educated man or woman. We assumed that such an educated person would naturally have the attributes, understanding, and wisdom that would enable him to occupy a superior place in the world. Today we completely reverse the process. We decide what are the attributes that education should provide—good citizenship, acquaintance with the scientific method, an adjusted personality, group consciousness, occupational adjustment, control of accidents, success in marriage, social dynamics, etc.—and then we set up special courses, for credit-hour study, to teach each of these specific features. We leave nothing to chance, save the possibility that the college or university graduate should acquire a little learning and wisdom while he is being groomed as a competent citizen or as a proficient technician." [13]

Then there was Alexander Meiklejohn, president of Amherst and later director of the experimental college of the University of Wisconsin, who started from an idealistic position that posited ultimate values and saw the main purpose of college as intellectual, but ended up in a pragmatic educational experiment which had all the earmarks of the "progressive" school.[14] Among others who saw merits on both sides was President Lewis Webster Jones of Rutgers. In his presidential address to the Association of Land Grant Colleges and Universities in 1955 Jones flatly asserted: "This country was not built by an elite, and it is inconceivable that it should ever be run by one, unless it deteriorates into a totalitarian society." John Dewey could have stated it no better. But President Jones did not approve, as do some of the Dewey disciples, of setting up formal courses and workshop guidance programs for every problem that comes along. On the contrary he insisted that there should be less intellectual baby-sitting and spoon-feeding.[15]

And so the controversy seesawed on. Perhaps the widest consensus of opinion in recent years came from the Commission on Higher Education appointed by President Truman in 1947, composed of representative figures in higher education from all parts of the country who were asked to formulate long-term objectives.[16] Their report begins with the major premise that any worthwhile comprehensive program for the colleges and universities must grow out of the needs of contemporary society. "Effective democratic education will deal directly with current problems." Then it pays its respect to the Great Tradition: "This is not to say that education should neglect the past—only that it should not get lost in the past." To try to apply "eternal" truths to every situation "is likely to stifle creative imagination" and "may blind us to new problems." Pure, undiluted Dewey! The goals of higher education that should come first in our time must be to bring to all the people of the nation: 1) Education for a fuller realization of democracy in every phase of living; 2) education for international understanding and cooperation; 3) education for the application of creative imagination and trained intelligence to the solution of social problems and to the administration of public affairs. This voluminous report represented the consensus of a large segment of professional opinion, but it did not satisfy everybody. There was a minority, whose criticism was directed chiefly along intellectual and economic lines. For one thing, the dissenters held, the hordes of students which the commission expected to throng the universities in the next decades would not be capable of real intellectual accomplishment on the college level and would therefore debase all standards. Any large-scale attempt on the other hand to provide vocational and manual training and "appreciation" courses beyond high school for all of these prospective students would saddle the taxpayers with a crushing burden. In anticipation of some of these criticisms, the commission had maintained, on the basis of army tests, that about one half of our population had the mental ability to complete junior college, and almost one third was intellectually qualified for advanced liberal and professional study; and they reiterated that the United States is the richest country in the world.

Exhilarating as these controversies may have been to the participants, their main purpose was to influence the college and university programs of study. The success of either the Hutchins or the Dewey idea would be measured by the extent and the amount of change that each could bring about in the curriculum. Both wanted change. Neither was satisfied with unlimited electives, or even with the distribution-concentration pattern. As might be expected, few colleges went all-out for either philosophy. Most educational institutions were too ponderous to turn intellectual somersaults. Quantitatively, the move in the direction of the Dewey viewpoint was stronger. In fact only one college of consequence adopted the Hutchins program in its entirety. This was St. Johns College in Annapolis. Here, in 1937 and under the presidency of Stringfellow Barr, with Hutchins himself standing by as chairman of the board of visitors, the elective system was rooted out and replaced by a four-year all-required course of study centering about the reading and discussion of a prescribed list of books, all of them world classics. Thus St. Johns returned to the liberal arts, "not necessarily the old curriculum but a modern equivalent." These arts were held to include reasoning, as the highest, but also memory, manual dexterity, calculation, and measurement. Mathematics figured prominently, languages were studied as needed, and there was laboratory science. And the end in view? "The production of good intellectual and moral habits which provide the basis for human freedom." Eighteen years later, in an evaluation report, St. Johns reaffirmed its faith in its controversial curriculum. Alumni seemed satisfied; almost 60 per cent of them had gone on to graduate work either in the arts and sciences or in the professions. Minor changes had been made. The list of books for one thing was constantly being retested, with resulting additions and deletions. Language study had been improved, music study extended, and laboratory experimentation given greater stress. By and large, however, St. Johns has held to its course. The ability to discern general principles in all the arts and sciences is still its goal. It stands on its record, but it stands alone.[17]

There was more activity in the other camp. Several new "progressive" colleges were founded in the 1920's and 1930's, and some older ones overhauled their schedules in an intellectual face-lifting operation. Prime examples of the former were the new women's colleges, Sarah Lawrence and Bennington, as well as smaller enterprises like the cooperative Black Mountain College in North Carolina. The second type was represented by Rollins, a Congregational college in Florida reorganized along progressive lines by its president, Hamilton Holt; and by Goddard College in Vermont, founded in 1863 under Universalist religious auspices but converted in 1937 to the gospel according to Dewey.

Though differing in detail, all these institutions had certain features in common. Higher education as they conceived it was not the transmission of an intellectual tradition, not the faith once for all delivered to the Saints, but total life experience. As such, it was constantly changing and in need of continual re-examination. In this re-examination and in the program planning which resulted from it, students, faculty, administration, in some cases wives, all had a share. These new-styled colleges had little use for required courses or standard majors; rules and prescriptions of all kinds were anathema to them. Instead, they made unusual efforts to discover the interests and abilities of each student and with the aid of copious advice to build for each a "tailor-made" and, if necessary, unique program of studies. In the execution of these individualized programs, customary teaching procedures, such as lectures, rigidly organized courses, conventional examinations, and all traditional formalizations, were, insofar as possible, discarded. Instruction was suited to the needs of the students. At least that was the ideal.

There is some indication today that these centrifugal forces have, at least for the time being, reached their outward limit, and that progressive colleges are in some respects beginning a cautious return in the direction of the norm. It would be correct to say also that the norm, over the past thirty years, has bent in the direction of the progressive colleges.[18]

For an understanding of the norm we must turn to the large and influential colleges and universities. Here the prevailing attitude was like St. Paul's: Prove all things, hold fast that which is good. Let the eager young progressive colleges do the former, and the substantial institutions with a reputation to sustain would take care of the latter. But if the giants moved more slowly, it was not for lack of intelligent comprehension of the issues. It simply took longer in a diversified, ponderous institution, where the brakes of tradition and vested interests were stronger.

Columbia was the trail-blazer with its famous course in contemporary civilization, introduced just after the first world war. Oddly enough, Columbia pioneered in the other direction too, for it was John Erskine of the English department there who organized the first colloquium, for select upperclass students, in Great Books of the Western World, years before Hutchins or St. Johns College took it up. In thus adventuring in both directions Columbia illustrated (as perhaps every university should) William James's philosophical corridor with the many rooms opening from it in each of which something different and even contradictory is going on. The contemporary civilization course *was* different. Though a history course in form, it did not treat a conventional historical period like the Middle Ages or the French Revolution, but was really contemporary in that it came down to the present and selected from the past those activities, ideas, and institutions that were most significant in explaining the present. The reason for doing it this way was simplicity itself: College graduates should understand their own world and know something of its origins. It differed from conventional courses in other ways. It was not, to borrow from professional terminology, subject-centered but student-centered. Unity was secured by the common purpose of explaining the present in terms of the past, and by a common reading program which consisted of long extracts from significant literary, political, and philosophical documents written during the various centuries covered by the course. In the second place it cut across departmental lines and thus tended to reverse the tendency toward overspecialization. Though essentially historical, it was not the property of the history department but a cooperative enterprise, in which instructors from history, government, economics, and philosophy participated. It was taught in small sections each with its own instructor. Since the instructors came from different fields, a variation in emphasis resulted, giving the course a flexibility that was intentional. Since, furthermore, most of the course was outside the field of specialization of any one instructor, it was impossible to use it as a vehicle for training specialists; instead it represented a joint faculty responsibility for that general education which must precede all specialization.

Most of the features of the "orientation" courses so familiar to college freshmen and sophomores today were found in this grandfather of them all. It has been much revised. Some years after its introduction it became a two-year sequence required of all freshmen and sophomores, with the first year still historical in approach and the second concerned with current political, economic, and social problems. Meanwhile a parallel sequence of two synthetic courses was set up in the humanities, meaning the departments of literature and the fine arts, with history and philosophy collaborating here too. The freshman year of this second sequence was a study of literature with wide-ranging reading, and the second devoted a term each to painting and music. Finally a similar two-year program was constructed by the natural sciences. All of these courses were part of a general education. And all were "musts" for every freshman and

sophomore. Columbia had thus radically departed from the free elective system. Its new program was quite different, too, from the group
electives of the distribution-concentration curriculum. In the name
of the needs of its students and the cultural and civic responsibilities
of the educated citizen, Columbia had returned to an almost complete prescriptive program for its junior college. In the two upper
years the student moved on to a major with electives in one of the
conventional liberal arts departments or shifted to one of the many
professional schools of the university.[19]

Scores if not hundreds of institutions have copied the Columbia
program or adapted it to their conditions. Orientation or survey
courses of a composite nature are now commonplace. If the Columbia plan did not wholly satisfy, a school looking for a model might
after 1945 study the innovations at Harvard. For in that year, a
quarter-century after Columbia had set the new direction, a Harvard
faculty committee surveyed the field and came out with a comprehensive analysis of the various contemporary plans and theories for
improving higher education, in the light of which they proposed
a program of reform for Harvard. The title of this study, *General
Education in a Free Society,* reveals both the philosophical basis and
the area in which most of the changes were to be made. It was not
the student's specialization, for which Harvard made ample provision, but his general education that left something to be desired.
The committee accordingly recommended that all departments of
Harvard College make a distinction, in planning their courses, between students who would want to specialize or "concentrate" in
that subject, and those who merely wanted to find out a few general
things about it by way of rounding out their education, and to offer
separate courses to each type of student. Once such courses were set
up all through the college, every student would be required to take
six of his total of sixteen courses in this type of "general education."
Some of the six were prescribed: one in the social sciences, one in
the humanities, one in natural sciences. The remaining general
courses, on what might be called a second level, could be taken at
any time before graduation, so that general education would not end
with the sophomore year, as at Columbia, but continue tapering off
until graduation. English composition was also required, not as a
separate course, but as a skill to be used in connection with the
general courses in the other subjects. This was the Harvard contribution.[20]

Still another variant was developed at Chicago. In the citadel of Hutchins, as one might expect, it became possible to graduate upon completion of a program almost entirely made up of required material. Sequences of three successive general education courses in each of three fields, the social sciences, the natural sciences, and the humanities, taking ordinarily three years, were topped off by a year of tutorial studies in a special field, culminating in a substantial essay. Or one could move to one of the professional schools for the fourth year. An alternative option was the conventional distribution-concentration curriculum.[21]

With increasing frequency the reorganized underclass programs were being referred to as general education, and after 1945, when Harvard chose this designation as the title of its report, the term had even wider currency. General education, then, meant the non-professional, nonspecialized part of a college program, that which all students had in common and which was completed, or nearly so, by the end of the sophomore year.

To avoid confusion, it should be noted that the same term also came to be used to designate a different kind of university activity altogether. Columbia's School of General Studies and the University of Minnesota's General College, both taking shape after World War II, were not the equivalent of the undergraduate programs just described. The Columbia school was an attempt to revive the medieval *studium generale* in modern dress for the benefit of more mature individuals who had not had the opportunity to go to college, but who wished to extend their education as best they could, choosing such courses and subjects as met their needs and convenience, without any immediate concern for a degree. Such students might eventually matriculate for a degree by demonstrating their competence and meeting the customary requirements. It was Columbia's program of adult education reorganized under this new label.[22] Adult education was nothing new. Many universities, especially in urban centers, had been offering such opportunities for years. They were usually given the name university extension or, when degrees were offered, university college.

Somewhat different in plan and purpose is the General College of the University of Minnesota. This was designed as a two-year junior college for young people who had not had a complete high school preparation or who had made poor grades. From the academic point of view it offered a diluted college education. Its sweeping survey courses were not constructed by cooperation of several academic departments as was the case with the Columbia contemporary civilization course and its numeous progeny. The Minnesota surveys were built around altogether different concepts, such as personal orientation, home life orientation, social and civic orientation. Known as functional courses, they represented an attempt to apply the Dewey philosophy to American society by offering additional educational opportunity beyond high school to those who had demonstrated neither ability for nor interest in the regular four-year academic program leading to the A.B. degree. Students in the General College may, however, transfer to the degree course if they "demonstrate they can meet the competition." [23] Minnesota has had some imitators; in fact there are colleges that have introduced functional courses of the Minnesota type into their regular undergraduate program.

Numerous individual variations of the patterns of change described thus far have appeared. Prominent among them is the directed study program of Yale, established in the 1940's as part of what Yale's historian has called "the magnificent invigoration of the curriculum" of those years. In this program a limited number of freshmen and sophomores take a carefully selected two-year sequence of courses which is to form a common intellectual basis for the two upper years, when the students go on to a conventional major subject. Philosophy courses are at the center of the program, and are used to draw together and illuminate the work of the other courses. There are also colleges which believe that general education, especially the kind that promotes civic responsibility, may well be continued to the end of the college course, and who have tried to insure this by various devices. Dartmouth's answer is the Great Issues course for seniors, whereby the graduating class is kept *au courant,* with the aid of visiting speakers, of changing conditions in the nation and the world. Colgate continues general courses in this field, diminuendo, into the senior year, while at the same time, by ingenious planning, giving the freshmen a foretaste of specialization.[24] And there are many others.

Recapitulating the curricular innovations of the twentieth century, we find the following varieties of the liberal arts college curriculum in force today: 1) the group-distribution and major concentration plan; 2) general comprehensive survey courses followed by major concentration in either the Columbia or Harvard pattern;

3) the functional curriculum of the Minnesota general college type; 4) the prescribed four-year curriculum focused on great books; 5) individual guidance and "personalized" majors of the more consistent progressive colleges; 6) variations and combinations of the other types. Categorizations such as this are useful but are only half the story. Whatever label the curriculum may carry, the quality of its end-product, the A.B. degree, depends on the quantity and quality of the work done, the ability and interest of the student, the interest and competence of the teacher, the range and depth of the library. Whatever the catalogue may promise, these are the imponderables that determine the outcome.

Chapter Eleven

The Liberal Arts College Today

Having followed the fortunes of the liberal arts college through its successive stages as an independent institution to its present most common form as part of a university, along with professional and vocational schools, we may now ask what is its current state of health and what are its chances of survival. A casual examination not only of educational journals but also of educational items in the better magazines and newspapers forces one to the conclusion that for all the changes it has suffered it is still vigorous. The interminable controversies over ends and means of higher education, the keen competition for public support, the chronic financial crisis, the flourishing alumni associations, the occasional brushes with public opinion and vested interests, the confident announcements of novel experiments, contrasting with abject breast-beating and gloomy predictions of failure and decay—all of these are symptoms of an institution that is alive. The twentieth century college has not gone to sleep like its mid-nineteenth century predecessor. It is willing to change when necessary, though not always agreed on the direction. It has solid achievements to record, as well as failures. But it is not complacent.

At the annual conference in 1955 of the Association of American Colleges six hundred college presidents and deans discussed the theme "Liberal Education and America's Future" for a solid week. College and university professors continually debate similar themes at their own professional meetings. The college, then, is aware of itself, conscious of its strengths and weaknesses, and alert to the dangers that threaten it. Its raw adolescence has been left behind, and it may even have reached the stage when, as Adlai Stevenson has said of the United States as a whole, it must learn to live with its ulcers and its arthritis. To use another analogy, the college has emerged from the stage of anarchic competition and become a public utility. But in that form, too, it is still productive.

New types of colleges continue to appear. No one set pattern can be discovered among the most recent establishments, but, as has always been the case, they are being molded to the needs of the community and the trend of the times. As one would expect, prominent among the newest ones are urban institutions designed to serve the rapidly growing metropolitan centers. Roosevelt University in Chicago is an example. With a hotel in the heart of the city as its "campus," its purpose is "to provide equal opportunity for all students who have the desire and the ability to learn the truth." It contains the traditional college of arts and sciences with the usual program leading to the A.B. degree, but also a variety of vocational schools, including a division of labor education with special classes for union members.[1] Another recent urban institution is Brandeis University near Boston, established under Jewish auspices in 1948 and committed to the liberal arts approach, aiming to "develop the whole man, the sensitive, cultured, open-minded kind of citizen." [2] Rapidly growing suburban areas also have new educational needs which in some cases have been met by the founding of new colleges. Fairleigh Dickinson in northern New Jersey, across the Hudson from New York City, began as a junior college but was expanded to a full four-year college in 1948. Its program is closely articulated with the public school system of the area.

Though the big cities have most of the new institutions, the simple country college of an earlier day has not entirely disappeared, has in fact showed signs of renewed vigor. Bard College in New York State, for a time a satellite of Columbia, has resumed its independence. Vermont, in a sense our last frontier, has produced some vigorous colleges, among them Marlboro College, founded in 1946, and housed on an old farm. With poets and novelists on its board of trustees along with the usual bankers and corporation directors, Marlboro is a place where the student is expected to develop "that intellectual flexibility which is the product of the liberal arts, and that social responsibility which is essential to self-government." In a program of general education it attempts to show the student the "full range of human experience and knowledge." Its government is the town meeting in which students, faculty and staff, and their wives all have equal votes. It has a work program reminiscent of the old manual labor colleges of the 1830's, and the students conduct an annual maple sugar project.[3]

Most pressing and immediate among the problems confronting colleges and universities today are those caused by their rapid growth. An unprecedented number of students are thronging our institutions of higher education, and, barring catastrophes, this number is almost certain to increase at an accelerated rate for years to come. During the academic year 1956-1957 about 250,000 instructors taught more than 3,000,000 students in the 1,855 institutions of higher learning of the country. The last figure is the total of all types of schools above the high school level: universities, independent liberal arts colleges, junior colleges, and professional schools.

To all those interested in the continued vitality of the liberal arts such growth is an opportunity and a challenge. At the same time it presents new difficulties, the most urgent of which is financial. With classrooms, laboratories, libraries, and dormitories overcrowded, the colleges and universities of the country, whether publicly or privately supported, are desperately searching for new and increased revenues. And with reason, for in spite of the increasing demands that the American people are making on higher education, the money they are spending for it has not increased, percentage-wise, in recent years. In 1956, according to the Carnegie Corporation's Report for that year, it amounted to four-fifths of one per cent of the gross national product, a smaller percentage than at any time since 1951.

The prospective freshman gets a preliminary glimpse of these complexities when he opens the catalogue of the university of his choice. There he is confronted by columns upon columns of names of faculty and administration. The former are graded into assistant instructors, instructors, assistant professors, associate professors, and professors. Above the teaching faculty, in bewildering assortment, rise tiers upon tiers of registrars, bursars, deans, with the president, sometimes seconded by a provost, at the apex. Beyond the president looms a shadowy final authority: the trustees.

The annual bulletins of a large modern university, with all its colleges and professional schools, run to thousands of pages of printed matter filling many inches of shelf space. They are for the most part drab and discouraging to look at. Now and then some more imaginative university officers manage to brighten them up. In the post-

Civil War years, for example, some of the resurgent southern colleges went through a phase of slick-paper catalogues in pastel shades and Spencerian script. And today many colleges issue illustrated pamphlets in addition to their catalogues. But as a rule it is a sobering experience for the expectant freshman to pick up one of these volumes and thread his way through the complex maze of directions, often couched in strange technical jargon that speaks of prerequisites, group requirements, major concentrations, and quality credits, and bristles with "provided thats," all of it the accumulation, seemingly, of ponderous professorial afterthoughts. Actually the catalogue represents much hard thinking and genuine concern for the student's welfare on the part of faculty and administration, but that is not always clear to the layman. Only an occasional college manages to extricate itself from academic abracadabra and to explain to its students in straightforward English what it expects of them.

Undaunted by limitations of space and funds, modern colleges and universities have continued to experiment with new methods and techniques, all designed to meet the new problems which a changing world continues to impose on them. Some of these must now be examined.

The Dewey-inspired emphasis on student-interest programs of general education as opposed to formal academic subject matter has percolated into the upper reaches of the colleges and resulted in new types of majors, which derive from actual life situations and do not consist of courses selected from one of the customary academic subjects. The argument for such a departure runs as follows: The average student, even if alert and intelligent, is not necessarily interested in history, or economics, or philosophy as such. Those subjects are artificial organizations formulated by experts for experts. But the student may very well be interested in the relations between the United States and the Soviet Union or Latin America; or in the problems of the Middle East; he may be curious about the influence of the immigrant on American civilization; or he may wish to discover the philosophical and psychological bases of Marxism or of fascism. Such perfectly natural interests and legitimate demands of our students are not always adequately met by the conventional academic majors. Out of this situation have grown the new kinds of majors usually known as regional or area studies. In their simplest form, in the smaller institutions, these may be just a list of courses selected from all relevant departments that might shed light on a given topic or area like those mentioned above. In larger universities where specialists and technical libraries are available, area studies have mushroomed into institutes and schools, often interlocking with the graduate school and granting certificates of proficiency as well as graduate degrees. All of them, however, are marked by an attempt to avoid the purely academic approach and to link the work of the classroom and seminar with the realities of the outside world which the students will soon have to face.

Not only the content of the liberal curriculum but also its length has again come under scrutiny in recent years. Why should every student be required to put in four years, no more and no less, to earn the bachelor's degree? It is argued by Deweyites and others that inasmuch as individuals differ in ability and interest the time they require to do a given piece of work may vary too. The Hutchins forces come to a similar conclusion but by a different road. Since the mental maturity and understanding which the reading of great books is supposed to produce is measured by examinations, such examinations, which must be both broad and thorough, might well be given whenever the student is ready for them. If he can pass them all in less than four years and thus demonstrate his maturity, there is no reason for delaying his graduation and holding up his degree. Accordingly, colleges are increasingly concerned with making it possible for exceptional students to graduate in less than the conventional four years.

It is also being suggested, with greater frequency, that all students, not just the most talented, might be able to complete both their college and high school courses in shorter time than is now required. This viewpoint was given an impetus by the second world war. Ever since the miltiary exigencies of that time forced accelerated programs of all kinds on the universities, educational leaders have been investigating the possibility of condensing and telescoping course requirements in order to save time. All acceleration is not necessarily a good thing. Though it is a truism that the finest values cannot be hurried, it is hardly to be denied that time for reflection is necessary for real learning, as opposed to the mere accumulation of information of the quiz kid variety. Nevertheless waste and duplication do exist. Various groups, usually including representatives of the colleges and the secondary schools, have in recent years been at work on this problem, and several plans are being tried out. A number of colleges have for some years past been admitting qualified high school students a year or more before their graduation, with gratifying results. Others have been giving examinations of college caliber to high school graduates. Those who pass are permitted to substitute advanced courses for the introductory ones, and may thus shorten their time in college.[4]

One of the consequences of the substitution of a major field of study for scattered, unrelated electives has been the comprehensive examination, in which the senior, or the sophomore at the end of the general education phase of college, is examined in the materials, not only of the course just completed, but of his whole major field. Comprehensive examinations have been widely adopted, but they came hard at first, for, as Harvard's historian points out, it took time to get used to "so revolutionary a step as requiring a student to remember something until he graduated."[5]

By way of supplementing the comprehensives, Harvard also introduced, in President Lowell's day, the tutorial system, under which students individually or in small groups talked over their reading with a tutor and received from him valuable suggestions and criticisms of a kind that was impossible in a large class. This new type of tutor must not be confused with the tutors of the old-time college; those were bright and pious young graduates who were kept on for a few years, with no special training, to teach underclassmen, maintain order in the dormitories, and do the dirty work of the professors. Harvard tutors today, like those of Oxford and Cambridge, can come from any faculty rank. The most distinguished professor may, if he desires, take on tutorial teaching for a while, being relieved of a corresponding amount of other work.

A logical consequence of the tutorials was the so-called residential college, or house system, also an adaptation of the centuries-old Oxford and Cambridge system. A residential college had quarters for students and tutors (one of the latter being the master of the college) as well as a dining room, a common room, and its own library. All this was designed to facilitate informal intellectual and social contacts between students and faculty. Both Harvard and Yale erected a number of such residential colleges in the 1920's. Princeton, meanwhile, has continued its preceptorial system, inaugurated in Woodrow Wilson's day.

Akin to comprehensives and tutorials are the various devices for enabling superior students to work to capacity by freeing them from some of the artificial limitations of classes and courses and putting them on their own responsibility to produce to the highest level of their ability. Generally known as honors programs, these arrangements began about 1920 as adaptations of British university practice. Oxford and Cambridge had long been distinguishing between their honors students and the pass men who coveted no more than a gentleman's grade. Most American colleges today offer honors work in one form or another. Swarthmore under President Frank Aydelotte, a former Rhodes scholar, was a pioneer; there the honors idea was carefully thought out, and a higher percentage of the student body enrolled in the program than in most other institutions. In President Aydelotte's words the essence of honors work was this: "The honors student has his work outlined for him not in terms of what he must do but in terms of what he must know. Instead of taking courses he studies a subject. He must (with what assistance he can get) organize his materials, set his own tasks, find out and strengthen his own weaknesses, develop his own strong points and, in general, take the responsibility for his own salvation." [6]

Tutorials, preceptorials, and honors programs are all devices to spur the ablest students to do their best. In an age of high enrollments and steadily mounting costs the chief objection to them is their expense. Their merits are great, but they require many professors to devote a large proportion of their time to comparatively few students. Not much expansion of these programs is to be expected in the near future, since they are likely to be regarded by budget-conscious administrators as a luxury beyond their reach.

One of the most pervasive changes in educational practice has come about in the character of tests and examinations. Examinations are as old as the university itself. They began in the Middle Ages when the scholar who thought he was ready to become a master in his profession presented himself before a group of his peers as a candidate for the degree of master of arts and gave an oral account of his knowledge and competence, whereupon the latter granted or withheld the degree, thereby admitting or rejecting him for membership in the guild. In the early American college final examinations, still oral, were public occasions to which prominent citizens were invited who might contribute questions of their own. Soon after the middle of the nineteenth century this practice was discontinued and examinations became the cloistered written exercises they are today. Ever since then we have had the types of questions so familiar to millions of college students and, for that matter, high school boys and girls:

What is . . . ; who was . . . ; give three examples of . . . ; explain and discuss . . . ; trace the causes . . . ; compare the influence. . . . Examinations of this "essay" type are still widely used in the best colleges both in introductory and advanced courses, and with satisfactory results. Yet they, and the grades that they produce, have always been the source of controversy and left much room for disagreement. The student had to accept the unsupported judgment of his teacher as to the merit of his performance and the grade he deserved. That judgment, even though the teacher was scrupulously fair, was bound to be a subjective estimate. This state of affairs bothered both students and conscientious teachers. Should it not be possible, so they thought, in this age of science and precision, to come up with something more objective and accurate? Educational administrators and theorists concentrated on the problem and in due time produced a new kind of examination which they recommended as completely scientific and objective, and altogether free from personal bias. Thus was introduced the mechanical objective test.

Very simple at first and designed for limited use, scientific testing and measuring has become a major industry serving business and government as well as educational institutions. In form and content as well as in extent of coverage the modern testing industry goes as far beyond the first simple true-false information tests as the latest V-8 automobile motor goes beyond the first simple internal combustion engine that Henry Ford mounted on carriage wheels. Not only information but recognition of relationships, likes and dislikes, aptitudes, and character traits are tested in this way. There are personality inventories and inventories of belief and opinion, and tests are now being devised to measure that most elusive and complex faculty, critical judgment.[7]

The increasingly widespread use of mechanical tests suggests that they satisfy a widespread need. To meet this need with ever more dependable measurements, they are being constantly retested and refined. For certain purposes they are of inestimable value. Popular as they are in many quarters, however, they have also met with considerable opposition from teachers and students. As everyone who has been to school since about 1920 knows, the essence of the objective test is a choice of alternatives. Among the materials on the mimeographed or printed sheet before him, whether they are the elementary single statement of fact or a series of alternative statements, the student must choose the correct one, or the preferred one, or the one which most nearly represents his opinion or belief, and indicate his choice by putting a mark in the numbered or lettered square provided for this purpose. Some tests add complications and embroideries, but always at the end the student marks a box. That is all he does. All the instructor does is check the right against the wrong and come up with an unerring mathematical score, free from bias or subjective opinion. If the institution is advanced enough, the instructor will hand his papers to the testing office to be machine-processed. There the electronic eye hands down a verdict which is precise, objective, and completely scientific.

Or is it? All the trappings of science are there. And yet the suspicion grows that for all their seeming inerrancy the tests can be manipulated. The adventurous student may decide to guess when he does not know, and even though the scoring system discourages this kind of gambling, he has a fifty-fifty chance, at least in the true-false type, of guessing right. To be fully scientific the final score should therefore allow for a variable: the degree of intensity of each student's gambling instinct. And there are other ways of working the oracle. Personality inventories can be manipulated, too. And, of course, the tests can also be abused by the instructor. When thousands upon thousands of students of about the same background and training take the same test in a given subject, the percentage of those whose work will be excellent and good and average and failing—assuming that there is agreement on the meaning of those four terms—can be predicted with considerable accuracy. Plotted on a graph, this becomes the probability curve. But when an instructor applies this curve a priori to his class of thirty and thus predestines a fixed percentage to failure regardless of the quality of their examination, he is making hash of statistics. Results thus obtained are nothing if not scientific, and they are not scientific.

But even when the tests are not manipulated or misused, the question remains: What do they test? The ability to detect error in a given set of statements. To be foolproof, the statements must be so obviously correct or incorrect as to leave no room for differences of opinion. Such statements, when they do not sink to the level of two times two is four, are still likely to oversimplify and distort actuality. They are made to order for the naïve average student who likes his world in simple blacks and whites, while the abler scholar who sees shadings and has learned to make distinctions is more apt to flounder in tests of this kind. Thus it happens that the best students—best in the opinion of the teachers who know them well—sometimes make disappointing grades in the standard tests, while mediocre ones do unusually well.

There is a more serious defect. In all standardized tests all the material is given in advance, and the student merely approves or rejects by marking his squares. He does not have to make or fashion or produce anything. The old-fashioned essay type examination, whatever its defects, at least had the merit of requiring a student to give an account of his knowledge or to justify his opinions by starting with an idea, organizing material around it, and presenting it with some clarity as a logical whole. This kind of activity resembles actual life situations far more closely than do the supposedly scientific objective tests. Men and women will continue to pass examinations long after they graduate from college. They will, true enough, be asked to distinguish the correct and the incorrect, and to choose among alternatives, but rarely will these alternatives be neatly placed before them by someone else; far more often they will have to identify the problems, arrange the alternatives, and make the choice themselves. When the college or high school graduate applies for a job, or the junior executive prepares a report for his superior, or the public-spirited man asks his fellow citizens to join him in a program of reform, he will have to assemble data, organize them logically, and present them convincingly in sentences which consist of subject and predicate. Life will not give any of these men a passing grade for checking little squares.

For all their shortcomings the mechanical tests will probably continue to flourish, for they have one great advantage: They save time. With ever-larger waves of students descending on him year after year, the college teacher, like his colleague in the high school, will continue to resort to this labor-saving device as the only means of keeping ahead of his work. He will console his professional conscience by observing that everyone else uses them too, and make believe that he really discerns the abilities of his students more clearly in the light of their pseudo-scientific glow.

The scope and variety of the problems with which the liberal arts college of today must come to grips is proof that the institution is still in process of change, as it has been throughout its history. One may ask for how much longer such an evolving institution is likely to retain its basic character, whether in fact it has not already changed beyond recognition. The answer is not easy because the term liberal arts is not very precise. A name applied to an institution that is constantly changing is itself subject to changes in meaning. Current catalogues usually refer to the undergraduate division of a university as the college of liberal arts, or of arts and sciences. Occasionally it is called the humanities college, though this is ordinarily a term of more limited meaning. Sometimes it is referred to as the college of general education. All these vague appellations only complicate the problem of definition.[8] One might get at the problem in a negative way by saying that liberal-general-humanistic is what is left after all vocational and professional subjects and courses have been abstracted. This affords clarity of a sort but explains nothing; it is merely a practical rule-of-thumb distinction.

If the liberal arts concept will not lend itself to definition, at least its content can be explored. To conservatives of the Hutchins school, the liberal arts are identical with the heritage of the Great Books. That heritage, they maintain, was properly communicated to American college students of earlier generations, at least in substance, until the day when Charles W. Eliot and other iconoclasts ripped the liberal curriculum apart and substituted their seductive program of free electives. That such a heritage exists and that our present civilization rests on it, no one would deny. Whether it was transmitted, even in substance, to earlier college generations, in a way that is now no longer the case, is open to question. A related question arises: Can this body of truth and values be transmitted only through the channel of a certain fixed number of subjects of study, which are properly called the liberal arts? An examination of the historic college curriculum will force us to answer both questions in the negative.

The liberal curriculum has come a long way since it began as the seven liberal arts salvaged from the wreckage of the Roman Empire. An accidental assemblage to begin with, it was pretty thin fare until enriched by the three philosophies of Aristotle in the high Middle Ages. The fifteenth and sixteenth centuries brought Greek into the program, and it became a standby from then on. The seventeenth century added mathematics, the eighteenth the first formalized instruction in science. It was at this stage in its development that the liberal curriculum reached America; this was substantially the curriculum that was hailed by the Yale report of 1828 as *the* liberal education, which was sound and good for all time. Yet even in that approved form it included no extensive study of the Great Books, for there was not much time left for those after grammar, syntax, and routine translation had been attended to. The Yale report failed in the long run to fix the content of the liberal arts, for subject after subject that the conservatives had thought secondary or quite unnecessary found its way into the college catalogues. Modern languages, English literature, and history all gained admission over bitter opposition and, once in the fold, became in turn staunch defenders of the revised *status quo*. By the end of the nineteenth century laboratory science had firmly established itself and even gained priority status; and the social sciences, economics, government, sociology, were gaining recognition as worthy bearers of the Great Tradition. Each of these subjects in turn was constantly changing in content and emphasis. And the process goes on; to this day newly organized areas of knowledge and novel combinations of subject matter are shouldering their way into the select circle and gaining the grudging approval of the custodians of the cultural heritage. A day may come when such relative newcomers as the behavioral sciences and American studies will be defended to the death as essential to the liberal tradition, against the impudent claims of the philistines of that day. The numbers of those who view this curricular evolution with alarm are declining, but the Hutchins school, for example, remains in opposition, and Catholic leaders are critical of the trend. At a recent meeting of the Association of American Colleges the Reverend Theodore M. Hesburgh, president of Notre Dame University, sharply denounced the submergence of the classics, that core of all liberal education, and deplored the resulting disintegration of the cultural unity of the Western world.[9]

But the disintegration, if that is what it is, goes on. Among the subjects currently in controversy are the creative arts. The drama has for some time been considered a legitimate part of the study of literature; and music and painting, once taught privately or in conservatories and trade schools, have found their way into the college catalogues. The artistic and especially the musical awareness of the average undergraduate today is vastly superior to what it was fifty years ago. For proof one need only compare college glee club and choir programs with those of the 1890's. The question remains whether the critics or the practitioners of the arts are the true carriers of the cultural tradition. Upton Sinclair lashed out forty years ago against the, to him, ridiculous practice of accepting a learned critique of a poem, a painting, or a symphony for college credit or even a Ph.D. degree, while the poet, the painter, the composer, and concert performer rated no such academic recognition.[10] This situation too is slowly changing. Academic recognition of the creative arts is not as far off as it once was. With increasing frequency, the demand is made that demonstrated mastery of painting, or an original musical composition, or a poem, or a novel, should be accepted as the equivalent of a doctoral dissertation, while poets, painters, and musicians in residence are no longer a rarity on college campuses.[11]

To assign a fixed content to the liberal arts turns out to be almost as difficult as to define them. Nor can we escape the difficulty by adopting a quantitative standard and saying the liberal arts are the four years of college which come after high school. As we have seen, there is nothing sacred about the American four-year college; it is not an eternal verity but a historic accident. Though on the whole it has proved a convenient division of time, yet it has always had its critics.

The inadequacy of the rigid four-year yardstick is pointed up by the growing intrusion of vocational and professional courses into the liberal quadrennium. The proportion of men who graduate with a straight arts and science major, such as literature, history, biology, economics, or philosophy, has steadily declined until today it is scarcely one in three.[12] In colleges for women, where direct professional preparation for a career is not so essential, liberal arts majors are more numerous. This drift away from the cultural core does not meet with the approval of the more thoughtful business leaders. In impressive numbers modern captains of industry are deploring the overspecialization and the lack of general cultural orientation of the young men entering the ranks of business and industry today. Lack of specific skills is not nearly so often the cause of failure on the job, they say, as character and personality defects which presumably could have been corrected by more broadly liberal courses in college. Unfortunately these laudable aims of the spokesmen for business are somewhat offest by their practice. When employment representatives of the larger corporations descend upon the college campuses in the spring to select their quotas from the season's crop of graduates, it is usually the vocationally trained seniors who are picked out first. Engineers, for the moment at least, can write their own ticket; business administration majors do well enough; but those who have chosen English or history, subjects with which one can "do nothing," still bring up the rear.[13]

Addressing himself to the general theme of bridging the gap between liberal and vocational aims, President Francis H. Horn of Pratt Institute denounced the belief in a fixed body of liberal truths and values, immutably set apart from the vocational, as "folklore." Most young people must prepare for a vocation in two to four college years, and liberal arts advocates display bad grace in berating them for this. The problem, as Horn sees it, is not liberal *versus,* but liberal *and* vocational. Furthermore he insists that a liberal education is not so much a matter of content as a way of looking at things. "Just as the so-called liberal subjects can be taught illiberally, likewise so-called vocational subjects can and should be taught liberally." [14] In other words a vocational subject can be taught in terms of its basic principles and underlying structure, as the Hutchins school would put it, while a liberal subject can degenerate into a mechanical drilling of skills and a hand-to-mouth acquisition of facts. There is much truth in this viewpoint, and yet, as President Horn no doubt would agree, it has its limitations. Not all subjects are equally valuable for all purposes. No matter how expertly or liberally it may be taught, a course in newspaper advertising or in plant pathology will not prepare its students as well for responsible participation in our democratic society as will a course in constitutional problems or a seminar in political behavior, equally well taught.

And this takes us to the heart of the matter. A liberal education is not a thing of precise definition like an isosceles triangle, nor is it a fixed list of courses in a college catalogue taken over a given period of years. It is rather a human quality and a personal achievement, which can be attained in a variety of ways. In wading through the voluminous literature on the subject, voluminous because it must remain imprecise, one needs to exercise caution. As William H. Cowley of Stanford, formerly president of Hamilton College, has said, "the literature of higher education slops over with effusions about sentimental purposes." [15] Pinning down the exuberant clichés and vaguely defined objectives in which it abounds is, as Theodore Roosevelt once said in another connection, like nailing currant jelly to the wall.

Nevertheless, the hundreds who have written about it and the hundreds of thousands who have experienced it are convinced there is *something* there, and that something is priceless. Its component parts, if anything so vague can have component parts, might be described somewhat as follows. A liberal education means knowledge:

verified and dependable information about the world of nature and its processes, and about human society both in its historic origins and its ever-changing contemporary forms. It means trained skills and abilities: to use one's own language effectively and one or more foreign languages adequately; to think critically—itself a cosmos of more specific skills; to judge intelligently among alternatives; to participate helpfully in social situations. It means appreciation of people; of the moral and spiritual quality of actions; of human imagination whether displayed in painting or music, in poetry or drama, or in mathematics, astronomy, or physics.[16] A liberal education is something like that. To one who has never experienced it, this attempt to dissect the intangible will be meaningless; to one who has, it is superfluous. Both groups will include bachelors of arts and doctors of philosophy, as well as men and women who have never set foot in a college.

Chapter Twelve

Academic Freedom

If the liberal values, which are after all the values on which our whole civilization rests, are to be preserved, colleges and universities must be allowed to function freely and without artificial restraints. It is difficult enough to keep the cultural tradition alive and to transmit it, undiluted and unadulterated, to future generations. To enlarge it by scientific research is perhaps even more difficult. Yet, both activities must go on, continuously and at their highest level of efficiency, if our nation is to remain healthy and our civilization to survive. All arbitrary interference with this work, in the form of censorship or intimidation of any kind, is therefore a blow at civilization itself. If colleges and universities are to be true to their trust, they must be safeguarded against such interference. In other words, they must be assured of academic freedom.

The term academic freedom is another of those easily manipulated educational labels which requires careful analysis to be fully understood. It is of recent origin. The old-time college of John Witherspoon and Timothy Dwight knew nothing of it. Not until the end of the nineteenth century did it gain currency, and then only as a result of the widening cleavage between some of the newly emphasized activities of the universities and the vested interests and inherited beliefs of their constituents. The insistence on academic freedom in the American version is an attempt to resolve this peculiarly American dilemma. Unlike Europe we have not had nationally supported universities of ancient vintage and international prestige, like those of Paris, Oxford, and Heidelberg.[1] A few are beginning to approach this status, but in the main, American colleges and universities still depend, as they always have, on their own alumni or other interested philanthropists, or on the church that sponsors them, or on the taxpayers of the state. In seeking this multiple support some institutions have gone to great lengths. One need only glance at the many groups of advisers and interested supporters, in addition to the trustees, which appear in various college catalogues. By way of example, Stetson University in Florida has a President's Board of Alumni Counselors, also the Stetson Associates, made up of "representative men and women who, although they did not attend Stetson, have identified themselves with the University and are supporting it both morally and financially," and finally the Stetson University Council, "an auxiliary board of distinguished business and professional leaders . . . to cooperate in planning future developments." [2] And this is fairly typical.

With this kind of planning and public relations programs, colleges can build up warm loyalties among diversified groups of followers, though in doing so they lay themselves open to sharp criticism from these same sources. The various groups of supporters of an institution, trustees and alumni, church officials, business well-wishers, and patrons of football games, all want to be proud of "their" college. But for that very reason they want it to be the kind of college that they can be proud of, and they are ready to criticize every action or expression emanating from their beloved campus that conflicts with their own notions of what a college ought to be. Unfortunately these notions are not always those of the faculty. The latter are inclined to believe that the great, the ideal, college is one in which all members are free to express and publish any idea, popular or unpopular, that they have honestly explored and which they consider true and important. They hold to the theory of intellectual leadership, which higher education has always professed as one of its principal reasons for existence. This is high ground and difficult to maintain. Practice has not always kept abreast of profession; when environmental pressures become too great, colleges sometimes behave like the army captain whose company got out of hand and who rushed after them, saying: "I must follow them, I am their leader."

Such conflicts of opinion between the practitioners of the liberal arts and their constituents were far less likely to arise in the earlier years of our history. Colleges then were few and small and their impact on public opinion correspondingly weak. Since in addition they were nearly all church-controlled, students, faculty, and trustees shared the same prevailing philosophy, which was Protestant Christianity leavened with the ideas of the Enlightenment. The colleges, finally, were not research institutions but teaching seminaries; as such, they contented themselves with transmitting the accepted tradition and spent little time discovering new and unpalatable truths. Faculties and governing boards in the days before Darwin and Eliot usually managed to sense public opinion and to set a course slightly, but not too far, in advance of the thinking of their constituencies. Harvard is an example of this, as it was gently wafted into Unitarianism early in the nineteenth century. In 1805 the Corporation chose, and the Overseers approved, a Unitarian, the Reverend Henry Ware, as Hollis professor of divinity. The presidency had meantime fallen vacant, too, and the governing boards, after first offering it to an Episcopalian who declined it because of "advanced age" (he was forty-seven) elected a Unitarian for this position also. Conservative objections to this lapse from Calvinist orthodoxy were met with the argument that orthodox simply meant "the general sentiments of the country." [3]

Nonconformist professors in the older colleges were not numerous. Among the few who were ousted from office, personality clashes were as much an issue as their unpopular opinions. Josiah Meigs, professor of mathematics and natural philosophy at Yale and an ardent Jeffersonian, fell under suspicion of subversion in that Federalist stronghold. To keep his position, he made a formal statement of his political beliefs as proof that he was sound, much in the manner of modern loyalty oaths; even so, he found the climate of New Haven uncongenial and left for Georgia, where he became president of the newly founded state university. In the opinion of his wife he was expatriated "for no earthly reason but his stern democracy." But even in the politically more congenial surroundings of Georgia he did not last long. His stern democracy and admittedly great ability happened to be coupled with a sharp tongue; accused, among other things, of calling the trustees "a damned pack of tories and speculators," he was forced to resign the presidency and accept a lower professorship, and eventually he was ousted from that too. [4]

Two other scholars who fell afoul of public opinion in the days of the old college were Horace Holley and Thomas Cooper. Holley, president of Transylvania University in Kentucky, and urbane religious liberal, succumbed to the opposition of the strait-laced and orthodox Presbyterian element of that state. Cooper was a distinguished English-born scientist and religious nonconformist. Through the good offices of Thomas Jefferson he became president of South Carolina College and made it, with the aid of an unusually competent faculty, one of the best colleges in the country. At first Cooper was held in high esteem in South Carolina, for besides his scholarly pre-eminence, he was "right" on slavery, the tariff, and nullification. In view of all this, his religious liberalism might have been overlooked had he not been so bitterly anticlerical and given to provocative pamphleteering. Charges were ultimately brought against him by the conservative religious forces of the state; in defense of his position he advanced elaborate, well-grounded arguments in favor of free expression of opinion both on and off the campus—which anticipated much of the legal and philosophical reasoning that underlies the case for academic freedom today. Though he was vindicated by the trustees, the unfavorable publicity and declining enrollments which resulted, brought about his resignation.[5]

Meigs, Holley, and Cooper were isolated cases which had little effect on the solid front of popular religious and political faith. The situation changed when the college was transformed into the university and the theologically trained professor gave way to the research scholar. With the latter's claim of the right to investigate all opinions and to proclaim his findings in public, the way was open to challenge all religious and philosophical authority. Before such an assault the old unity of belief crumbled, and the area of potential friction between the university as an exponent of free research and its more conservative supporters was materially enlarged.

At first this friction was most noticeable in the field of science, where the evolutionary philosophy was making deep inroads into accepted beliefs. Its by-product was a series of disputes over the right of scientists to teach and publish their heterodox views. For a while the more outspoken ones found it difficult to obtain teaching positions or secure reappointments. There were a few heresy trials. Andrew Dickson White cites the more celebrated ones in his apologia for theological tolerance: *The Warfare of Science and Theology*.[6] Church-controlled institutions, naturally enough, were most sensitive to changing winds of doctrine. Thus when the geologist Alexander Winchell, who had written a tract on the pre-Adamite origins of man, was expelled from Vanderbilt University in 1878, the Tennessee Methodist Conference exulted: "Our university alone has had the courage to lay its young but vigorous hands upon the mane of untamed speculation and say, 'we will have no more of this.' "[7] But

Winchell soon found another position, this time at Michigan. Winchell's experience was not typical, for by and large the scientists were acclimated and their right to publish their findings accepted as part of the function of a university.

It was a different story with the social scientists. They, too, like the geologists and biologists, were enlarging their sphere of interest, but in doing so they ran head-on into another already existing vested interest, one to which the university was increasingly beholden. This was the interest of business and industry, and it was important, for as the universities grew and their activities diversified, costs mounted in proportion. Church support was no longer adequate, and student tuition fell a long way short of filling the gap. Tuition fees to this day account for considerably less than half of the cost of higher education, and in many state universities they are negligible. There was only one other source to turn to, namely the chief creators of American wealth and chief beneficiaries of its prosperity, the business community.[8] It responded with munificence. The businessman contributed to the support of higher education in various ways. If he sent his sons and daughters to a private college, he paid tuition like everybody else; at the same time he was taxed for the support of his state university; as an alumnus, he was expected to pledge continued support to his alma mater, and if, finally, he reached the higher economic brackets, he was likely to be solicited for large donations to the building or endowment fund. It was this last activity that forged the strongest link between the communities of business and the university. When Abbott Lawrence gave Harvard the unprecedented sum of $50,000 in 1847, he set in motion a chain reaction which in time effected a revolution in American higher education. Abbott's contribution was topped, thirty years later, by the $3,500,000 gift of Johns Hopkins. The Stanford bequest near the end of the nineteenth century ran to $24,000,000 all told, and Rockefeller's gifts to the University of Chicago in the same decade totaled $34,000,000. The twentieth century ushered in the great foundations: the General Education Board of the Rockefellers, the Carnegie Corporation, the Harkness and Guggenheim trusts, and most recently the Ford Foundation. They all are now part of the American scene, and among university administrations and faculties they are household words.[9]

As the businessman's financial contacts with the colleges increased, so did his interest in what the colleges were doing. What they were doing was investigating the businessman with all his works and all his ways. At least the economists and sociologists and historians and political scientists were investigating him, and they were the ones who from now on drew the lightning of his criticism and censure. Here was the new area of friction which in time produced a new crop of heresy trials: economic and social heresy this time. For the social scientists spurned the ivory tower and operated in the world of reality. Out of the seminar of Richard T. Ely at Johns Hopkins came new-styled economists who were not content to mouth the a priori formulations of their classical *laissez faire* predecessors but insisted on making empirical studies of monopoly and social control, of money problems, of labor relations and other economic actualities. Historians gave up shouting glory and turned with Woodrow Wilson and Charles A. Beard to a re-examination of American institutions in the light of current shortcomings and abuses. Political scientists were exposing governmental weaknesses and smelling out noisome political machines, while sociologists on the basis of systematically collected evidence were calling for improvement of the lot of the underdog. In fact it was largely university professors who formulated the problems and collected the evidence on the strength of which that group of reform-minded journalists known as the muckrakers touched off the Progressive movement, which in turn we associate with the names of LaFollette, Bryan, and Theodore Roosevelt.

In the process of exposure some distinguished toes were stepped on and some sacred cows handled with disrespect. The business community did not take the attack lying down. As in the early days of the evolution controversy, charges were brought, this time involving some nationally known leaders of the profession. Among those investigated were Ely himself, dean of American economists, and Edward A. Ross, pioneer sociologist. There were other cases, less prominent than those of Ely and Ross, in which the issue of academic freedom was at stake. They occurred at Chicago, Brown, Syracuse, Indiana, Northwestern, Kansas State, Marietta, and elsewhere. Among the charges leveled against the scholars in these institutions were the following: encouraging strikes, defending Eugene Debs the labor leader and native socialist, advocating municipal ownership of utilities, favoring free silver, opposing monopolies, opposing a protective tariff, and opposing the imperialism that resulted from the war with Spain. From the perspective of the second half of the twentieth century some of these issues of fifty years ago seem dated and innocuous;

at the time they were real enough. Significantly, it was not an ideological struggle, as the evolution controversy had been. The offending social scientists were not attacking any American ideals but were on the contrary, in the name of those ideals, insisting on the right to examine all aspects of American life and to express publicly their critical findings. In doing so, they found themselves questioning many current business and political practices and attacking many vested interests.

The charges against the professors were handled by the universities in various ways. Sometimes the president acted alone and decided the issue by virtue of his authority as chief executive; at others the trustees investigated and made the final decision. The latter bodies, by the way, had also undergone a transformation that corresponded to the larger social changes of the time. In the days of the old college the clergy, though even then a minority, had been the most influential element in the governing boards. Now business and financial leaders were most numerous, with lawyers, representing the same general interest, next. The remainder were scattered among various professions; state universities had a few farmers on their boards; labor was virtually unrepresented.[10] It was before boards thus constituted that the offending academicians were haled to give an account of their doings.

Out of the trials of Ely, Ross, and the others, at the turn of the twentieth century, a belief built up in university faculty circles that the business interests of the nation were cooperating, even conspiring, to suppress all investigation and publication injurious to themselves. Presidents and trustees, knowing what side their bread was buttered on, seemed to be selling out to these interests. Though no statistics are available, it is hardly to be questioned that this stereotype of predatory wealth as opposed to dedicated scholarship came to have considerable vogue among college professors. As a bit of academic folklore, it has not entirely disappeared even yet, for the business community adds just enough fuel to the fire from time to time to keep it burning. The latter had its folklore, too. Again without counting heads one may safely say that there was—and is—a widespread feeling among businessmen that college professors were irresponsible crackpots who were out to corrupt the morals of youth and undermine the system of free enterprise (the two were apparently synonymous) and who had to be watched at every step.

Both views are open to question, to say the least. Stereotypes generally are. The black and white, or devil, theory of social change is too simple to make the necessary allowance for the complexity of the problems facing human societies. Rich businessmen as a class are not necessarily reactionaries and malefactors nor are professors in the aggregate either crackpots or patient martyrs for Truth. On closer examination the particular group of celebrated cases cited above displayed considerable individual differences. Though clash of opinion over a social or economic issue was a constant element in all, personality factors complicated each case, and the outcomes were not all the same. Heroes and villains do not emerge clearly, and all the affairs were not simple epic struggles between the "good guys" and the "bad guys."

Ely, now at Wisconsin, and the most famous of the group, was completely vindicated by the board of regents of the state university after an elaborate public hearing, and all charges against him were dismissed.[11] On that occasion the regents of the university accompanied their verdict with the following statement of principles: "We cannot be unmindful of the fact that many of the universally accepted principles of today were but a short time ago denounced as visionary. . . . We could not for a moment think of recommending the dismissal or even the criticism of a teacher even if some of his opinions should, in some quarters, be regarded as visionary. . . . We cannot for a moment believe that knowledge has reached its final goal, or that the present condition of society is perfect. . . ." This statement came from a board whose membership was essentially political in character.

Edward W. Bemis of the University of Chicago, on the contrary, was dismissed out of hand by President Harper without trial or specification of charges, after he had made a speech attacking the railroad companies during the Pullman strike. Yet other economic nonconformists on the Chicago faculty, including Charles Zeublin the socialist, and the iconoclastic Thorstein Veblen, were left undisturbed.[12] The dismissal at Stanford of Edward A. Ross came about because his economic views offended Mrs. Stanford, who held the purse strings. "I am weary of Professor Ross," wrote Mrs. Stanford to President Jordan, who played an equivocal role in the whole affair, and Ross had to go. Yet he had come out to the coast in the first place with a chip on his shoulder. Perhaps he was reacting against his own youth and college days which were spent, as he put it, in a "tight little intellectual world . . . bounded by Presbyte-

rianism, Republicanism, perfectionism and capitalism." At any rate
he was determined, when coming to Stanford, to "test this boasted
academic freedom; if nothing happened to me others would speak
out. . . . If I got cashiered, as I thought would be the case, the
hollowness of our role of independent scholar would be visible to
all." Ross went on to fight many another battle. Among other things
he wrote one of the fundamental tracts of the Progressive movement,
Sin and Society, for which he was roundly denounced by conservatives generally. Rising eventually to the top of his profession, first
at Nebraska, then at Wisconsin, he believed to the end of his distinguished career that big business was out to get his scalp.[13]

Still another version of the story was the case of John Spencer Bassett, outstanding historical scholar and professor at Trinity College
in North Carolina. Bassett had written an article on the Negro
problem in which he pleaded with his fellow Southerners to substitute conciliation for intimidation and, among other things, called
Booker T. Washington the greatest Southerner, next to Robert E.
Lee, of the last hundred years. A storm of abuse descended on him
from the southern press, and public opinion demanded his dismissal. But the president of the college stood firmly behind his professor, and the lay-clerical board of this Methodist institution supported the president, stood its ground against popular clamor, and
refused to discharge Bassett. Though disagreeing with his views, the
trustees, its business members more liberal than its ministers, declared, by a vote of 18 to 7: "We are unwilling to lend ourselves to
any tendency to destroy or limit academic liberty." Benjamin N.
Duke, leading trustee and financial patron of the institution, fully
supported this view.[14]

Militating further against the oversimplified theory of the aggressive, reactionary business tycoon versus the underdog liberal professor is another fact. The social scientists, or at any rate the economists, were by no means unanimous in support of the "liberal" side
of the questions of the day. Most of them favored the gold standard
and thus agreed with conservative business opinion, and many favored a protective tariff. Nor is there much evidence that insidious
radicalism was contaminating the undergraduates. A straw in the
wind as to student opinion was a poll of the students of the University of Wisconsin, taken in the autumn of 1900, at the height of Ely's
prestige and the beginning of LaFollette's career, when 674 students
voted for McKinley, 148 for Bryan, and two for Debs. Among the

coeds, the Republican majority was even higher. The boys and girls at Wisconsin, at least in 1900, were successfully resisting the intrusion of ideas, subversive or otherwise.[15]

Leftist elements, in the rare cases when they gained political control, did not show a particularly tender regard for academic freedom. When the Populists, native radical party of the West and South, won the Kansas state elections in 1896, they gained control of the board of regents of the state agricultural college. The latter promptly fired the entire faculty, then rehired those professors who were "sound," by Populist standards, on land nationalization and monetary reform and added new ones of the same persuasion, thus insuring an "unprejudiced" examination of all economic problems in favor of Populism and an "unbiased" stand against Republicanism.[16]

Somewhat more plausible than the outright conspiracy theory was a variant which held that although the businessman was not personally hostile or wicked, he represented a philosophy of life so fundamentally different from that of the scholar that the two groups were, and always would be, culturally incompatible. Chief exponent of this view was Thorstein Veblen, and he developed it in his *The Higher Learning in America*. In Veblen's estimate the only purpose of the university was to train and encourage scholars and scientists; it had no call to dispense general education to the man in the street. Yet it was governed by boards of trustees made up of this type of man—who lived, furthermore, by the profit motive for which the single-minded scholars of the campus had no use whatever. Thus a deep gulf was fixed between the practitioners of higher education and its governors. "If scholarly and scientific training . . . unfits men for business efficiency, then the training that comes of experience in business must also be held to unfit men for scholarly and scientific pursuits, and even more pronouncedly for the surveillance of such pursuits." All that trustees are good for is "bootless meddling with academic matters which they do not understand." Presidents, deans, and university administrators generally, Veblen believed, had unfortunately taken on the color of their financial environment and succumbed to the ideals of business. Their goals were efficiency and success, measured by external standards, not scholarly achievement and scientific advance.[17]

Here in Veblen's thesis we have once again the dedicated scholar on a lonely eminence surrounded by philistines, jealous and afraid, who try to drag him down to their level because they do not understand the principles and standards he so nobly upholds. Like the conspiracy charge, the theory of cultural incompatibility is a stereotype that contains some grains of truth. The large universities have taken on many of the aspects of business and industry. Whatever else it may be, an institution that numbers its buildings by the scores, its faculty by the hundreds, its students by the thousands, and its productive endowment by the millions is a business institution. This is a fact which trustees, president, and comptroller can ignore only at their peril. They are engaged in a competitive enterprise, competing for students, gifts, and good will. How to approach the oil tycoon with a million dollars to donate, and where to find the proper person to head the university's public relations office, are questions that will give the president more gray hairs than the questions over which the faculty stews: whether American literature is to be taken in the sophomore year or whether geology is to be added to the group requirement in science. An occasional president has succumbed to this pressure, and has become a super-salesman and nothing more.

The competition for funds and favors has taken many a curious turn. When President Eliot hesitated about accepting the conditions of Joseph Pulitzer's offer of $1,000,000 to found a school of journalism at Harvard, Nicholas Murray Butler "snatched the proposition from under his nose" and the Pulitzer School of Journalism went to Columbia. Edward S. Harkness, graduate of Yale, had offered his alma mater $3,000,000 for something in the way of an honors college, but the Yale authorities argued and delayed, and Harkness transferred his offer to Harvard. "It took Mr. Lowell about ten seconds to accept"; in fact he got Harkness to raise the ante to $10,000,000 to build and equip seven residence colleges. For Yale it may have been some consolation to remember that four years before it had secured the George Pierce Baker drama workshop from Harvard, when the latter found it impossible to build a university theater.[18] Success in conducting a university did seem to depend on an alert business sense, on promotion and salesmanship.

Few university presidents were so venal as to accept funds from just any source or under any conditions. Nicholas Murray Butler, himself a political conservative and an intimate of wealthy men, said in one of his annual reports: "Under no circumstances should, or can, any self-respecting university accept a gift upon conditions which fix or hamper its complete freedom in the control of its own educational policies."[19] Woodrow Wilson rejected William Cooper Procter's offer of a graduate school for Princeton on the high ground of institutional independence and integrity, and President Lowell of Harvard reputedly turned down $10,000,000 offered on condition that a certain professor be dismissed.[20] By way of confirmation of such an independent stand on the part of educational leaders came the announcement, in 1956, of an eight-point set of principles adopted by seven privately supported universities as a guide for accepting gifts from corporations. Of particular relevance is point five: "Corporation gifts for any purpose other than the advancement of learning through independent teaching and research should not be accepted." The statement was signed by the presidents of Chicago, Columbia, Cornell, Harvard, Princeton, Stanford, and Yale.[21] It suggests that university presidents, though perforce turning a ready ear to financial opportunities, have not forgotten the real purposes for which their institutions exist. By and large college and university presidents are still, as they always have been, the principal spokesmen for the aims and ideals of their profession. The educational theories discussed throughout this book have, for the most part, been the thought and expression of college and university presidents.[22]

With the coming of the first world war the question of collegiate independence, or academic freedom, took a new form. It became a matter of patriotism and loyalty. At what point did unpopular classroom utterances and publications of college teachers dealing with the war cease to be merely the expression of minority or individual opinion and become subversive of national safety? To what extent does loyalty in wartime justify suppression of free speech? It was an issue involving not only the universities but the entire school system, the churches, newspapers, and political parties. It led to soul-searching by the Supreme Court and was the occasion for some trail-blazing political philosophy emanating from the pen of Mr. Justice Oliver Wendell Holmes. Once again, as in the evolution and business controversies, a number of academic individuals fell afoul of the issue, though most college professors went their way unmolested, perhaps because they did not step out of line or had no occasion in their subject of instruction to test the issue. In various localities, accusations of disloyalty were made and some dismissals resulted. The furor was most intense in the Middle West, where a disillusioned isolationism had swung over into an intense pro-war anti-German sentiment and where an ostentatious patriotism was demanded of all. At the University of Nebraska the regents investigated twelve professors at the instigation of the State Council of Defense and discharged three of them. The University of Minnesota dismissed the chairman of the department of political science, only to reverse itself twenty years later and reinstate him as professor emeritus.[23]

But the eastern states had their flare-ups too. The director of the school of journalism of the University of Virginia was dismissed for suggesting in a speech that the war would not make the world safe for democracy and that Russia would be the spiritual leader of the next generation. A flagrant instance occurred at Columbia. Here Professor J. McKeen Cattell, outstanding psychologist, was dismissed for disloyalty. He had written to three congressmen urging them not to approve a bill to send American conscripts to Europe to fight. The trustees of Columbia, not content with dismissing Cattell, went further and ordered an investigation of the faculty to determine whether any of them were disseminating doctrines that "are subversive of, or tend to the violation or disregard of the Constitution or the laws of the United States . . . or which tend to encourage a spirit of disloyalty." And President Butler specifically warned the history department not to teach anything that might promote disrespect for American institutions. The historians wondered whether he was including such institutions as the congressional pork barrel or Tammany Hall. Cattell was apparently a difficult person, and many of his colleagues felt that he might well deserve dismissal on the grounds of incompetence or total incompatibility. But to deprive a man of his livelihood for exercising his clear constitutional right of writing to his congressman was another matter! In indignation some of the biggest men on the faculty resigned, among them Charles A. Beard, the historian, who by the way was not out of sympathy with American war aims. In his letter of resignation Beard laid the blame for the entire situation on a small and active group of trustees, reactionary and visionless and with no standing in the world of education, and went on to complain that America, of all countries, should have made the status of a professor lower than that of a manual laborer, who at least had his union to back him up.[24]

The second world war saw comparatively little interference with freedom of research or expression on the campuses, although, to be sure, security restrictions applied to some kinds of research. This may have been in part because the academic world supported the war against the Nazis with greater unanimity than it had the war against the Kaiser a quarter-century earlier. American Firsters and other critics of the second war were not numerous in university circles. But when at its close the chasm opened between the United States and its former Soviet ally, the situation changed once again. The "cold war" brought a renewal of attacks on the colleges. Loyalty, as vaguely defined as in the first war, was again proposed as a test of professorial fitness. Loyalty oaths multiplied, and loyalty investigations disturbed the serenity of the largest universities and the smallest colleges, from the College of the City of New York on the eastern seaboard to the University of California on the west coast. Again there were dismissals of professors unable or unwilling to clear themselves or to convince their judges of the patriotic propriety of their behavior. Since at the time this is written some of these cases are still pending and appear in the headlines as unfinished business, any attempt to judge them or assess their significance would be premature.

A few general comments are in order, nevertheless. The "cold war" and our resulting preoccupation with international Communism have given the old question of freedom and loyalty a new and baffling dimension. Formerly charges were brought against a professor for something he had said or done, and the question was, did he have the right to say or do it. About the fact itself there was usually no dispute. But now it became increasingly a matter of membership in, or deliberate or even unwitting association with, a crafty and slippery political conspiracy—a state of affairs much more difficult to prove or disprove. In such a murky atmosphere, suspicions and rumors, half-truths and half-denials, grew rank. Yet it all came about naturally enough. In the light of the events of the past two or three decades one can see why certain types of individuals became entangled in the Communist philosophy, and also why the public in general has so overwhelmingly turned against it. The idealistic young college graduate of the depression years, jobless through no fault of his own, might well become interested in the panaceas of Marx and Lenin; he was joined by the social misfit and the congenital failure, who entered the party to attain status or to get even with society; there was also the occasional undergraduate who went along out of curiosity or just for a thrill; all groups were held in line by the small hard core of professional revolutionary Communists who are the same the world over. During the war years, too, it was quite respectable to be pleasantly tolerant of Communism. Our best people attended dinners of Soviet-American friendship and lent their names to relief drives for our Russian allies. An examination of the guest and sponsor list of some of these affairs might conceivably prove embarrassing to some of our most righteous present-day flag-wavers.

Then came the end of the war and complete disillusion; for the Soviet leadership soon made it clear that they still considered capitalism the enemy and had not given up their dream of world revolution. The obnoxious Communist tactics of infiltration and underground machination, and the perverted morality which sanctions deceit, treachery, brain-washing, and cold-blooded murder, were all again in evidence. Saddened and angered at having been played for suckers, many of the idealists who had strayed into the party moved out again. Some had left earlier on intellectual grounds, having found the devious twists of the party line an insult to normal intelligence. Some of these repentant idealists were scholars of considerable ability who found their way into college teaching positions. Possibly a very few of the hard-core regulars also got in. The overwhelming majority of college and university faculties and administrations were not fooled by the Communist siren song, either before the war or after. For this reason they resent the charges so frequently and carelessly leveled at the profession in general, of being soft on Communism and hotbeds of subversion and disloyalty. One or two suspected Communists in a faculty of four or five hundred apparently make a hotbed.[25]

That the American public should become alarmed at the unpleasant turn of events since the end of the second world war is understandable too. The Communist world conspiracy is an alarming thing, and a democratic society owes its members every legal and constitutional safeguard against it. Decent citizens have the right to protest if their sons and daughters are being indoctrinated with subversion at tax-supported and tax-exempt institutions of higher learning, and to demand appropriate action of university authorities. But they should first make sure that such indoctrination is actually going on and that they are not being victimized by irresponsible rumor-mongers. The abuse of the Fifth Amendment by guilty conspirators in no way invalidates its proper use as a protection for the innocent; it was for the latter that the Founding Fathers put it into the Constitution in the first place.[26] Confused situations like this are of grave concern to every responsible citizen. Unfortunately they are also made to order for certain types of human scum: the greedy professional informer who fishes in troubled waters; the disillusioned conspirator who salves his conscience by smearing equally repentant former associates; and the gutter politician who wraps himself in the flag to cover his moral nakedness. As to whether a given academic specialist has been abusing his privilege and is guilty of disloyalty, hysterical agitators and malicious gossips are hardly the best judges. His own academic colleagues and superiors, the faculty and administration of the university, are more likely to reach a sound conclusion in such cases, for they have the integrity and good name of the university at heart, and, besides, they know the nature of the problem.

By way of consolation for his current harassments the university professor may reflect that it is all a symptom of his growing importance. Today the public pays attention to what he says and does. He is no longer the harmless absent-minded simpleton he was once held to be, except in caricature. Since the time of the Progressive movement of fifty years ago, and even more since the days of the New Deal, the university specialist has been drawn into consultation in examining social problems, formulating policies, and directing opinion. Even the Republican campaign managers in the Presidential campaign of 1956 considered it necessary to cultivate the "eggheads."

Contemporary attacks on academic freedom have been difficult to cope with because they have been so nearly indistinguishable in the public mind from measures which should legitimately be taken in the interests of the national security. Meanwhile, the academic profession has been strengthened in its defense by two achievements within the last forty years. It has in that time succeeded in formulating and delimiting the term academic freedom itself, and it has formed an association whose main purpose is to clarify the issue, keep it alive, and come to the support of its members when unjustly accused. The term itself is German in origin, though the concept has much older, and primarily English, roots. When George Ticknor and Edward Everett, the first Americans to study abroad, went to Germany in 1815, they were impressed with the freedom of both students and professors, when compared with the regimented life in the American college. The German student was free to attend any university, for as long as he liked, sign up for any course, attend classes or not as he pleased, and take the final examinations whenever he was ready. The Germans called this *Lernfreiheit*. The professor meanwhile, once he had mastered his subject and been installed in his career, was secure in his position, could offer any course of lectures and publish any opinion in the field of his competence, and try with all the power of his intellect to convince his students of the rightness of his views. That was *Lehrfreiheit*. It was not considered indoctrination since the student was under no obligation to come to class or listen to the lectures. If he did, it was presumably with his eyes open. As a result the ponderous pedant read his findings before audiences of three or four sometimes, while the dynamic lecturer performed before full houses.

By the end of the nineteenth century the number of the American scholars in Germany was mounting into the thousands, and when these thousands came back to take positions in the universities and colleges, they disseminated the German idea of academic freedom throughout the American world of scholarship. Though the admiration of German practices ended after 1914, a standard of academic behavior was thus established which proved useful in defending oneself or one's colleagues against charges of theological or economic or political heresy, and it was so used in the instances that have been recounted in this chapter. At the same time it became evident that such defense, to be effective, must rest on wide agreement as to exactly what those professional rights and privileges were and that, furthermore, an organization would have to be formed to maintain them effectively. The first call for such an organization went out from Johns Hopkins. After some preliminary exchange of views, chiefly among the social scientists, agreement was reached in 1915, and the American Association of University Professors, with eight hundred and sixty-seven members, came into being. Its present membership is 42,000.[27] Its chief functions in the forty years of its existence have been to formulate the principles of academic freedom, to work for the acceptance of these principles by the universities of the land, to achieve greater security of tenure for competent and experienced teachers and scholars, and to bring to bear whatever influence the group possessed in support of any professor who lost his position and asked for help and who, after careful investigation, was considered worthy of help. This help was usually not of a material kind, for the association had no administrative authority, nor was it a union engaged in collective bargaining. It could operate only through publicity. It does so today by publishing its findings in its *Bulletin* and by declaring every institution which, in its opinion, has wrongfully ousted a professor and refuses to make amends, or has otherwise flagrantly violated academic freedom, a "censured administration."

Immediately upon its organization in 1915, the association proceeded to formulate its conception of academic freedom and to draw up a code of action for making it effective. The basic principle on which the whole idea rested was clearly and simply expressed: "Institutions of higher education are conducted for the common good and not to further the interest of either the individual teacher or the institution as a whole. The common good depends upon the free search for truth and its free exposition." There follows the key statement as to the rights and duties of a college teacher, here reproduced in full:

> The teacher is entitled to full freedom in research and in the publication of the results, subject to the adequate performance of his other academic duties; but research for pecuniary return should be based upon an understanding with the authorities of the institution.
>
> The teacher is entitled to freedom in the classroom in discussing his subject, but he should be careful not to introduce into his teaching controversial matter which has no relation to his subject. Limitation of academic freedom because of religious or other aims of the institution should be clearly stated in writing at the time of the appointment.
>
> The college or university teacher is a citizen, a member of a learned profession, and an officer of an educational institution. When he speaks or writes as a citizen, he should be free from institutional censorship or discipline, but his special position in the community imposes special obligations. As a man of learning and an educational officer, he should remember that the public may judge his profession and his institution by his utterances. Hence he should at all times be accurate, should exercise appropriate restraint, should show respect for the opinions of others, and should make every effort to indicate that he is not an institutional spokesman.[28]

This statement has become the credo not only of the association but of American university professors in general. It will be noticed that it deals not only with rights and privileges but also with corresponding duties and obligations. Although much of it derived from Germany, there was one German practice that was never accepted here. The German professor's claim of the right to persuade and indoctrinate his students was rejected, and it was held instead that the professor, whatever his personal views, had no right to impose these on his students; rather he was under obligation to present all controversial matter relevant to his subject as fairly as possible and with due attention to all sides of the question, so that the student, in possession of all available opinion, would be able to reach his conclusions in an atmosphere as free from bias as it was possible to make it.

When first made public, the statement of the association, together with its accompanying provisions for the making and terminating of appointments, met with considerable antagonism and some misrepresentation. The parallel organization of college presidents, the Association of American Colleges, denounced it as impractical and presumptuous. But over the years this attitude changed, and by 1940 a revised version of the code, which had been worked out jointly, received the full endorsement of both bodies. Since then, increasing numbers of university governing boards have adopted it in whole or in part and incorporated it, in one form or another, into the statutes of their institution.

The future of the liberal arts is staked on the continued vitality of the principle of academic freedom. Understanding and acceptance of this principle are doubly important for the decades immediately ahead, when, if present trends continue, the enrollment of the country's institutions of higher education is likely to double. A liberal education does not depend on the form of college organization or the content of the curriculum, both of which have changed and will change again, but on the open mind. To survive, the liberal arts college must continue to produce men and women of disciplined intelligence, appreciative of old and hospitable to new truths, and responsive to the problems of the day. With this end in view it must remain free to investigate all relevant controversial issues. That is the *sine qua non* which needs reassertion in all ages but particularly today; for ever since the beginning of the "cold war" a smothering blanket of timidity has settled on the land and we have been backing away from controversy. We want to be informed, yes, entertained, certainly, "but nothing controversial." With such an attitude there is no point in going to college; it would be an expensive waste of time and far too unsettling. The young person who wants to avoid all controversy and play it safe would do much better to stay at home and curl up with a good telephone directory. Yet without controversy a government of, by, and for the people cannot exist. The truths in a political or social issue cannot be discovered, nor the wisest national policy adopted, without free and open discussion of all alternatives. And higher education in any real sense cannot survive in such an atmosphere of faint-hearted avoidance or actual suppression of discussion. When dissenters are liquidated, the citadel of learning is captured.[29] The Nazis and the Soviets throttled controversy with results that everybody knows. The great names in our history on the contrary are those of men who took a firm stand on controversial issues and defended their stand with their lives, their fortunes, and their sacred honor.

The liberal philosophy is threatened not only from without, but also by unwitting foes in its own household. The reactionary professor who resists every innovation in courses or methods as destructive of the liberal arts is himself antiliberal. At the other extreme, exponents of novelty such as, for example, composite interdepartmental and functional survey courses, run the danger of ladling out subject matter in such weak dilution as to debase the quality of the educational product. Such courses may look modern, yet fail to offer solid intellectual food. A bright package is poor consolation if all nourishment has been processed out of the contents. Neither do we want to bog down in the preliminaries of why's and wherefore's or become entangled in the machinery of methods and techniques, to the detriment of knowledge itself. One can overdo the hairsplitting distinctions between the ends, the goals, the aims, the purposes, and the objectives of education, for all this is preliminary to the real business of learning. And that begins at the moment when the teacher, whatever his subject, manages to inspire, shame, or bludgeon the individual student to recognize his inherited clichés, face new facts and ideas honestly, and begin to think his own thoughts.

In its final form the problem is a moral one. When Columbia University celebrated its bicentennial in 1954, it chose as its motto "man's *right* to knowledge and the free use thereof." [30] Whence does this right derive and how far does it extend? Dewey and his school contended that the purpose of knowledge is to solve problems as they arise in the everchanging flux of events. Well and good; but which way shall we solve them? Most problems lend themselves to several solutions. The scientist's understanding of nuclear fission may be used for the storing and ultimate dropping of bombs—which could end all controversy and all education—or it may be turned to the construction of power plants which will make life easier for all the inhabitants of the globe. Fascist and Communist nations have solved some of their problems quite effectively, but their solutions are not the kind that we could for a moment approve. Problems, we say, must be solved right. The necessary knowledge must be accompanied by an ethical purpose. The Hutchins thesis is no more satisfactory in this respect than that of Dewey. True, the Great Tradition of our civilization furnishes us with many examples of beauty and wisdom and nobility of conduct, but it has also saddled us with poverty, cruelty, intolerance, and war. Again we must select that which is good by making an ethical choice, and must judge the facts in the light of some kind of dependable principles and lasting values.

But who is to decide what these values are? The churches? They have contributed deep insights, but they do not always agree. More than one religious organization in the course of human history has set itself up as the chief arbiter of morals and sole channel of divine revelation and has, when possible, throttled all rival claims. The results have not been edifying. A political party? That is the Communist way. The government? The Fascists and Nazis have demonstrated the disastrous consequences of that. A board of scientists, or a committee of professors? God forbid! What remains, for practical purposes, is that vague general consensus, "the sense of the meeting," which grows slowly, by trial and error, out of human experience, so that eventually the majority arrives at a conviction that certain courses of action are right and others wrong. Expressed in its widest terms, it is a conviction that the individual human being is an end in himself, never a means to an end. Thomas Jefferson called it the unalienable right to life, liberty, and the pursuit of happiness. A religious philosopher might formulate it as the infinite value of every human soul, or agree with Paul on Mars' hill: God "hath made of one blood all nations of men for to dwell on all the face of the earth." On some such common doctrine theologians and scientists can agree; here is a platform that religion and scholarship can share. Out of this general proposition grow all individual and social rights and obligations: the family, private property, government. Scholarship, or the right to know, rests upon it also. The basis of liberal education then is an ethical assumption or value judgment, which does not grow automatically out of science or the practice of scholarship but is antecedent to them.

If this major premise is correct, if knowledge is morally preferable to ignorance, certain conclusions are inescapable. For one, knowledge must be accurate and authentic. From this corollary stem all the paraphernalia of scholarship: the weighing of sources, the amassing of critical bibliographies, and the proper use of footnotes; and their counterpart in the sciences, the precision of laboratory techniques and the rigorous testing of hypotheses. Intellectual honesty is the essence of all scholarly activity. Honor pledges on student examinations and honor boards maintained by student government associations derive from the same source and are the students' way of saying that they will abide by the moral obligations of scholarship. On the same moral grounds the college must resist censorship in all its forms and keep open the avenues to truth. Academic freedom, in other words, is a moral obligation.

It is an obligation to acknowledge honestly the *status quo* and pay due respect to conventional behavior, but also to permit expression to the nonconformist crying in the wilderness and not to suppress his message. He may be preparing the way of the Lord. The great names of those who have pushed civilization forward are the names of nonconformists. Socrates was one, and Franklin, and Jefferson. The nonconformity of Jesus has had the profoundest influence on all subsequent history. "Ye have heard that it was said by them of old time . . . but I say unto you." There is the old and the new. We need both, for one supplements the other. What was said by them of old time contains the wisdom of the ages, which the liberal college must preserve and transmit to posterity. But whenever a prophet of new ideals arises to speak with the authority that rests on fullness of knowledge and conscientious conviction, it is the duty of the liberal college to give him a hearing.

Notes

1. Massachusetts Bay Records, I, 183, quoted in Samuel E. Morison, *The Founding of Harvard College* (Cambridge, 1935), p. 168. Morison's volume is a most detailed and scholarly account, not only of the founding of Harvard, but of the European background, and the transit of college and university from its medieval beginnings at Paris, Oxford and Cambridge, to the New World.

2. This generalization would, on closer inspection, prove subject to many qualifications; but these are beyond the scope of this book. The standard work on medieval universities is Hastings Rashdall, *The Universities of Europe in the Middle Ages* (London, 1936). See also Paul Monroe, *Cyclopedia of Education* (New York, 1915). On the question of scholars' privileges see Pearl Kibre, "Scholarly Privileges: Their Roman Origin and Medieval Expression," *American Historical Review*, LXX, No. 3 (1954).

3. Morison, in *The Founding of Harvard College*, p. 122, describes the steps in this watering-down process from Paris to Harvard.

4. Samuel E. Morison, *Three Centuries of Harvard* (Cambridge, 1936), pp. 160, 170.

5. Herbert B. Adams, "Thomas Jefferson and the University of Virginia," *U. S. Bureau of Education Circular of Information*, No. 1, 1888, p. 74.

6. The nine in chronological order are Harvard 1636, William and Mary 1693, Yale 1701, Princeton 1746, Pennsylvania 1749 (or 1740), Columbia 1754, Brown 1764, Rutgers 1766, Dartmouth 1769.

7. Morison, *Founding*, p. 234 and ch. 17. Many a college was to recapitulate, in substance, these experiences of Harvard.

8. The story is told in Edward P. Cheyney, *History of the University of Pennsylvania, 1740-1940* (Philadelphia, 1940).

9. Dixon Ryan Fox, *Union College, an Unfinished History* (Schenectady, N. Y., 1945).

10. Claude M. Fuess, *Amherst, the Story of a New England College* (Boston, 1935).

11. Thomas J. Wertenbaker, *Princeton, 1746-1896* (Princeton, 1946), p. 36.

12. Cornelia R. Shaw, *Davidson College* (New York, 1923).

13. Edward D. Eaton, *Historical Sketches of Beloit College* (New York, 1928).

14. *Records of the University of Michigan, 1817-1837* (Ann Arbor, 1935).

15. The precise number for the first half of the nineteenth century is difficult to fix. *The American Almanac and Repository of Useful Knowledge* for 1841 lists an even hundred, with the caution that some of these are probably academies; the *Seventh Census of the United States* (1850) counts 234, but probably includes many short-lived schools; Donald G. Tewksbury, *The Founding of American Colleges and Universities before the Civil War* (New York, 1932), a careful and informed study, counts 182 surviving institutions, by 1860.

16. Tewksbury, p. 28.

17. Wertenbaker, p. 36. W. H. S. Demarest, *A History of Rutgers College* (New Brunswick, N. J., 1924), pp. 32, 78. *Catalogue of Rutgers College, 1843-1844,* and other years.

18. Fox, p. 11. Louis C. Hatch, *The History of Bowdoin College* (Portland, Me., 1927), p. 2.

19. Philander C. Chase, *A Plea for the West* (Philadelphia, 1826).

20. *Historical Sketch of Antioch College* (no author or date, but internal evidence indicates it was written about 1876). Arkansas Conference College *Bulletin,* 1911. David D. Banta, *History of Indiana University, 1820-1920* (Bloomington, Ind., 1921), p. 41.

21. *Report of a Committee of the Trustees of Columbia College* (New York, 1854).

22. Jonas Viles, *The University of Missouri—A Centennial History* (Columbia, Mo., 1939), p. 19. Daniel W. Hollis, *South Carolina College* (Columbia, S. C., 1951), ch. 1. James H. Morgan, *Dickinson College, 1783-1933* (Carlisle, Pa., 1933), p. 10. Fuess, p. 62. Alfred W. Anthony, *Bates College and Its Background* (Philadelphia, 1936). Charles H. Rammelkamp, *Illinois College—A Centennial History, 1829-1929* (New Haven, 1929), p. 67.

23. Wertenbaker, p. 181. Cheyney, p. 226. Morison, *Three Centuries,* p. 295.

24. Thomas Fitzhugh, *The University of Virginia in Texas and the Southwest* (pamphlet, Lynchburg, Va., 1897).

25. Morison, *Founding,* p. 246. E. M. Coulter, *College Life in the Old South* (New York, 1928), p. 12, and chs. 1 and 2. Demarest, chs. 8 and 9.

26. Rammelkamp, p. 457.

27. *U. S. Bureau of Education Circular of Information,* No. 1, 1890. *Proceedings of the Board of Regents* (University of Michigan), 1837-

1864, p. 977. *Historical and Statistical Record of the University of the State of New York* (Albany, N. Y., 1885). Henry M. Bullock, *A History of Emory University* (Nashville, Tenn., 1936), pp. 66, 69. Hollis, pp. 4, 16. Viles, ch. 2. Coulter, chs. 1 and 2.

28. Wertenbaker, p. 31. Philip G. Nordell, "The Rutgers Lotteries," *Journal of the Rutgers University Library*, XVI, No. 1 (1952).

29. The story is told in Fox, p. 29.

30. Theron Baldwin, head of the Society for the Promotion of Collegiate and Theological Education at the West, quoted in Tewksbury, p. 5.

31. *Transactions of the American Philosophical Society* (Philadelphia, 1799), IV. For a general discussion of the educational views of the late eighteenth century see A. O. Hansen, *Liberalism and American Education in the 18th Century* (New York, 1926).

32. James D. Richardson (comp.), *Messages and Papers of Presidents, 1789-1907* (Washington, D. C., 1896-), I, 202.

33. Richardson, I, 409, 485; II, 312.

34. Bowdoin and Brown are two examples.

35. Morison, *Three Centuries*, p. 159.

CHAPTER TWO

1. Thomas J. Wertenbaker, *Princeton, 1746-1896* (Princeton, 1946), p. 3.

2. Quoted in Samuel E. Morison, *The Founding of Harvard College* (Cambridge, 1935), p. 160.

3. Herbert B. Adams, "The College of William and Mary," *U. S. Bureau of Education Circular of Information,* No. 1, 1887. See also the article on Commissary Blair in the *Dictionary of American Biography*.

4. F. B. Dexter, *Documentary History of Yale University* (New Haven, 1916).

5. Wertenbaker, ch. 1. W. H. S. Demarest, *A History of Rutgers College* (New Brunswick, N. J., 1924), ch. 1.

6. Morison, *Founding*, p. 247. V. L. Collins, *President Witherspoon* (Princeton, 1925), II, 222, 229. *The American Almanac . . . for 1850.*

7. Morison, *Founding,* p. 161. *General Catalogue* of William and Mary, 1660-1874. Wertenbaker, p. 397. Demarest, p. 75. "Advertisement of Kings College," in *Charters, Acts of the Legislature, Official Documents and Records,* John B. Pine, compiler (New York, 1920), p. 32. W. C. Bronson, *The History of Brown University* (Providence, 1914), p. 29. E. C. Parsons, *Educational Legislation and Administration of the Colonial Governments* (New York, 1899), contains the charters of the colonial colleges.

8. Morison, *Three Centuries of Harvard* (Cambridge, 1936), p. 139. Wertenbaker, pp. 57, 65. Demarest, p. 49. Bronson, p. 66. Horace Coon, *Columbia, Colossus on the Hudson* (New York, 1950), p. 50.

9. *Bureau of Education Circular of Information*, No. 1, 1888.

10. J. S. Patton, *Jefferson, Cabell, and the University of Virginia* (New York, 1906), p. 76.

11. Timothy Dwight, *Theology Explained and Defended* (New Haven, 1843), I, 20. Morison, *Three Centuries*, p. 184. Wertenbaker, p. 77.

12. Woodbridge Riley, *American Thought* (New York, 1915), p. 121.

13. Lyman Beecher, *A Plea for Colleges* (Cincinnati, O., 1836).

14. Allen E. Ragan, *A History of Tusculum College, 1794-1944* (Bristol, Tenn., 1945), ch. 1.

15. Joseph Smith, *History of Jefferson College* (Pittsburgh, Pa., 1857).

16. The Asbury quotation is in W. W. Sweet, *Indiana Asbury-DePauw University, 1837-1937* (New York, 1937), p. 21. Durbin's article is in the *Quarterly Register and Journal of the American Education Society*, IV, No. 1 (1832).

17. Albea Godbold, *The Church College of the Old South* (Durham, N. C., 1944), p. 55.

18. *U. S. Bureau of Education Circular of Information*, No. 4, 1888. F. W. Shepardson, *Denison University, 1831-1931* (Granville, O., 1931), pp. 1, 73.

19. F. P. Cassidy, *Catholic College Foundations and Development in the United States, 1677-1850* (Washington, D. C., 1924).

20. Edward D. Eaton, *Historical Sketches of Beloit College* (New York, 1928), p. 24, note. Cornelia R. Shaw, *Davidson College* (New York, 1923), p. 45. Sweet, p. 37. *Catalogue* of Baylor University for 1868-69. Shepardson, p. 373.

21. Daniel W. Hollis, *South Carolina College* (Columbia, S. C., 1951), p. 173, ch. 6 *passim*. Jonas Viles, *The University of Missouri—A Centennial History* (Columbia, Mo., 1939). *Catalogue* of the University of Cincinnati for 1881-82. *Proceedings of the Board of Regents* (University of Michigan), 1837-1864, p. 1054.

22. The claim that nine out of ten presidents were theologians is based on actual count. I checked the careers of 288 pre-Civil War college and university presidents and found that 262 of them were ordained ministers. The entire colonial period did not produce a single non-theological president. The first lay president was John Wheelock of Dartmouth, in 1779. Then followed William Samuel Johnson of Columbia, in 1787. The next was John McDowell, provost of Pennsylvania, in 1803. Josiah Quincy was the first layman to be president of Harvard, in 1829. All of these were again followed by clergymen. Webster's remark about the children of Adam is in Claude M. Fuess,

Amherst, the Story of a New England College (Boston, 1935), p. 30.

23. Robert S. Fletcher, *A History of Oberlin College* (Oberlin, O., 1943), I, 9, 84, 178, and *passim. Laws and Regulations of the Oberlin Collegiate Institute,* 1840.

24. *Historical Sketch of Antioch College* (pamphlet, no author, date, place, internal evidence suggests about 1876).

25. Edward Beecher, *Narrative of the Riots at Alton* (Alton, Ill., 1838). Jonathan Blanchard, *Sermons and Addresses* (Chicago, 1892); *Rights of Congregationalists in Knox College* (Chicago, 1859). Charles T. Morgan, *The Fruits of This Tree* (Berea, Ky., 1946).

26. Hollis, p. 164 and ch. 13. Fuess, p. 111.

27. Fletcher, pp. 209, 435. Charles G. Finney, *Memoirs* (New York, 1876), p. 5.

28. Morison, *Three Centuries, passim. Catalogue* of Bucknell for 1852. Estelle F. Ward, *The Story of Northwestern University* (New York, 1924), p. 29. Shaw, p. 45.

29. Article in the *New Englander,* quoted in Charles H. Rammelkamp, *Illinois College—A Centennial History, 1829-1929* (New Haven, 1929), p. 189.

30. The Jesuit credo is found, for example, in the *Catalogue* of St. John's College, Fordham University, for 1913-14.

CHAPTER THREE

1. R. Freeman Butts, *The College Charts Its Course* (New York, 1939). Samuel E. Morison, *The Founding of Harvard College* (Cambridge, 1935), chs. 2 and 3, gives a detailed account of the transit of the curriculum from the medieval continental beginnings via sixteenth century Cambridge to Harvard. The official sanction for the Oxford and Cambridge programs of study is discussed in Phyllis Allen, "Scientific Studies in 17th Century English Universities," *Journal of the History of Ideas,* X (April, 1949).

2. L. F. Snow, *The College Curriculum in the United States* (n.p., 1907), p. 23. Morison, *Founding,* pp. 248, 434. The quotation from the president's speech at Columbia is in *Addresses at the Inauguration of Mr. Charles King as President of Columbia College, New York* (New York, 1849).

3. The generalizations of this paragraph are based largely on the examination of hundreds of college catalogues of the early, middle, and late nineteenth century.

4. Ernest Earnest, *Academic Procession* (New York, 1953), p. 19.

5. Phyllis Allen, *Journal of the History of Ideas,* X. I. Bernard Cohen,

Some Early Tools of American Science (Cambridge, 1950). Samuel E. Morison, *Three Centuries of Harvard* (Cambridge, 1936), pp. 58, 80, 92. Thomas J. Wertenbaker, *Princeton, 1746-1896* (Princeton, 1946), ch. 3.

6. For an extended discussion of the Scottish philosophy, which has necessarily been oversimplified in this capsule presentation, see G. A. Johnston, *Selections from the Scottish Philosophers of Common Sense* (Chicago, 1915).

7. The following are the principal American texts: Samuel Johnson (first president of Columbia), *Elementa Philosophica* (Philadelphia, 1752). This appeared before the opening of Columbia, and was intended as a manual for beginners. It had a Berkeleyan orientation. John Daniel Gros (professor at Columbia), *Natural Principles of Rectitude.* . . . (New York, 1795). John Witherspoon (first president of Princeton), *Lectures on Moral Philosophy,* in his *Works,* ed. by V. L. Collins (Princeton, 1912). Samuel S. Smith (president of Princeton), *The Lectures . . . in the College of New Jersey on . . . Moral and Political Philosophy* (Trenton, N. J., 1812). See also Smith's essay before the American Philosophical Society on "The Causes of the Variety of Complexion and Figure in the Human Species." Frederick Beasley (provost of Pennsylvania), *A Search of Truth in the Science of the Human Mind* (Philadelphia, 1822). Beasley tried to rehabilitate Locke, who, he felt, had been misinterpreted by the Scottish school. Francis Wayland (president of Brown), *The Elements of Moral Science* (New York, 1835). John L. Dagg (president of Mercer), *The Elements of Moral Science* (New York, 1860). Asa Mahan (president of Oberlin), *Abstract of . . . Mental and Moral Philosophy* (Oberlin, O., 1840); *A System of Intellectual Philosophy* (New York, 1845). Mahan was one of the few who did not hold with the Scottish philosophy but introduced German idealism, acknowledging his debt to Kant, Coleridge, and Cousin. Mark Hopkins (president of Williams), *Lectures on Moral Science* (Boston, 1868). Hopkins was not in full accord with the Scottish school either. The Channing statement of indebtedness to the Scottish philosophy is in William H. Channing, *The Life of William Ellery Channing* (Boston, 1899).

8. *Catalogue* of Randolph-Macon for 1860-61.

9. George R. Poage, "The College Career of William Jennings Bryan," *Mississippi Valley Historical Review,* XV, No. 2 (1928).

10. James McCosh, *Philosophy of Reality* (New York, 1894), section 1.

11. I have seen such manuscript notes of the lectures of Provost John Andrews of Pennsylvania, Presidents Timothy Dwight, the elder, of Yale, Charles Nisbet of Dickinson, Eliphalet Nott of Union, and Charles G. Finney of Oberlin; and have read numerous biographical

and autobiographical references to these and other favorably remembered professors of this course.

12. For Nott's course I used the notes of two students, W. Saul and H. Baldwin, taken in 1829. See also Nott's commencement addresses and occasional lectures.

13. Silliman's diary, quoted in Edward P. Cheyney, *History of the University of Pennsylvania* (Philadelphia, 1940), p. 210.

14. Lyman Beecher, *Autobiography* (New York, 1864), I, 39. W. C. Bronson, *The History of Brown University, 1764-1914* (Providence, 1914), pp. 370, 397.

15. Johnson quoted in John B. Pine, comp., *Charters . . . and Records* (New York, 1920), p. 32.

16. The *Quarterly Register and Journal of the American Education Society* in its first volume, in 1829, contains a survey of courses of study and texts used in twenty-two colleges from Maine to Tennessee, and it shows a remarkable uniformity.

17. George R. Crooks, *The Life of Bishop Matthew Simpson* (New York, 1890), p. 126, has the Allegheny story. The warning to Transylvania is in the *Western Review* for October, 1820, quoted in F. L. Mott, *A History of American Magazines* (Cambridge, 1938), I, 146. E. T. Sanford, *Blount College and the University of Tennessee* (Knoxville, Tenn., 1894), p. 22. Beloit catalogue cited in Edward D. Eaton, *Historical Sketches of Beloit College* (New York, 1928), p. 50.

18. The report is printed in full in the *American Journal of Science and Arts*, XV (1828), 297.

19. Abraham Flexner, *Universities* (New York, 1930), p. 177.

20. Lyman Beecher, *A Plea for Colleges* (Cincinnati, O., 1836). Stephen Olin, *Works* (New York, 1852), II, 271. Simpson's position is in Crooks, p. 171 and appendix.

21. Frederick A. P. Barnard, *Report on a Proposition to Modify the Plan of Instruction in the University of Alabama* (New York, 1855). See also his *Improvements Practicable in American Colleges* (Hartford, Conn., 1856). Kemp P. Battle, *History of the University of North Carolina* (Raleigh, N. C., 1907), I, 95, 98. Daniel W. Hollis, *South Carolina College* (Columbia, S. C., 1951), frontispiece, pp. 167, 174.

22. William Smith, *Discourses on Public Occasions in America* (London, 1762), Appendix II.

23. Philip A. Bruce, *History of the University of Virginia* (New York, 1920), I, 322, 333.

24. C. Van Santvoord, *Memoirs of Eliphalet Nott* (New York, 1876), p. 153. Dixon Ryan Fox, *Union College, an Unfinished History* (Schenectady, N. Y., 1945), p. 12. For the size of classes at Union, see, for example, enrollment figures in the catalogues of 1823 and 1845.

25. "Two Reports of the Faculty of Amherst College to the Board of Trustees," in Snow, p. 155. James Marsh, *Inaugural Address, 1826; System of Instruction . . . in the University of Vermont* (Burlington, Vt., 1831).

26. Philip Lindsley, *Inaugural Address, 1825; Commencement Address, 1826.*

27. *Autobiography of Andrew Dickson White* (New York, 1905), I, 27.

28. See note 2, chapter 4.

29. Wayland's views are found in the following treatises, from which the ensuing discussion and quotations are drawn: *Thoughts on the Present Collegiate System in the United States* (Boston, 1842), p. 83 and *passim; Report to the Corporation of Brown University* (1850), pp. 12, 51; *The Education Demanded by the People of the United States* (1854), p. 29 and *passim; Lecture before the American Institute of Instruction* (1854).

30. Henry Philip Tappan, *University Education* (New York, 1851), pp. 47, 50, 64, 90.

31. Earnest, ch. 2.

32. Quoted in Charles M. Perry, *Henry Philip Tappan* (Ann Arbor, 1933), pp. 200, 202.

33. David D. Banta, *History of Indiana University, 1820-1920* (Bloomington, Ind., 1921), p. 68. Charles H. Rammelkamp, *Illinois College— A Centennial History, 1820-1929* (New Haven, 1928), p. 65.

34. For an excellent analysis of this phenomenon see Merle Curti, "Intellectuals and Other People," presidential address to the American Historical Association, in *American Historical Review,* LX, No. 2 (1955).

35. Bronson, p. 321.

36. Claude M. Fuess, *Amherst, the Story of a New England College* (Boston, 1935), p. 99. Philip Lindsley, *Commencement Address, 1829.* Morison, *Three Centuries,* p. 225. Josiah Quincy, *Remarks on the Present State of the Latin Department* (Cambridge, 1841). *Catalogue of . . . the University of North Carolina,* 1851-52. *Report of a Committee of the Trustees of Columbia College* (New York, 1854). *Annual Catalogue of Columbia College,* 1862-63.

37. Robert N. Corwin, *The Plain Unpolished Tale of the Workaday Doings of Modest Folk* (New Haven, 1948), p. 76.

38. John McLean, *History of the College of New Jersey* (Philadelphia, 1877), II, 421, 427. *Proceedings Connected with the Semi-Centennial . . . of Rev. Charles Hodge* (1872).

39. Quoted in Morison, *Founding,* p. 433.

40. *Statutes of Rutgers College,* 1825, 1845; *Catalogues* for 1863-64, 1868-69, 1869-70.

41. Ohio University (Athens) *Annual Catalogue,* 1858-59. Union College *Catalogue,* 1845. The letter of the Yale student is in Herbert B. Adams, *The Life and Writings of Jared B. Sparks* (Boston, 1893), I, 45.

42. Philip A. Bruce, *History of the University of Virginia, 1819-1919* (New York, 1920), I, 334. *Register* of Geneva College (Hobart), 1840-41.

43. This expression was first used, I believe, by Robert L. Kelly in *The Effective College* (New York, 1928), p. 54.

44. *Catalogue* of Bethany College (West Virginia), 1867-68.

45. *Catalogue* of William and Mary, 1839-40. *Catalogue* of St. John's College (Fordham), 1913-1914.

46. The library practices cited here were those of Bowdoin, Columbia, Dartmouth, Illinois College, Princeton, with dates ranging from 1825 to 1892. The account of South Carolina's separate library building is in Hollis, pp. 4, 45. The Harvard book total is in Morison, *Three Centuries,* p. 267.

47. Francis W. Hirst, *Life and Letters of Thomas Jefferson* (New York, 1926), p. 37.

48. W. H. Hallock, *A Sketch of the Life and Labors of the Rev. Justin Edwards* (New York, 1855), p. 18. William G. Hammond, *Remembrance of Amherst* (New York, 1946). Giles G. Patterson, *Journal of a Southern Student, 1846-1848* (Nashville, Tenn., 1944).

49. *Register* of Hobart, 1840-41.

50. They are in the *Calendar of the College of New Jersey,* 1870-71.

51. It appeared in the examination for the following year, ranging from Shakespeare to Tennyson.

CHAPTER FOUR

1. Louis C. Hatch, *The History of Bowdoin College* (Portland, Me., 1927), p. 24.

2. *The American Almanac and Repository of Useful Knowledge* occasionally published figures of college attendance and related data between about 1830 and 1860. The figures which I give below are samplings from this source, which, in turn, took many of them from the *Quarterly Register and Journal of the American Education Society.* Insofar as I have been able to check them against the respective college catalogues, the *Almanac* figures are reliable. If anything, they run a little lower than catalogue claims.

COLLEGE ATTENDANCE STATISTICS FOR 1828-29, FROM THE
"AMERICAN ALMANAC" FOR 1830

College	Academic Faculty	Under-graduates	College Library	Student Library
Yale	16	324	8,500	6,500
Harvard	15	254	30,000	4,600
Union	9	223	5,000	8,000
Amherst	9	211	2,300	3,140
Virginia	8	131	8,000	
Dartmouth	8	128	3,500	8,000
Bowdoin	7	107	8,000	4,300

A few at the lower end of the scale:

College	Academic Faculty	Under-graduates	College Library	Student Library
Dickinson	6	62	2,000	5,000
Princeton	6	43	8,000	4,000
Wash. & Jeff.	3	31	400	525

Princeton was in one of its sinking spells; its enrollment did not remain that low for long. Its catalogue for 1828 claimed 71 rather than 43.

COLLEGE ATTENDANCE STATISTICS FROM THE "AMERICAN ALMANAC" FOR 1860, FOR THE PREVIOUS YEAR

College	Academic Faculty	Undergraduates	Libraries
Yale	21	502	67,000
North Carolina	15	450	21,000
Virginia	14	417	30,000
Harvard	24	409	123,400
Union	15	326	15,500
Dartmouth	16	304	33,699
Princeton	17	300	21,400
Michigan	14	287	10,000
DePauw	6	266	12,000
Amherst	14	235	24,700
Williams	9	224	18,355
South Carolina	8	202	24,000

Trailing these, in order, were Brown, Columbia, Pennsylvania, Rutgers, Georgia, Vermont, William and Mary. Among those that apparently did not report that year was Oberlin, which would have been well up in the list.

Some Random Figures of Student Expenses

Here 1830 and 1860 are compared. The figures for the earlier date are taken directly from the *Register* of the American Education Society, the later ones are from the *Almanac*. For the early year over-all estimates are given, which usually include tuition, room, board, light, fuel, washing, sometimes books. They are not too accurate but are valuable principally for comparison of the various institutions. Unless two figures are given, they indicate minima.

1830: Hamilton $72-$91; Williams $79.50-$104.75; Dartmouth $101.22; Dickinson $122; Hampden-Sydney $146; Harvard $179; Yale $140-$190.

1860: Tuition from $24 (Bowdoin) and $26 (Hamilton) to $75 (Harvard and Virginia). Board from $50 (Western Reserve) to $110 up (Virginia); $140 (North Carolina); $110-$150 (Yale); $110-$160 (Harvard).

Geographical Distribution of Students in Several Colleges

The most national institution, in terms of geographic origin of its student body, was Princeton, with Yale and Union next. Among the most provincial, in this respect at least, were Harvard and Virginia. The figures here sampled are for 1839, but the same proportions held for several decades before and after this date.

Princeton		Yale		Union	
Total	237	Total	411	Total	286
N. J.	65	Conn.	159	N. Y.	170
Pa.	38	Rest of New		New England	30
N. Y.	35	England	82	Pa.	5
New England	2	South	40	South	77
South (Del. to		Northwest	20	Northwest	4
La.)	94				

Harvard		Virginia		Oberlin	
Total	216	Total	247	Total	115
Mass.	161	Va.	161	Ohio	33
New England	21	Rest of South	83	N. Y.	45
N. Y. & Pa.	13	Pa.	3	Pa.	3
South	14			Mich.	3
Northwest	5			Canada	4
				New England	27

3. Oberlin *Catalogue* for 1890-91. Samuel E. Morison, *Three Centuries of Harvard* (Cambridge, 1936), p. 200. Daniel W. Hollis, *South Carolina College* (Columbia, S. C., 1951), p. 129. Albea Godbold, *The Church College of the Old South* (Durham, N. C., 1944), p. 151. Thomas J. Wertenbaker, *Princeton, 1746-1896* (Princeton, 1946), pp. 192, 331. Claude M. Fuess, *Amherst, the Story of a New England College* (Boston, 1935), p. 138. Henry M. Bullock, *A History of Emory University* (Nashville, Tenn., 1936), p. 66. *Autobiography of Andrew Dickson White* (New York, 1905), I, 18.

4. Occasional references in college laws and comments in numerous biographies of college presidents and college graduates bear this out. To cite a few examples: At the University of Georgia the minimum age of admission was thirteen down to the 1830's. The entrance age at the newly established University of Michigan in 1837 was fixed at fourteen. The same limit was in force at Knox College as late as 1863. A student graduating at Indiana in 1826, at the age of seventeen, was not the youngest in his class. Of the first eight students to enroll at Bowdoin seven were under sixteen and one was thirteen. Josiah Quincy, the younger, who attended Harvard from 1817 to 1821, remarked that the average age at entrance was fifteen, and that some were only thirteen. At the University of Pennsylvania the entrance age in the early nineteenth century was fourteen. At Brown as late as 1856 it was fifteen, lower with faculty permission. E. M. Coulter, *College Life in the Old South* (New York, 1928), p. 47. E. M. Farrand, *History of the University of Michigan* (Ann Arbor, 1885), p. 68. *Annual Catalogue* of Knox, 1863. David D. Banta, *History of Indiana University, 1820-1920* (Bloomington, Ind., 1921), p. 28. Hatch, p. 21. Josiah Quincy, *Figures of the Past* (Boston, 1892), p. 23. Eliphalet Nott, ms. of senior course. Edward P. Cheyney, *History of the University of Pennsylvania* (Philadelphia, 1940), p. 179. *The Laws of Brown University*, 1856.

5. W. B. Sprague, *Annals of the American Pulpit* (New York, 1857), II, 23.

6. A. V. Raymond, *Union University* (New York, 1907), I, 83. C. Van Santvoord, *Memoirs of Eliphalet Nott* (New York, 1876), p. 120. "Statutes of the College in 1792," in *William and Mary Quarterly*, XX, No. 1. *Catalogue* of Baylor University, 1868-69. *Annual Catalogue* of Swarthmore, 1872-73. Godbold, p. 109. *Catalogue* of Bethany College, West Virginia, 1867-68. R. and J. Peter, *Transylvania University* (Louisville, Ky., 1896), p. 92. Coulter, p. 81.

7. *William and Mary Quarterly*, XVIII, No. 3 (1911); XIV, No. 3 (1907). *Laws of the College of New Jersey*, 1870.

8. Cheyney, p. 93. Giles G. Patterson, *Journal of a Southern Student* (Nashville, Tenn., 1944), p. 55. William G. Hammond, *Remembrance of Amherst* (New York, 1946), p. 256.

9. Julian M. Sturtevant, *Autobiography* (New York, 1896), pp. 84, 91, 94.

10. College histories abound in these stories, and memoirs and biographies confirm them. The particular incidents recorded here and in the two succeeding paragraphs are found in *Autobiography of Andrew Dickson White*, I, 18. W. L. Tobey and W. O. Thompson, *The Diamond Anniversary Volume—Miami University* (Hamilton, O., 1899), p. 130. Kemp P. Battle, *History of the University of North Carolina* (Raleigh, N. C., 1907), I, 199. Philip A. Bruce, *History of the University of Virginia* (New York, 1920), II, 309. Quincy, *Figures*, p. 20. *Memoir of the Rev. David Tappan Stoddard* (New York, 1858), p. 41. J. Marion Sims, *The Story of My Life* (New York, 1894), p. 89. Hollis, p. 168. Cornelia R. Shaw, *Davidson College* (New York, 1923), p. 77. Wertenbaker, p. 138. Morison, *Three Centuries*, p. 231.

11. Horace E. Scudder, *James Russell Lowell* (Boston, 1901), I, 47. The Harvard Laws of 1734 are cited in Morison, *Three Centuries*, p. 112.

12. Quincy, p. 23. G. E. Woodberry, *Nathaniel Hawthorne* (Boston, 1902), p. 19. *Laws of Dartmouth College*, 1828. W. S. Tyler, *A History of Amherst College* (New York, 1895), p. 81.

13. *Report on a Proposition to Modify the Plan of Instruction of the University of Alabama* (New York, 1855). See also Frederick A. P. Barnard, *Letters on College Government* (New York, 1855), p. 10.

14. Morison, *Three Centuries*, p. 252.

15. Hatch, p. 96. Leonard Woods, *An Essay on Native Depravity* (Boston, 1835), preface.

16. A general critique of the manual labor experiment is found in *Quarterly Register and Journal of the American Education Society*, VI, No. 1 (1833). The alumnus quoted is President Tuttle of Wabash College, a graduate of Marietta, in *Addresses and Proceedings Connected with the Semi-Centennial Celebration of Marietta College*.

17. *Catalogue* of Ohio Wesleyan for 1852-53.

18. John K. Lord, *A History of Dartmouth College* (Concord, N. H., 1913), p. 329.

19. Timothy Dwight, *Travels in New-England and New-York* (London, 1823), IV, 361. Hollis, p. 164.

20. Lyman Beecher, *Autobiography* (New York, 1865), I, 43. Silliman is quoted in Wright, Reynolds, and Fisher, *Two Centuries of Christian Activity at Yale* (New York, 1901), p. 65. The journal is the *Quarterly Register and Journal of the American Education Society*, IV, Nos. 2 and 3 (1832).

21. George R. Crooks, *The Life of Bishop Matthew Simpson* (New York, 1890), pp. 164, 190. C. Durfee, *History of Williams College* (Boston, 1860), p. 221. Robert S. Fletcher, *A History of Oberlin College* (Oberlin, O., 1943), pp. 211, 438.

22. Cornelia R. Shaw, p. 31. Charles H. Rammelkamp, *Illinois College—A Centennial History, 1820-1929* (New Haven, 1928), pp. 77, 81. Hammond, p. 231.

23. Sturtevant, p. 161.

24. The Harvard *Catalogue* for 1820 lists a morning, a forenoon, and an afternoon class period, the first two running six days a week. The Princeton *Calendar* for 1870-71 mentions three morning and two afternoon class periods, each an hour long. By 1870 Princeton's schedule had become sufficiently cluttered to require more hours than Harvard, and almost everybody else, had been able to get along with in 1820.

25. Dwight, *Travels,* I, 167.

26. Battle, I, 160.

27. Wertenbaker, p. 137. The Rutgers *Catalogue* for 1843-44.

28. Here are a few random figures on salaries of college presidents who, it will be remembered, were also members of the teaching faculty. Salaries of ordinary, run-of-the-mill professors ran 10 to 20 per cent lower. At Columbia salaries advanced from $1,000 in 1787 to $3,500 in 1857. The president of Harvard was getting $2,550 in 1826, and 10 per cent less than that in 1840. In 1840 the president of Rutgers was getting $2,500. At South Carolina College, one of the best-paying schools, the presidential salary was $3,000 in 1836. At the other end of the scale: Kenyon, $800 in 1830; Denison, $600 in 1830. College histories furnished most of these figures.

29. V. L. Collins, *Princeton* (New York, 1914), p. 115. Jonas Viles, *The University of Missouri—A Centennial History* (Columbia, Mo., 1939), ch. 2. Bruce, II, 50. *Resolutions Passed by the Trustees of Columbia College from 1820 to 1868.*

30. *Autobiography of Andrew Dickson White,* I, 27. W. H. S. Demarest, *A History of Rutgers College* (New Brunswick, N. J., 1924), ch. 9.

31. Cheyney, p. 247. *Report of a Committee of the Trustees of Columbia College* (New York, 1854). George F. Smythe, *Kenyon College* (New Haven, 1924), p. 169.

32. Morison, *Three Centuries,* p. 138. Wertenbaker, pp. 100, 201.

33. Hollis, p. 230.

34. This discussion is distilled from many college histories. Concrete illustrations and specific citations are from the records of Harvard, Princeton, Amherst, Bowdoin, Georgia, South Carolina, Emory, Missouri, Pennsylvania, Oberlin, Columbia, Tusculum.

35. Cheyney, p. 85.
36. A few southern schools had commencement in December.
37. Henry James, *Charles W. Eliot* (Boston, 1930), I, 50. Coulter, p. 176. Carl F. Price, *Wesleyan's First Century* (Middletown, Conn., 1932), p. 79. A broadside containing the Rutgers commencement program of 1838 mentions the janitor as leader of the procession.
38. Fuess, p. 120.

CHAPTER FIVE

1. Sir Alexander Grant, *The Story of the University of Edinburgh* (London, 1884), I, 155, 199. Charles E. Mallet, *A History of the University of Oxford* (London, 1924), I, 43. Albert Mansbridge, *The Older Universities of England* (Boston, 1923), ch. 3.
2. *Laws of Harvard College* for 1814. A very similar table of duties and grant of authority is found, for example, in the *Laws of the College of New Jersey* (Princeton) for 1802, and for 1851, exactly identical for both years. *The Statutes of Columbia College* for 1811 and 1851 show the same unchanging grant of powers, except that Columbia in 1811 divided the authority between the president and the newly created provost's office, which was a subterfuge devised to get John Mason, a prominent Presbyterian clergyman, to run the school and yet not lose the valuable property donated by Trinity Church with the understanding that the president of Columbia always be an Episcopalian. For a southwestern college, see the *Laws of the University of Nashville in Tennessee* for 1835.
3. William M. Meigs, *Life of Josiah Meigs* (Philadelphia, 1887), pp. 45, 48. Eleazar Wheelock, *A Plain and Faithful Narrative of the . . . Indian Charity-School* (Boston, 1763), VII, 3. W. C. Bronson, *The History of Brown University* (Providence, 1914), p. 96.
4. C. Durfee, *History of Williams College* (Boston, 1860), p. 198. Claude M. Fuess, *Amherst* (Boston, 1935), p. 124. *History of Higher Education in South Carolina, U. S. Bureau of Education Circular of Information*, No. 1, 1888. Charles H. Rammelkamp, *Illinois College—A Centennial History, 1820-1929* (New Haven, 1928), p. 85. Jonathan Blanchard, "My Life Work," in *Sermons and Addresses* (Chicago, 1892). J. Fulton, *Memoirs of Frederick A. P. Barnard* (New York, 1896), p. 199. W. L. Tobey and W. O. Thompson, *The Diamond Anniversary Volume—Miami University* (Hamilton, O., 1899), p. 82. *Correspondence of Thomas Ebenezer Thomas* (n.p., 1909). Thomas was an admirer of President Bishop of Miami.
5. Thomas J. Wertenbaker, *Princeton, 1746-1896* (Princeton, 1946), p. 75.

6. John Witherspoon, *Lectures on Moral Philosophy,* in *Works,* ed. by V. L. Collins (Princeton, 1912). Witherspoon's son-in-law and immediate successor as president of Princeton, Samuel Stanhope Smith, did not use his father-in-law's text but wrote and published his own lectures which, to me, were more interesting than Witherspoon's. The general story of Witherspoon's life is in V. L. Collins, *President Witherspoon* (Princeton, 1925). See also the account of Witherspoon in Wertenbaker, chs. 2 and 3.

7. Timothy Dwight, *Theology Explained and Defended* (New Haven, 1843). *Greenfield Hill* (New York, 1794), Part 2, line 707. *Travels in New-England and New-York* (London, 1823), preface; II, 456; IV, 513.

8. Herbert B. Adams, *The Life and Writings of Jared B. Sparks* (Boston, 1893), I, 46. Meigs, p. 38. "Glimpses of Old College Life," *William and Mary Quarterly,* VII, No. 4 (1900).

9. Dwight, *Travels,* I, 473; *Greenfield Hill,* Part 4, line 138, is the source of the line: "till little. . . ." The class comments are based on a set of manuscript notes of Dwight's lectures, taken by L. Daggett of the class of 1808.

10. The diatribe against the closet scholar is in Dwight's *Sermons* (New Haven, 1828), I, 394; the student's eulogy is in Herbert B. Adams, *Life of Jared Sparks,* I, 46.

11. Codman Hislop, "Eliphalet Nott," in *Union Worthies,* No. 9 (1954). C. Van Santvoord, *Memoirs of Eliphalet Nott* (New York, 1876), pp. 30, 156, 167, 173.

12. Van Santvoord, appendix C. Dixon Ryan Fox, *Union College, an Unfinished History* (Schenectady, N. Y., 1945), p. 16.

13. "Instructions delivered to the senior class in Union College, Schenectady, in 1828-29, by the Reverend Eliphalet Nott." This is a transcript of the class notes of William Soul and Henry Baldwin. Though no doubt there are misinterpretations, these notes seem a fairly dependable account of Nott's rambling and vivacious lectures. At any rate they indicate what two students thought he said.

14. F. and H. L. Wayland, *A Memoir of the Life and Labors of Francis Wayland* (New York, 1867), I, 36.

15. Nisbet's story is based on some of his manuscript letters; on Samuel Miller, *Memoir of the Rev. Charles Nisbet* (New York, 1840), pp. 116, 141, 287; on James H. Morgan, *Dickinson College* (Carlisle, Pa., 1933), pp. 16, 24, 32, 35.

16. For the general situation in Tennessee: Thomas P. Abernethy, *From Frontier to Plantation in Tennessee* (Chapel Hill, N. C., 1932). For Lindsley's views and career: *Inaugural Address,* 1825; *Commencement Address,* 1826; *Baccalaureate Address,* 1827; *Cause of the Farm-*

ers and the University, 1832; *Speech about Colleges,* 1848; see also Leroy J. Halsey, "A Sketch of the Life and Educational Labors of Philip Lindsley," in *American Journal of Education,* September, 1859.

17. The principal sources for Holley are Charles Caldwell, *A Discourse on the Genius and Character of the Rev. Horace Holley* (Boston, 1828); R. and J. Peter, *Transylvania University* (Louisville, Ky., 1896); and a recent work, Niels H. Sonne, *Liberal Kentucky* (New York, 1939).

18. The most recent life of Hopkins is Frederick Rudolph, *Mark Hopkins and the Log* (New Haven, 1956).

CHAPTER SIX

1. Thomas Woody, *A History of Women's Education in the United States* (New York, 1929), I, 330. This is a thorough and scholarly study, the standard work on the subject.

2. Woody, I, 345.

3. Arthur C. Cole, *A Hundred Years of Mount Holyoke College* (New Haven, 1940), pp. 4, 8.

4. Cole, pp. 14, 72.

5. William G. Hammond, *Remembrance of Amherst* (New York, 1946), p. 108.

6. Cole, pp. 103, 141, 144, 164. For the transition from seminary to college see the *Annual Catalogue* for 1889-90, and compare it with earlier issues.

7. Woody, II, 154, ch. 4.

8. Gilbert Meltzer, *The Beginnings of Elmira College* (Elmira, N. Y., 1941), pp. 10, 89.

9. James M. Taylor, *Before Vassar Opened* (Boston, 1914), chs. 1 and 2.

10. Matthew Vassar's statement to the trustees is quoted in the Vassar *Catalogue.* The rest of the information in this paragraph comes largely from a pamphlet prospectus by its president, John H. Raymond, *Vassar College, Its Foundation, Resources, and Course of Study,* May, 1873.

11. Alice Payne Hackett, *Wellesley—Part of the American Story* (New York, 1949), pp. 32, 41. See also George H. Palmer, *The Life of Alice Freeman Palmer* (Boston, 1908). *Official Circular,* No. 6 (Smith College), October, 1879.

12. *Bryn Mawr College Program,* 1885-86. Edith Finch, *Carey Thomas of Bryn Mawr* (New York, 1947), pp. 83, 87, 137, 140. See also Cornelia Meigs, *What Makes a College* (New York, 1956).

13. A. H. Knipp and T. P. Thomas, *The History of Goucher College* (Baltimore, 1938); see also the Goucher *Bulletin* for March, 1910. *Randolph-Macon Woman's College Catalogue,* 1905-06. *Milwaukee-Downer College Bulletin-Catalog,* 1955-56. *Rockford College Catalogue,* 1955. *Bulletin of Mills College,* March, 1955. *Catalogue of Sweet Briar College,* 1955.

14. The Beecher quotation is in Robert S. Fletcher, *A History of Oberlin College* (Oberlin, O., 1943), p. 377. The comment from Brown is in W. C. Bronson, *The History of Brown University* (Providence, 1914), p. 452.

15. James M. Taylor, p. 41.

16. *Historical Sketch of Antioch College* (n.p., n.d., probably written in the late 1870's).

17. Kent Sagendorph, *Michigan, the Story of the University* (New York, 1948), pp. 28, 111.

18. Merle Curti and Vernon Carstensen, *The University of Wisconsin, 1848-1925* (Madison, Wis., 1949), I, 369. Finch, p. 53.

19. Virginia Gildersleeve, *Many a Good Crusade* (New York, 1954), p. 40. Samuel E. Morison, *Three Centuries of Harvard* (Cambridge, 1936), p. 391. Bronson, p. 449. *Douglass College Bulletin,* 1956-57.

20. Woody, II, 151. Cole, pp. 50, 181.

21. Henry N. McCracken, *The Hickory Limb* (New York, 1950), pp. 28, 90. Gildersleeve, p. 98. Cole, pp. 171, 199. Fletcher, p. 377.

22. For the Thomas comment see Finch, p. 1. Sophia Smith's views are quoted in the Smith College *Catalogue.* Gildersleeve, p. 70. Cole, p. 181. Curti and Carstensen, I, 623: photograph of the class. McCracken, p. 5.

23. Figures for Smith in the *Catalogue.* The incident of the disappearing teacher is told by McCracken in *The Hickory Limb,* p. 9.

24. *Many a Good Crusade,* p. 98.

25. Alice Duer Miller and Susan Myers, *Barnard College* (New York, 1939), p. 25. Bronson, p. 451.

26. Taylor, ch. 4.

27. Finch, pp. 182, 209. McCracken, p. 24.

28. Woody, II, 204.

29. Hackett, p. 31. *Official Circular,* No. 6 (Smith, 1879). Knipp and Thomas, p. 88, appendix; *Eighth Annual Program* (of Goucher), 1896.

30. Cole, p. 241. McCracken, p. 59.

31. See current catalogues of Mills and Sarah Lawrence.

CHAPTER SEVEN

1. *Autobiography of Andrew Dickson White* (New York, 1905), I, 272.
2. Kent Sagendorph, *Michigan, the Story of the University* (New York, 1948), pp. 62, 116, 154, 227. *General Catalogue* of the University of Michigan, 1837-1901.
3. *Catalogue* of the University of Wisconsin, 1869. Merle Curti and Vernon Carstensen, *The University of Wisconsin, 1848-1925* (Madison, Wis., 1949), I, 60, 83, 316, 400.
4. Bushnell's part and the story of the first college is told in a pamphlet, *Movement for a University in California* (San Francisco, 1857). The remaining data are in the *Register of the University of California, 1874-75,* and the *Annual Report of the Board of Regents,* May 31, 1875.
5. *Report of the President,* for 1879. *Catalogue,* 1882-83. James E. Pollard, *History of The Ohio State University* (Columbus, O., 1952), ch. 1.
6. Clyde K. Hyder, *Snow of Kansas* (Lawrence, Kans., 1953), pp. 107, 170.
7. *President's Report* of the University of Arizona, 1906. *Third Annual Register* of the University of Arizona, 1893-94. Roy Gittinger, *The University of Oklahoma, 1892-1942* (Norman, Okla., 1942), pp. 5, 8, 11, 16, 59. University of Texas *Catalogue,* 1956-57, Part 5.
8. The best account of this movement that I know is Earle D. Ross, *Democracy's College: the Land-Grant Movement in the Formative Stage* (Ames, Ia., 1942). See also the U. S. Office of Education's *Survey of Land-Grant Colleges and Universities* (1930).
9. For an example of the effect of the initiative and referendum on the fortunes of a state university see Henry D. Sheldon, *History of the University of Oregon* (Portland, Ore., 1940), pp. 144, 154.
10. Allan Nevins, *Illinois* (New York, 1917), p. 43. Hyder, pp. 105, 173. Curti and Carstensen, I, 408.
11. Illinois, Nebraska, and Michigan have a popular vote, the last-named in odd years on a nonpartisan ballot. Everywhere else appointment is by the governor, with or without legislative consent, or by the legislature directly. Sample sizes of boards are: Indiana 8, Iowa 9, Michigan 9, Nebraska 6, New Jersey (Rutgers Board of Governors) 11, Ohio State 7, Texas 9. All the above information, except the Rutgers data, is from Hubert P. Beck, *Men Who Control Our Universities* (New York, 1947), esp. pp. 120, 175.
12. George E. Howard, "The State University in America," *Atlantic Monthly,* LXVIII (1891), p. 332.

13. Edward A. Ross, *Seventy Years of It* (New York, 1936), p. 27.

14. James Morgan Hart, writing in 1878, quoted in Richard Hofstadter and Walter P. Metzger, *The Development of Academic Freedom in the United States* (New York, 1955), p. 376.

15. *Year-Book of the Catholic University of America, 1895-96*. John T. Ellis, *The Formative Years of the Catholic University of America* (Washington, D. C., 1946), ch. 1.

16. Charles Francis Adams, "The Sifted Grain and the Grain Sifters," address at the dedication of the State Historical Society building of Wisconsin, October 19, 1900, in *American Historical Review*, VI (January, 1901). Thomas Cooper, *On the Connection Between Geology and the Pentateuch*, a letter to Benjamin Silliman of Yale (Boston, 1833). Samuel S. Smith, *The Lectures . . . on . . . Moral and Political Philosophy* (Trenton, N. J., 1812), I, 46.

17. Gray's articles ran for three issues of the *Atlantic Monthly*, VI (July, August, October, 1860). Asa Gray, *Darwiniana* (New York, 1876), p. 378. Joseph LeConte, *Evolution* (New York, 1922, first ed., 1887), p. 276.

18. John Fiske, *A Century of Science* (Boston, 1899). "The Progress from Brute to Man," *North American Review*, CVIII (October, 1873). The circulation figure of *Popular Science Monthly* and comment on it is from F. L. Mott, *History of American Magazines* (Cambridge, 1938), III, 497. The Wright quotation is from his review article on Darwin and Wallace in *North American Review*, CIII (July, 1871). See also James B. Turner, ed., *Letters of Chauncey Wright* (Cambridge, 1878).

19. Charles Hodge's *What is Darwinism?* was one of the more influential polemics. For Agassiz's ideas see Elizabeth Carey Agassiz, *Louis Agassiz, His Life and Correspondence* (Boston, 1886), I, 372, 388; II, 510, 777. See also Frank H. Foster, *The Modern Movement in American Theology* (New York, 1939), pp. 40, 47, 54.

20. Among the presidents on whose pronouncements this generalization is based were Noah Porter of Yale, Frederick A. P. Barnard of Columbia, James McCosh of Princeton, William H. Campbell and Merrill E. Gates of Rutgers, W. A. Stearns and Julius Seelye of Amherst, William G. Ballantine of Oberlin, James B. Angell of Michigan, Ethelbert D. Warfield of Lafayette, and Francis H. Snow of Kansas.

21. Hofstadter and Metzger, pp. 334, 335-38.

22. *The President's Report* for 1881.

23. John Fulton, *Memoirs of Frederick A. P. Barnard* (New York, 1896), pp. 346, 361. *Annual Report of the President of Columbia College* for 1865. Sidney Ratner, "Evolution and the Rise of the Scientific Spirit in America," *Philosophy of Science*, III (January, 1936). See also Barnard's *Address Delivered before the American Association for the Advancement of Science* (Salem, Mass., 1869).

24. Hyder, ch. 11.
25. William M. Sloane, *The Life of James McCosh* (New York, 1897), p. 234. James McCosh, *Christianity and Positivism* (New York, 1875), p. 8; *Twenty Years at Princeton College* (1888).
26. For Seelye's treatment of his science professors see Claude M. Fuess, *Amherst, the Story of a New England College* (Boston, 1935), p. 218. The Billy Sunday episode is in Charles H. Rammelkamp, *Illinois College—A Centennial History, 1820-1929* (New Haven, 1928), pp. 386, 475.

CHAPTER EIGHT

1. Henry James, *Charles W. Eliot* (Boston, 1930), I, 318. *Autobiography of Andrew Dickson White* (New York, 1905), I, 342; *A History of the Warfare of Science and Theology* (New York, 1896), I, introd. and p. 318. David Starr Jordan, *Footnotes to Evolution* (New York, 1898), p. 341.
2. Abraham Flexner, *Daniel Coit Gilman* (New York, 1946), p. 35. *Autobiography of Andrew Dickson White*, I, 335, 380. William Rainey Harper, *The Trend in Higher Education* (Chicago, 1905), p. 30. Edward M. Burns, *David Starr Jordan, Apostle of Freedom* (Stanford, Calif., 1953), p. 133.
3. James, I, 50, 58, 68, 107. Samuel E. Morison, *Three Centuries of Harvard* (Cambridge, 1936), ch. 14.
4. Morison, *Three Centuries*, p. 324.
5. For the Law School see the *Catalogue* of 1867-68; also James, I, 266. Adams' comment is in *The Education of Henry Adams* (New York, 1931), p. 60.
6. The inaugural address is in Charles W. Eliot, *Educational Reform* (New York, 1898), ch. 1.
7. *Annual Report* of President Thomas Hill for 1867-68.
8. James, I, 196.
9. Morison, *Three Centuries*, p. 346.
10. Morison, *Three Centuries*, pp. 387-390.
11. Thomas J. Wertenbaker, *Princeton, 1746-1896* (Princeton, 1946), p. 306.
12. Robert N. Corwin, *The Plain Unpolished Tale of the Workaday Doings of Modest Folk* (New Haven, 1948), p. 76.
13. Frederick A. P. Barnard, "The Studies Proper to be Pursued Preparatory to Admission to College," in *Proceedings of the Third Anniversary of the University Convocation of the State of New York* (Albany, 1866). See also Fulton, p. 379.
14. Flexner, *Daniel Coit Gilman*, ch. 1.

15. The inaugural address is in Daniel Coit Gilman, *University Problems in the United States* (New York, 1898).
16. John C. French, *A History of the University Founded by Johns Hopkins* (Baltimore, 1946), p. 33. *Register* of Johns Hopkins for 1877-78, and for 1882-83. The enrollment figures are taken from Flexner, *Daniel Coit Gilman*, p. 96.
17. White's ideas and measures are paraphrased in part from his inaugural address, which is in the Cornell University *Register* for 1868-69, and from other data in that and later *Registers* and *Catalogues*. See also his *Autobiography*, I, 42, 355, 402, 429. Carl Becker's comment is in his *How New Will the Better World Be?* (New York, 1945), p. 133.
18. These ideas are summarized in Shirley W. Smith, *James Burrill Angell, an American Influence* (Ann Arbor, 1954), p. 93. See also Angell's *Reminiscences* (New York, 1912); and Kent Sagendorph, *Michigan, the Story of the University* (New York, 1948), and the several annual reports of Angell's, cited earlier in this chapter.
19. Burns, ch. 1. Orin L. Elliott, *Stanford University, the First Twenty-five Years* (Stanford, Calif., 1937).
20. Letter cited in Burns, p. 155.
21. Jordan's ideas are collected, in part, in his *The Voice of the Scholar* (San Francisco, 1903). See also Burns, ch. 7.
22. You can read it all in the first *Annual Register* of the university, for 1892-93.
23. Thomas W. Goodspeed, *History of the University of Chicago* (Chicago, 1916), p. 133. See also Goodspeed's *William Rainey Harper* (Chicago, 1928).
24. William Rainey Harper, *The Trend in Higher Education* (Chicago, 1905), pp. 4, 7, 97.
25. Horace Coon, *Columbia, Colossus on the Hudson* (New York, 1947), chs. 3 and 4.
26. Ray Stannard Baker, *Woodrow Wilson, Life and Letters* (New York, 1927), II, 130, 144, 166. Wertenbaker seems to assign Wilson a somewhat less important role in the building of the university.
27. George W. Pierson, *Yale College, an Educational History*, 1871-1921 (New Haven, 1952), pp. 81, 129, 167, 258.

CHAPTER NINE

1. The statements about Bascom and Jordan are in their respective biographical sketches in the *Dictionary of American Biography*. Shaler's

exploit is recounted in Rollo Walter Brown, *Harvard Yard in the Golden Age* (New York, 1948), p. 111.

2. The following data relating to the number, kind, and type of control of institutions of higher education in 1955 are taken from the *Educational Directory, 1955-56*, Part 3, put out by the U. S. Office of Education, beginning on page 8. The terms and designations are those of the *Directory*.

A. The total number of institutions offering two or more years of education or training beyond the twelfth grade was 1,855. Of these, 510 were junior colleges of all kinds, that is, institutions offering programs of at least two but less than four years; 267 were professional and technical institutions, some with, some without departments of teacher training; 98 were institutions primarily for the training of teachers; 83 were devoted to liberal arts and general education only. All the rest, or 897, were described as liberal arts institutions which included professional, terminal-occupational, and teacher-training programs in varying amounts and degrees.

Broken down in another way, 510 were less than four-year schools; 732 were four-year schools granting the bachelor's degree; 415 granted the master's degree in addition; 180 granted the Ph.D. or equivalent. All others: 18.

B.	Control	Two-year	Four-year and Beyond
	State institutions	34	337
	Municipal institutions	260	21
	Private institutions	89	391
	Protestant	94	376
	Roman Catholic	33	215
	Jewish	0	5

C.	Type	Two-year	Four-year and Beyond
	Men's colleges	38	178
	Women's colleges	63	181
	Coeducational	409	986

The statistics of enrollment which follow are taken from *American Universities and Colleges* (7th ed., American Council on Education, Washington, D. C., 1956).

A.

	U. S. Population	Students Enrolled in Higher Education
1870	Over 38 million	52,286
1880	" 50 "	115,817
1890	" 62 "	156,756
1900	" 75 "	237,592
1910	" 91 "	355,213
1920	" 105 "	597,880
1930	" 123 "	1,100,737
1940	" 131 "	1,494,203
1950	" 150 "	2,296,592
* 1955	" 164 "	2,720,929

(p. 32)

* In 1956-57 the total enrollment rose above 3,000,000.

B. Ten largest institutions

University of California (all campuses) 38,594
State University of New York (all campuses) ... 33,623
New York University 31,867
College of the City of New York 26,426
 (If the four City Colleges of Greater New York
 were taken as one, as is done with California,
 they would make the largest total: about 80,-
 000 in 1956-57)
Columbia University 25,887
University of Illinois 24,129
University of Michigan 23,756
University of Minnesota 23,393
Ohio State University 21,744
University of Wisconsin 20,119

(p. 13)

C. Enrollment in Graduate Schools

1890	2,382	
1900	5,831	
1910	9,370	In 1890 about one sixth of these
1920	15,612	were women; today it is about
1930	47,255	one third
1940	106,119	
1950	237,208	
1954	280,155	

(p. 52)

D. Earned Doctor's Degrees (of all kinds except M.D.)		Earned Master's Degrees
Before 1870	16	None
1870-1880	227	6,506
In 1880	54	879
1890	149	1,015
1900	382	1,583
1910	443	2,113
1920	615	4,279
1930	2,299	14,629
1940	3,290	26,731
1950	6,633	58,219
1955	8,840	58,204

(p. 66)

Since about 1900 one tenth of the doctors and one fifth to one third of the masters have been women.

The following figures for the total number of full-time teaching faculty in all institutions of higher learning are in the *Statistical Abstract of the United States* for 1955, p. 125.

1940   131,552 (37,016 of these were women)
1950   210,359 (52,658 of these were women)

3. Samuel E. Morison, *Three Centuries of Harvard* (Cambridge, 1936), p. 370.
4. Nicholas Murray Butler, *Across the Busy Years* (New York, 1939), I, 197.
5. *Catalogue* of Michigan for 1892; see also Kent Sagendorph, *Michigan, the Story of the University* (New York, 1948), p. 150.
6. An excellent account of the development of the credit system is in Dietrich Gerhard, "The Emergence of the Credit System in American Education Considered as a Problem of Social and Intellectual History," *Bulletin of the American Association of University Professors,* XLI, No. 4 (1955).
7. The Van Amringe story is told in Horace Coon, *Columbia, Colossus on the Hudson* (New York, 1947), p. 343. The quotation relating to Dexter is in George W. Pierson, *Yale College, an Educational History, 1871-1921* (New Haven, 1952), p. 140 note.
8. Biographical sketch of Harper in *Dictionary of American Biography.*
9. Ray S. Baker, *Woodrow Wilson, Life and Letters* (New York, 1927), II, ch. 17. Among those who think higher education lost its soul is Van Wyck Brooks, *New England: Indian Summer* (New York, 1940), p. 105.

10. For Custer's last stand and similar expressions see Sagendorph, p. 154. The observation on new and old styles is in Russell Lynes, *The Taste Makers* (New York, 1954).

11. The generalizations of this paragraph are based on an extensive examination of catalogues and course announcements of some ninety institutions, large and small, public and private, east, west and south. In most instances I sampled a catalogue or two of the early seventies, of the nineties, and around 1913-14, and compared all these with the institution's latest, current catalogue.

12. Clyde K. Hyder, *Snow of Kansas* (Lawrence, Kans., 1953), pp. 105, 243.

13. Herbert Spencer, *First Principles of a New System of Philosophy* (New York, 1872), p. 396.

14. Henry S. Canby, *Alma Mater* (New York, 1936), p. 188.

15. *Catalogue of Allegheny College* for 1865-66, and for 1891-92. *Report of the President of Bowdoin College* for 1891-92. *Report of the President of Trinity College* for 1887-88.

16. The change is clearly set forth in W. Stull Holt, "The Idea of Scientific History in America," *Journal of the History of Ideas*, I (June, 1940). Professor Wheeler's lecture at Yale is described in Pierson, p. 279. The various Adamses were Henry at Harvard, Herbert Baxter at Johns Hopkins, and Charles Kendall at Michigan.

17. Lester Ward's course at Brown is mentioned in Samuel Chugerman, *Lester Ward, the American Aristotle* (Durham, N. C., 1939), pp. 36, 192; and in Richard Hofstadter, *Social Darwinism in American Thought* (Philadelphia, 1944), p. 54. When examined in the catalogue in the context of its purpose and outline, the course is not as silly as the title sounds. Sumner's comments on philosophy at Yale are in Pierson, p. 148. Edward A. Ross's education and social philosophy are set forth in his autobiographical *Seventy Years of It* (New York, 1936), pp. 40, 55.

18. The samples of Ward's vocabulary are in Hofstadter, p. 53. The claim of four hundred new words is in the biographical sketch of G. Stanley Hall in the *Dictionary of American Biography*.

19. Merle Curti and Vernon Carstensen, *The University of Wisconsin, 1848-1925* (Madison, Wis., 1949), I, 409. The very first university to make this move was the University of Virginia, which had voluntary chapel from the beginning, in 1826.

20. *Autobiography of Andrew Dickson White* (New York, 1905), I, 402. The reference to chapel at Johns Hopkins is in Abraham Flexner, *Daniel Coit Gilman* (New York, 1946), p. 87.

21. Morison, *Three Centuries*, p. 366. Pierson, pp. 13, 103. Coon, p. 85.

22. Thomas J. Wertenbaker, *Princeton, 1746-1896* (Princeton, 1946), p. 360. Baker, II, ch. 15.

23. Pierson describes this aspect of Yale life in chs. 1, 2, 13. Canby, p. 49.

24. Sagendorph, p. 180. Edward M. Burns, *David Starr Jordan: Apostle of Freedom* (Stanford, Calif., 1953), p. 19. Curti and Carstensen, I, 674.

25. Henry C. Hubbard, *Ohio Wesleyan's First Hundred Years* (Delaware, O., 1943), p. 117. Wertenbaker, p. 363.

26. William R. Baird, *Baird's Manual of American College Fraternities* (Menasha, Wis., 1940), pp. 2, 4. This is the standard work of reference.

27. Baker, II, ch. 16.

28. Sagendorph, pp. 73, 147, 160. James A. Pollard, *History of The Ohio State University* (Columbus, O., 1952), p. 58. Roy Gittinger, *The University of Oklahoma* (Norman, Okla., 1942), p. 26.

29. Louis C. Hatch, *The History of Bowdoin College* (Portland, Me., 1927), ch. 8. Wertenbaker, p. 356. Curti and Carstensen, I, 432.

30. An excellent analysis of the role of fraternities and their historic development on a particular campus is in Thomas LeDuc, *Piety and Intellect at Amherst College* (New York, 1946). Recent criticisms are Alfred M. Lee, *Fraternities Without Brotherhood* (Boston, 1955); and William S. Carlson, "Fraternities: Evil Force on the Campus," *Saturday Review,* September 10, 1955.

31. Nora C. Chaffin, *Trinity College, 1839-1892* (Durham, N. C., 1950), p. 443.

32. Wertenbaker, p. 325. Coon, p. 293. Morison, pp. 316, 404.

33. Sagendorph, p. 150. Morison, *Three Centuries,* p. 409. Wertenbaker, pp. 329, 344. Baker, II, ch. 14. Gittinger, p. 25. Thomas W. Goodspeed, *William Rainey Harper* (Chicago, 1928), p. 159. Burns, p. 169.

34. Pierson, pp. 33, 348.

35. Coon, p. 298.

36. A graphic account of a game in late November, 1950, at Ohio State, which was played in the snow and became a complete farce, is in the *New Yorker* for December 16, 1950, by John McNulty. Curti and Carstensen, I, 696, describes conditions at Wisconsin. See also Allen Jackson, "Too Much Football," *Atlantic,* CLXXXVIII (October, 1951).

37. Paul Bourget, *Outre Mer* (London, 1895), pp. 304, 330.

38. *The President's Report* (Northwestern) for 1893-94.

39. Morison, *Three Centuries,* p. 409.

40. Robert M. Hutchins, *The Higher Learning in America* (New Haven, 1936), p. 22.

41. *Washington University Magazine,* October, 1956.

42. Van Cleve Morris, "Football and the University," *A.A.U.P. Bulletin,* XXVIII, No. 3 (1952).

43. Pierson, p. 347. Morison, *Three Centuries,* p. 402.

44. Brown, p. 15.

CHAPTER TEN

1. For Yale's reaction to the Eliot system see, for example, George W. Pierson, *Yale College, an Educational History, 1871-1921* (New Haven, 1952), p. 258.

2. Samuel E. Morison, *Three Centuries of Harvard* (Cambridge, 1936), p. 344.

3. A. Lawrence Lowell, *At War with Academic Traditions in America* (Cambridge, 1934), pp. 36, 39, 238.

4. Abraham Flexner, *Universities* (New York, 1930), p. 177.

5. Mitchell Wilson, *American Science and Invention* (New York, 1954), p. 309.

6. In trying the almost impossible task of conveying here, in briefest outline, something of the flavor of Dewey's teaching I have drawn at random from his writings. Of his many published works I have found the following especially useful: *Democracy and Education* (New York, 1916); *Reconstruction in Philosophy* (New York, 1920); *Experience and Education* (New York, 1938). For an excellent analysis of both the "progressive" and the "conservative" position see R. Freeman Butts, *The College Charts Its Course* (New York, 1939), esp. chs. 15, 16, 17. Butts admittedly holds with the former.

7. The essence of Hutchins' views is found in his *The Higher Learning in America* (New Haven, 1936), and in a collection of his addresses published in the same year by the University of Chicago under the title, *No Friendly Voice.*

8. Hutchins, p. 48.

9. Hutchins, p. 56.

10. Hutchins, p. 78.

11. Harry D. Gideonse, *The Higher Learning in a Democracy* (New York, 1937), pp. 2, 5, 7, 12, 26.

12. Butts, pp. 360, 361.

13. Herbert P. Woodward, "The Ends of Education," *A.A.U.P. Bulletin,* XL, No. 3 (1954).

14. Butts, p. 304. Alexander Meiklejohn, *The Experimental College* (New York, 1932), esp. ch. 4.

15. Quoted in Benjamin Fine's column, "Education in Review," *New York Times,* November 20, 1955.

16. *Higher Education for American Democracy, a Report of the President's Commission on Higher Education* (Washington, D. C., 1947). This six-volume report is a mine of information and stimulating suggestions. Among the topics treated are required courses as opposed to electives, general as opposed to vocational education, methods and

techniques of teaching, liberal arts colleges and schools of education, research as opposed to teaching, statistics of all kinds. The statements quoted or paraphrased here are from Vol. I, 6, 8, 41.

17. The direct quotations are from the St. John's *Catalogue* for 1939-40. An account of the evaluation report is in the *New York Times* for May 22, 1955. See also the St. John's *Catalogue* for 1955-56.

18. Constance Warren, "The Plan for Sarah Lawrence College," *Progressive Education*, IX, No. 7 (1932). See also the current catalogue issue, *Sarah Lawrence College*, 1955-56. *The Educational Plan for Bennington College* (New York, 1931). See also Bennington's current catalogue. *Black Mountain College Bulletin* for 1933-34 and for 1952-53. *The Goddard Bulletin*, August, 1954. Rollins College current catalogue. *Marlboro College:* original announcement of 1946.

19. *Columbia College Announcement*, 1954-55. Horace Coon, *Columbia, Colossus on the Hudson* (New York, 1947), p. 350, ch. 12.

20. *General Education in a Free Society* (Cambridge, 1945), esp. ch. 5.

21. *University of Chicago Undergraduate Programs*, 1956-57.

22. *Columbia University School of General Studies Announcement*, 1955-56.

23. *Bulletin of the University of Minnesota—the General College*, 1956-57. Ruth E. Eckert, *Outcomes of General Education* (Minneapolis, Minn., 1943). See also Paul L. Dressel and Lewis B. Mayhew, *General Education Explorations in Evaluation* (Washington, D. C., 1954), esp. chs. 3 and 6.

24. See the catalogues of these institutions; see also Pierson, II, 398.

CHAPTER ELEVEN

1. Roosevelt University *Bulletin*, 1954-56.

2. Brandeis University *Bulletin*, 1953-54.

3. All the quotations are from the Marlboro College *Catalogue*, 1954-55.

4. For an example of this kind of planning see *General Education in School and College* (Cambridge, 1952), esp. chs. 1 and 5.

5. Morison, *Three Centuries*, p. 446.

6. Frank Aydelotte, *Honors Courses in American Colleges and Universities, Bulletin of the National Research Council* (April, 1925), p. 15.

7. For a sampling of the range and character of recent activities in the field of testing see Paul L. Dressel and Lewis B. Mayhew, *General Education Explorations in Evaluation* (Washington, 1954).

8. The origins and the logic of the conflicting uses are effectively analyzed in William H. Cowley, *The Heritage and Purpose of Higher Education*, an address before the Western College Association at Los Angeles, March 25, 1955.

9. The statement was made in a paper read at the 1955 meeting of the Association of American Colleges in Washington, D. C., reported in the *New York Times* of January 16, 1955, by Benjamin Fine.

10. In *The Goose Step* (Pasadena, Calif., 1923), p. 16.

11. The following examples may indicate the direction of thinking in this field. At the eastern regional American Studies conference, held in connection with the Columbia University bicentennial in 1954, Francis Fergusson, dramatist and critic, and professor at Rutgers, suggested that the experimental theater properly belongs in the college curriculum; Virgil Thompson, composer and music critic, pointed out the advantages of a university school of music over the conventional music conservatory; and Robert Goldwater, professor of art at Queens College, New York, praised college art departments for making possible the association of criticism and theory with technical skill and practical craftsmanship. Agnes DeMille has written on this subject. So has Alfred Kazin, author, and professor at Amherst. These are straws in the wind, but the acceptance of the principle is still far from universal.

12. Statistics indicating this figure are cited in an editorial, "Should a Business-man be Educated?" *Fortune* (April, 1953).

13. Numerous examples of the businessman's concern for real educational values are collected in an article by President Harry D. Gideonse of Brooklyn College: "On Re-thinking Liberal Education" (1953). See also the *Fortune Survey on Higher Education*, September, 1949; and the symposium on business and education in the *Saturday Review*, January 19, 1957.

14. Francis H. Horn, "The Folklore of Liberal Education," inaugural address at Pratt Institute.

15. Cowley address. To the general reader who wishes to know more about the recent thinking in this field I can only suggest a few works that I have found useful: *General Education in a Free Society* (Cambridge, 1945), by a Harvard faculty committee; *General Education in School and College* (Cambridge, 1952), by a joint committee of faculties of three universities and three preparatory schools; Theodore M. Greene, *Liberal Education Reconsidered* (Cambridge, 1953); Clarence B. Randall, *Freedom's Faith* (Boston, 1953); Huston Smith, *The Purposes of Higher Education* (New York, 1955); Harold Taylor, *On Education and Freedom* (New York, 1954). The Huston Smith book in particular is lively, specific, analytical, and avoids the usual platitudes.

16. In this analysis I have borrowed from many sources as well as incorporated my own thinking over the years; in form my summary leans heavily on Huston Smith, chs. 8, 9, 10.

CHAPTER TWELVE

1. I do not want to push this contrast too far. Even ancient universities of great prestige can decline, as the German universities did under Nazi rule, and as those of eastern Germany are suffering today under the Communists.
2. Stetson University *Annual Catalogue,* 1955-56.
3. Samuel E. Morison, *Three Centuries of Harvard* (Cambridge, 1936), p. 187.
4. William M. Meigs, *Life of Josiah Meigs* (Philadelphia, 1887), pp. 42, 52. E. M. Coulter, *College Life in the Old South* (New York, 1928), p. 23.
5. Daniel W. Hollis, *South Carolina College* (Columbia, S. C., 1951), chs. 5 and 6. See also Dumas Malone, *The Public Life of Thomas Cooper* (New Haven, 1926).
6. Vol. I, ch. 10.
7. Quoted from *Popular Science Monthly* in Sidney Ratner, "Evolution and the Rise of the Scientific Spirit in America," *Philosophy of Science,* III (January, 1936).
8. For much of the ensuing discussion I am indebted to the excellent study by Richard Hofstadter and Walter P. Metzger, *The Development of Academic Freedom in the United States* (New York, 1955), a contribution to Columbia University's bicentennial, particularly chapters 8, 9, and 10. This is the best analysis and interpretation of the problem that I know. The authors have been most thorough, using among other things legal decisions, and collections of unpublished correspondence which have rarely been tapped for this purpose.
9. The *New York Times* for June 25, 1956, carried a news article giving the following endowment figures of some of the leading universities today (which I have reduced to round millions): Harvard $229 million; Yale $151 million; Chicago $144 million; Columbia $113 million; Cornell $80 million; Princeton $79 million; Stanford $53 million.
10. A useful study of this situation is in Hubert P. Beck, *Men Who Control our Universities* (New York, 1947), particularly the statistics on pp. 173, 178.
11. Merle Curti and Vernon Carstensen, *The University of Wisconsin, 1848-1925* (Madison, Wis., 1949), I, 508, 525.
12. Hofstadter and Metzger, p. 427.
13. Ross's views are quoted from his autobiography, *Seventy Years of It* (New York, 1936), pp. 15, 44, 46, 64, 288. See also O. L. Elliott, *Stanford University* (Stanford, Calif., 1937), p. 340, and Edward M. Burns, *David Starr Jordan: Apostle of Freedom* (Stanford, Calif., 1953), p. 14.

14. Hofstadter and Metzger, p. 445.
15. Curti and Carstensen, I, 681.
16. Hofstadter and Metzger, p. 424.
17. *The Higher Learning in America* was written in 1916. I have used the edition of 1954, published in Stanford, Calif., pp. 20, 66, 75.
18. The Pulitzer incident is told in Horace Coon, *Columbia, Colossus on the Hudson* (New York, 1947), p. 107. The Harkness offer is told in Morison, p. 477; and the move of the drama workshop to Yale in Rollo Walter Brown, *Harvard Yard in the Golden Age* (New York, 1948), p. 171.
19. *Annual Report* quoted in Hofstadter and Metzger, p. 499 note.
20. For Wilson and the Proctor offer see Ray S. Baker, *Woodrow Wilson, Life and Letters* (New York, 1927), II, ch. 17. Lowell's action is in H. A. Yeomans, *Abbott Lawrence Lowell* (Cambridge, 1948), p. 314.
21. Reported in the *New York Times,* June 25, 1956.
22. John Dewey is an outstanding modern exception and the Yale faculty of 1828 an earlier one.
23. Hofstadter and Metzger, p. 497.
24. Coon, p. 125; Hofstadter and Metzger, p. 498.
25. It has been said that professors are naïve about such matters, being so tolerant themselves that they do not recognize the symptoms. I doubt it. I think that they are competent on the whole to police their profession. There are of course a good many who believe that membership in the Communist party, when not used for proselyting, should not be held against an otherwise competent scholar. Others on the contrary believe that membership *ipso facto* renders a man incapable of objective scholarship and is in flat contradiction to the principles of academic freedom. For an example of intelligent awareness of the situation see the article by Helen C. White, "Freedom in the University," in the *Key Reporter,* Phi Beta Kappa (July, 1956).
26. For an instance of the experience of an innocent person with the Fifth Amendment see the letter of Dean Paul Shipman Andrews of Syracuse University College of Law to the *New York Herald Tribune,* October 26, 1953, and an account of the same affair in the *New York Times,* November 14, 1953. A thoughtful comment on the whole situation is Alan Barth, "Universities and Political Authority," *A.A.U.P. Bulletin* (Spring, 1953).
27. Hofstadter and Metzger, p. 477 and ch. 10 generally.
28. *A.A.U.P. Bulletin* (Spring, 1955), p. 34.
29. James B. Conant, *The Citadel of Learning* (New Haven, 1955).
30. Italics mine.

Bibliographical Note

The sources for a study of this kind are varied and scattered, and a search for them sets one rummaging in many libraries. Most useful to me was the superior collection of college and university documents in Teachers College, Columbia University, and I am grateful to the library authorities of Teachers College for giving me the run of the place. If this were the history of one particular college, the faculty minutes, the trustees' minutes, and the annual reports of administrative officers would have been the first line of investigation. But when one is examining the fortunes of hundreds of institutions for the purpose of discovering some valid generalizations, exhaustive treatment of sources of this kind is hardly possible, nor is it necessary. They appear in the notes, but as samples or by way of confirmation. I have relied primarily on four different kinds of sources: college catalogues; the educational writings of college presidents and faculty members; biographies, autobiographies, and memoirs of the same group of men; college histories. I have also drawn on earlier published studies of my own.

The catalogues have gone through an interesting evolution. In their earliest form they were four- or eight-page pamphlets, octavo usually, containing the names of students, faculty, and trustees, with an occasional, perhaps decennial, publication giving alumni rosters as well. Down to about the second decade of the nineteenth century they were in Latin, with Latin endings provided for all the names. Next to appear were the college laws laying down rules of student behavior; these sometimes ran to many pages and were in time incorporated with the catalogues of officers and students. Expense figures also came to be included, for tuition, room, board, fuel, and the like, and so did student activities, like the debating societies. The curriculum was added too, of course. In some of the early catalogues one or two pages sufficed for all the courses of all four years. With the introduction of electives and professional schools late in the nineteenth century, the catalogues began to grow in bulk, and from then on a steady expansion set in until they became the complicated Sears-Roebuck-like tomes that puzzle the prospective freshman today. Directly or by inference the catalogues are an invaluable source for college life in all its phases.

The educational writings of college presidents and professors vary considerably in importance. The best of them are indispensable for an understanding of the changes in educational theory and practice over the years, but the average output is dull and repetitive. The well-worn platitudes of the ordinary inaugural and commencement addresses make dreary reading, so these addresses are useful mainly to determine the extent and prevalence of a given viewpoint or procedure.

Autobiographies, like those, for example, of Andrew Dickson White or Nicholas Murray Butler, are extremely important sources for the events and the educational climate of the times that they recall; the things they emphasize and the things they leave out are, furthermore, a significant commentary on the character of the writer. They must be supplemented by modern scholarly biographies, which are appearing in increasing numbers. We now have good studies of such leaders as Eliot, Gilman, and Jordan, as well as of earlier professor-presidents like Dwight, Witherspoon, and Hopkins.

College histories are also multiplying in number and improving in quality. They usually appear in anniversary years, to commemorate the fiftieth or hundredth or two hundredth year since the founding or the granting of the first charter. Earlier college histories were often little more than annals of successive presidential administrations, leavened with accounts of catastrophes like the burning of the main building or with anecdotes of the quainter professors and the more picturesque student pranks, and rounded out by lists of fraternity members and the scores of football games. The intellectual history of a presumably intellectual enterprise was usually conspicuous by its absence. There were honorable exceptions. A new standard was set by the volumes of Samuel E. Morison prepared for the Harvard tercentenary in 1936. Their thorough scholarship and historical and philosophical breadth raised college history writing to new levels and made it a legitimate and dignified contribution to the record of American culture. Harvard was not alone; more and more recent college and university histories have met this higher standard. Among others there is today an excellent two-volume history of Yale from

1871 to 1937. In anticipation of the bicentennial in 1954, historians at Columbia have written a series of volumes covering all phases of the history of that institution. There are shorter but no less scholarly histories of Princeton and of Pennsylvania, written by historians on their respective faculties. There are good histories of Amherst, Georgia, Oberlin, South Carolina, Stanford, Virginia, Wisconsin, and others. Unfortunately the older kind of scissors and paste job, hastily put together to meet an anniversary deadline by some loyal alumnus or professor emeritus who happened to have time on his hands, has not entirely disappeared. Good or bad, the college history is almost invariably written by someone connected with the institution. This ensures appreciation and sympathetic understanding, but not always the necessary critical detachment. The only exception I know of is Mount Holyoke, where the committee preparing the centennial of 1936 handed over the task of writing the college history to a social historian of known competence and prestige, a man, who had no direct connection with Mount Holyoke.

INDEX

Index

Phillips, Wendell, 40
Populists, 252
Porter, Noah, 164, 173
Potter, Alonzo, 96
Pratt Institute, 241
Presbyterian church, 25, 30, 35, 109, 121
President, college: recruited from clergy, 35; nature of office, 103-106; and evolution theory, 164
President's Commission on Higher Education, 219
Priestley, Joseph, 19
Princeton University: location, 11, 14; alumni, 13; and ministry, 24; secularism, 27; conservatism, 54, 67; examinations, 74; costs, 77; student behavior, 80, 82; debating societies, 98, 196; under Witherspoon, 107-109; under McCosh, 165; and electives, 173; under Wilson, 180; decline in scholarship, 192; honor system, 194; fraternities and eating clubs, 196; football, 198, 200; preceptorial system, 233
Procter, William C., 254
Psychology, 190, 211
Pulitzer School of Journalism, 253
Purdue University, 154

Queens College. *See* Rutgers University
Quincy, Josiah, 86

Radcliffe College, 134
Randolph-Macon College, 32, 49
Randolph-Macon Women's College, 132, 143
Ranke, Leopold von, 160
Raymond, John H., 141
Reformation, 23, 125
Reformed church, 8, 11, 25
Reid, Thomas, 47
Religion: theological students, 24; revivalism, 28; nature of church college, 33-35, 40; ministers on college faculties, 35; as means of discipline, 87-91; in women's colleges, 143; in state universities, 157; and evolution theory, 161-167; end of compulsory chapel, 182, 191; and college sponsorship, 287 (n. 2). *See also* individual religious denominations
Remsen, Ira, 175
Revivals. *See* Religion
Rittenhouse, David, 18
Rockefeller, John D., 178, 200
Rockefeller Foundation, 247
Rockford College, 132, 143
Rockne, Knute, 201
Rollins College, 221

Roman Catholic church, 33, 42, 132
Roosevelt, Theodore, 241
Roosevelt University, 229
Ross, Edward A., 190, 250
Rowing, 198
Rush, Benjamin, 18, 116
Rustication, 83
Rutgers, Henry, 14
Rutgers University: location, 11; lottery, 16; charter, 25; admission requirements, 68; and Douglass College, 135; becomes state university of New Jersey, 155; football, 198
Rutledge, John, 77

St. John's College, 221
Santayana, George, 218
Sarah Lawrence College, 144, 221
Science: in 18th century, 46; subordinated to classics, 50-51; and theory of evolution, 162, 167; expansion and dominance, 188. *See also* Curriculum, Evolution
Scottish realism, 47
Secularism, 167, 168, 192
Seelye, Clark, 139
Seelye, Julius, 166
Seneca Falls Convention, 137
Shakespeare, 188, 192
Shaler, Nathaniel, 181
Sheffield Scientific School, 139, 155
Shipherd, John H., 36
Silliman, Benjamin, 51, 89
Simpson, Matthew, 57, 89
Sims, J. Marion, 82
Sinclair, Upton, 239
Smith, Samuel H., 19
Smith, Samuel S., 49, 77
Smith, Sophia, 131
Smith, William, 7, 58
Smith, William A., 49
Smith College, 131, 139
Smith-Lever Act, 154
Snow, Francis H., 165, 187
Socrates, 91, 264
Sororities, 196. *See also* Fraternities
South Carolina, University of: location, 13; founding, 15; religion at, 34; and slavery, 38; library, 72; costs, 78; student behavior, 82; debating societies, 99; state support, 148
Sparks, Jared, 170
Spencer, Herbert, 143, 161, 187
Stagg, Amos A., 200
Stanford, Leland, 177, 247
Stanford University, 178, 193
State universities, 15, 148, 156-158. *See also* individual universities